WANDERING GREEKS

WANDERING GREEKS

The Ancient Greek Diaspora from the Age of Homer
to the Death of Alexander the Great

Robert Garland

PRINCETON UNIVERSITY PRESS

PRINCETON AND OXFORD

Published by Princeton University Press, 41 William Street, Princeton, New Jersey 08540
In the United Kingdom: Princeton University Press, 6 Oxford Street, Woodstock, Oxfordshire OX20 1TW

press.princeton.edu

Coin photography © Andy Daddio. Jacket design by Karl Spurzem.

Library of Congress Cataloging-in-Publication Data

Garland, Robert, 1947–

Wandering Greeks : the ancient Greek diaspora from the age of Homer to the death of Alexander the Great / Robert Garland.

pages cm

Summary: "Most classical authors and modern historians depict the ancient Greek world as essentially stable and even static, once the so-called colonization movement came to an end. But Robert Garland argues that the Greeks were highly mobile, that their movement was essential to the survival, success, and sheer sustainability of their society, and that this wandering became a defining characteristic of their culture. Addressing a neglected but essential subject, Wandering Greeks focuses on the diaspora of tens of thousands of people between about 700 and 325 BCE, demonstrating the degree to which Greeks were liable to be forced to leave their homes due to political upheaval, oppression, poverty, warfare, or simply a desire to better themselves. Attempting to enter into the mind-set of these wanderers, the book provides an insightful and sympathetic account of what it meant for ancient Greeks to part from everyone and everything they held dear, to start a new life elsewhere—or even to become homeless, living on the open road or on the high seas with no end to their journey in sight. Each chapter identifies a specific kind of "wanderer," including the overseas settler, the deportee, the evacuee, the asylum-seeker, the fugitive, the economic migrant, and the itinerant, and the book also addresses repatriation and the idea of the "portable polis." The result is a vivid and unique portrait of ancient Greece as a culture of displaced persons"—Provided by publisher.

Includes bibliographical references and index.

ISBN 978-0-691-16105-1 (hardback)

1. Greeks—Migrations—History—To 1500.   2. Greece—Social conditions—To 146 B.C.   3. Greece—Civilization—To 146 B.C.   I. Title.

DF222.2.G37 2014

938—dc23

2013034456

British Library Cataloging-in-Publication Data is available

This book has been composed in Sabon Next LT Pro and Ideal Sans

Printed on acid-free paper.

Printed in the United States of America

10 9 8 7 6 5 4 3 2 1

for Paul with lasting affection

γαῖα δ' ἔτι ξυνὴ πάντων—
Earth is common to all—

—HOM. *IL.* 15.193

CONTENTS

ILLUSTRATIONS

All coins are reproduced with kind permission of an anonymous collector.

MAPS

PREFACE

To put things in a modern perspective: there are 42.5 million displaced persons in the world today. More people were displaced in 2012 than at any other time during the past decade. There are 12 million refugees, 3.2 million of whom are living in Africa. According to the United Nations' estimate, "Every year, more than 5 million people cross international borders to go and live in a developed country," while "the number of people who move to a developing nation or within their country is much greater" (*Human Development Report* 2009, 9). Some 2.5 million people are being trafficked around the world. There are a million asylum-seekers, 80 percent of them housed in developing states. They comprise the tortured, political dissidents, the starving poor, and oppressed religious and ethic minorities. It has only been over the past century that the international community has attempted to regulate migration and to define those who should be accorded the special title of "refugees." An important step was the establishment in 1951 of the Office of the United Nations High Commissioner for Refugees, initially intended to address the refugee problems consequent upon World War II.

In the ancient world, by contrast, displaced persons weren't even a statistic. Though a few migrant groups caught the headlines, often due to the Odyssean circuitousness of their wanderings, the majority disappeared without trace once they had severed ties with their homeland. Citing the numerous accounts of Greek heroes being driven into exile as the result of murder, jealousy, and other exigencies, Gilbert Murray (1934, 207) perceptively observed, "All Hellas was *anastatos*, driven by [*sic*] its home [by the] constant war paths and uprootings of peoples." This, as I shall seek to demonstrate, was no less true of Greece in historical times.* It is also the case that scholars have largely overlooked the scale of the humanitarian crises that regularly occurred consequent upon war, famine, and political upheaval—not that humanitarian crises that occurred thousands of years ago could be expected to stir much passion today. Many Greeks found themselves displaced and on the move, condemned to live out the rest of their lives in moldy shacks and frosty tents. This said, our sources tell us very little about refugees in particular and not much about migrants in general. Their existence, though widespread at all periods of history, receives but cursory mention and then only when it happens to alter the political landscape.

It has only been relatively recently that scholars have become interested in migrants, refugees, *Gastarbeiter*, asylum-seekers, and the urban homeless. Over the past twenty-five years, however, migration studies has become a burgeoning field of inquiry that incorporates a wide range of disciplines including demography, economics, geography, history, sociology, anthropology, psychology, and cultural studies. Those who work in migration studies are concerned not only with process but also with the personal experiences of migrants and refugees. Much of its focus, as well as its theoretical underpinning, however, lies outside the scope of the present investigation. Questions such as, "What is the desired relationship between refugees and asylum-seekers on the one hand, and human rights and domestic law on the other? How should one weigh the right of the state unilaterally to prevent potential immigrants from crossing its borders against the right of individuals to freedom of international movement? Should the economic and cultural gains of migration to society be prioritized before the strains that migration imposes on its social fabric?" have little or no relevance to the ancient world. Likewise concepts such as multiculturalism, cosmopolitanism, globalism, and so on, which feature so prominently in discussions of contem-

---

* For the meaning of *anastatos* in a migratory context, see Hansen and Nielsen (2004, 123). The instability of medieval, as well as ancient, communities has been emphasized by Osborne (1991, 139–67), here in the context of village life. Walzer (1981, 1–35), though dated, provides an excellent introduction to many issues relating to migration, particularly the human toll on both migrants and receiving community.

porary diasporas, cannot usefully be applied to the ancient world. Even the notion of a border as a (semi-)permanent marker of territory has to be revised when we think of the ancient world. Arguably a more appropriate concept is that of a frontier consisting of neutral territory, which was available for livestock grazing but not for settlement or agriculture (Diener and Hagen 2012, 29–30).

Interest in exilic literature in classical antiquity has been growing over the past half-century, concentrating primarily on the three most famous exiled Roman authors, Cicero, Ovid, and Seneca the Younger. More recently it has expanded to include Greek literature, a notable example being Jan Felix Gaertner's edited volume *Writing Exile: The Discourse of Displacement in Greco-Roman Antiquity and Beyond* (2007b). By contrast the investigation of diaspora as a historical phenomenon in the Greek (and Roman for that matter) world continues to be sparse, other than in the case of overseas settlements, where the emphasis is primarily on this phenomenon as a galvanizing force in Greek history. One of the first works to spotlight the refugee was Elemer Balogh's *Political Refugees in Ancient Greece: From the Period of the Tyrants to Alexander the Great* (1943). Balogh was motivated to undertake his study by the refugee crisis occasioned by World War I. Paul McKechnie's *Outsiders in the Greek Cities in the Fourth Century BC* (1989) first alerted scholars to the fact that "the description and analysis of Greek life as the life of an aggregation of city-states is in essence and origin the Greeks' own"— and he went on to examine the many groupings to whom that narrow self-definition did not apply. His primary focus was on large-scale population movement, but he also examined the condition of mercenaries, brigands, pirates, itinerant workers, and traders. Other scholars have illuminated individual topics covered in the present survey. Silvia Montiglio's *Wandering in Ancient Greek Culture* (2005) demonstrates how wandering was conceptualized in literary and philosophical texts. "Colonization" in particular has generated intense interest. Recent pioneering work includes Robin Osborne's *Greece in the Making 1200–479 BC* (2nd ed., 2009) and Irad Malkin's *A Small Greek World: Networks in the Ancient Mediterranean* (2011). Nancy Demand's *Urban Relocation in*

Archaic and Classical Greece: Flight and Consolidation (1990) emphasized the degree to which the Greeks envisioned the city-state as a transportable entity. Hans-Joachim Gehrke's *Stasis: Untersuchungen zu den inneren Kriegen in den griechischen Staaten des 5. und 4. Jahrhunderts v. Chr.* (1985) pioneered the investigation of the political squabbles that frequently led to mass expulsion. The asylum-seeker has generated considerable interest particularly among German scholars, including Lienhard Delekat (*Katoche, Hierodulie und Adoptionsfreilassung*, 1964); Martin Dreher (*Das Antike Asyl. Kultische Grundlagen, rechtliche Ausgestaltung und politische Funktion*, 2003); and Ulrich Sinn (1990, 1993, and *ThesCRA* III, pp. 217–32). The importance of the economic migrant in Athenian society, first highlighted by Michel Clerc in *Les métèques athéniens* (1893), was brought into sharper relief by David Whitehead's *The Ideology of the Athenian Metic* (1977) and Edward Cohen's *Athenian Nation* (2000). Sara Forsdyke's *Exile, Ostracism, and Democracy* (2005), though chiefly focused on Athenian democracy, demonstrates how political power in the Greek world was intimately connected with the power to drive one's opponents into exile. Finally, Mogens Hansen's and Thomas Nielsen's edited volume *An Inventory of Archaic and Classical Poleis* (2004) has been invaluable, both for its comprehensiveness and for its discussions of cities that experienced civil war, underwent wholesale enslavement, formed a synoecism, and so on.

The principal questions that have fueled my inquiry are "What did it mean in the Greek world to be a migrant, a refugee, a settler, an evacuee, a deportee, an asylum-seeker, and so on? What physical and psychological challenges did such people face? What was the human cost of unsettlement? What kind of interactions did migrants have with those whom they encountered abroad? What were the consequences of dislocation for their sense of belonging and identity?"—even though, given the nature of the sources, I have rarely been able to answer them adequately (see later, "Envoi"). That is in part because there was no particular interest in what we would call the "human interest story."

I have subtitled this book "The Ancient Greek Diaspora from the Age of Homer to the Death of Alexander the Great" because "diaspora," an ancient Greek word, best describes the multifarious types of movement that I seek to investigate.* The term is not, however, unproblematic, and its meaning has generated much debate among anthropologists, sociologists, cultural critics, geographers, environmental psychologists, political scientists, and literary theorists, to name but a few, all of whom are engaged in the relatively new field of diaspora studies. Primarily "diaspora" has been used to describe the mass movements that took place in the second half of the twentieth century, "particularly in reference to independence movements in formerly colonized areas, waves of refugees fleeing war-torn states, and fluxes of economic migration in the post–World War II era" (Braziel and Mannur 2003, 4). More recently, however, its usage has been widened to include "any and every nameable population category that is to some extent dispersed in space" (Brubaker 2005, 3). It is thus "a universal nomenclature applicable to displaced peoples" (Barkan and Shelton 1998, 5). Another burgeoning field of multidisciplinary inquiry that has bearing on this investigation is border studies, which focuses on the importance of borders for social interaction, local identity, state sovereignty, and the exercise of power.

When I initially began my research, I intended to confine it to those who had been forcibly deprived of their homelands, their belongings, and their communities. It quickly became apparent, however, that the Greek refugee is not an isolatable category, since our sources often fail to give a precise explanation for population displacement. In addition, many of the individuals and groups who were exiled or who went into voluntary exile disappear from the record without trace, once mention has been made of their departure. There are other difficulties. We do not know what percentage of Athens's large metic—that is, long-term resident—population comprised economic migrants who were seeking

---

* The verb *diaspeirô* is first used in Pl. *Laws* 3.699d. The earliest occurrence of the noun *diaspora*, "that which is sown or scattered across," occurs in the Book of Deuteronomy (Septuagint, third century BCE), where the Lord warns the Hebrews that if they do not hearken to him, they "will be a diaspora in all kingdoms of the earth" (28.25). "Diaspora" later came to refer specifically to the expulsion of the Jews from Jerusalem after the destruction of the Second Temple in 586 BCE. It first entered the English language in 1876. For a condensed history of human migration, see Goldin, Cameron, and Balarajan (2011, 11–38).

a better life, and what percentage was driven abroad by compulsion, though their circumstances and motivation would have been very different from one another. Last but by no means least, Greek uses the same word to describe both an exile and a refugee (see appendix A).

It follows that the subject of this inquiry, *tout court*, may be defined as the dispersal, removal, and relocation of the Greeks, whether in groups or singly, either by choice or by compulsion, in the period from ca. 800 to the death of Alexander the Great in 323. Because of the difficulty in drawing hard and fast distinctions within the Greek diaspora, my chapters cannot be self-contained. I have simply done the best I can to organize the testimonia comprehensibly. The fact is that it is often impossible to distinguish the asylum-seeker from the fugitive, the evacuee from the deportee, or the economic migrant from the itinerant. One might justifiably claim from this that it is impossible to have an encounter with the Greek migrant. While respecting that opinion, I have done my level best to force one.

This investigation has been a long time in the conception and gestation. About a decade ago Paul Cartledge suggested that I might write a book on refugees, and although the finished product is less circumscribed than I had originally intended, I owe the initial inspiration to him. Paul had traveled back and knew what I had overlooked. He also painstakingly read the manuscript and corrected countless inaccuracies and infelicities, though the book has gone some distance since then and all the remaining errors and imprecisions are mine. So I would like to take this opportunity yet again to express my deep and abiding gratitude for his unfailing encouragement and incomparable friendship.

I owe an equal debt of inspiration to Vergil. The *Aeneid*, through its empathetic depiction of a man who is *profugus fato* (a refugee by fate), has provided us with an unparalleled resource for exploring the mental world of those who experienced deracination and did their best to live out its consequences. No Greek text comes close in explicating and laying bare the barrage of fears and false hopes that a person seeking a new homeland experienced day after endless day. In short, the *Aeneid* helped me to appreciate the predicament of those who lived in a world that was, almost by definition, perpetually *anastatos*.*

I am most grateful to Rob Tempio and to all the editorial staff at Princeton University Press, and to the anonymous Press readers for their invaluable suggestions. My research was greatly facilitated by a stipend attached to the Roy D. and Margaret B. Wooster chair of the Classics. David Whitehead expertly read at short notice chapters 9 and 10. I should like to express my appreciation to the Research Council at Colgate University for covering the cost of the maps and illustrations. My thanks go to Michael Holobowsky for drawing the maps, and to Andy Daddio for photographing the coins. Mick Jagger and my son, Richard Garland, have been an invaluable strengthening presence throughout the long journey of this book. My friends Peter Balakian and John Naughton and my daughter, Ling Ling, have been constantly at my side.

---

* Livy, too, in his early books consistently emphasizes the fact that Rome's growth owed everything to transfers of peoples. The abduction of the Sabine women is merely the most celebrated instance of this phenomenon (1.9).

WANDERING GREEKS

1

PROLEGOMENA

Ancient and Modern Responses to Migration

"Millions of Migrants Flood in and There's Nothing We Can Do to Stop Them!" screamed the headline in a British tabloid newspaper recently. The metaphor of flooding, which is particularly favored by the popular press, evokes the image of Britannia sinking beneath the waves under the weight of a migrant stampede.

There is, however, nothing novel in the sentiment. In 1601 Queen Elizabeth I had called for the banishment of "the great numbers of negars and Blackamoores, most of them infidels, who are fostered and fed here to the great annoyance of [my] people." Even so, it was not until 1905 that the British Parliament finally introduced legislation that gave the Home Secretary the power to restrict immigration. The so-called Aliens Act primarily targeted criminals and paupers; an attempt to incorporate a restriction on Jewish immigration under the same act was heavily defeated. This was also the first piece of legislation to provide asylum in Britain for those fleeing from religious or political persecution.

In the United States, too, racism has played its part in the legislative process. In 1790, a few months after the Constitution had been ratified, the Naturalization Act granted immigrant status to any "free white person" of "good moral character" who had been resident in the country for two years. How these persons of good character were to be identified was not spelled out, but they no doubt had to belong to the proper social class. The so-called white person prerequisite remained in force in every naturalization act passed by Congress until 1952. The Chinese Exclusion Act of 1882, which banned Chinese laborers from immigrating to the United States, was repealed only in 1943. It had been fueled by the anxiety that the Chinese were taking jobs from Americans—the persistent fear in a host population toward an energetic immigrant group.

The twentieth century witnessed a dramatic increase in the numbers of refugees, asylum-seekers, and migrants. This came about largely as a result of the rise of communism and fascism and the occurrence of two world wars. Around 1.5 million Anatolian Greeks and 500,000 Muslims became refugees in 1923 as a result of the "Convention Concerning the Exchange of Greek and Turkish Populations," which the governments of Greece and Turkey cosigned. As many as 12.5 million people were displaced from their homes following the partition of India and Pakistan in 1947. It has recently been determined that at the end of World War II between 12 and 14 million residents of mainly Czechoslovakia, Hungary, and Poland were expelled from their homelands to occupied Germany (Douglas 2012). Some 600,000 Jews fled to Israel from Arab states and from Iran in the late 1940s. Between 5.5 and 8.5 million migrants moved to Britain, France, Italy, Belgium, and Holland from their respective colonies in search of work in the period from 1945 to 1973. Hundreds of thousands of refugees fled to Thailand and Vietnam when the Khmer Rouge came to power in Cambodia in 1975. About 4.6 million Palestinians currently fall under the protection of the United Nations Relief and Work Agency for Palestinian Refugees in the Near East. Some one and a half million Chinese have been relocated from the region in Hubei Province around the Three Gorges Dam, which was begun in 1993 to provide energy for the world's biggest hydroelectric power plant. At the time of writing more than two million refugees have fled from Syria as a result of the civil war that began in 2011, around half of them children, while another 4.5 million have been internally displaced inside the country according to estimates from the United Nations High Commissioner for Refugees. Not the least troubling consequence of the events of September 11, 2001, has been a global tightening of policies aimed at immigrants, refugees, and asylum-seekers, who are seen as potential threats to national security and as a possible cause of armed terror.

Upheavals in early modern times include the expulsion of the Jews from Spain in 1492, the Moors from Spain in 1609, the Huguenots from

France in 1685, the early settlers to America, the émigrés of the French Revolution, and the Loyalists who fled to Canada and the Caribbean at the time of the American War of Independence. In addition, more than half a million Portuguese and Spaniards settled in Central and South America, while about 700,000 British subjects immigrated to the American colonies. It is estimated that between eleven and twelve million Africans were shipped as slaves across the Atlantic from the fifteenth to the nineteenth centuries. Approximately 2.3 million Chinese and 1.3 million Indians traveled to Southeast Asia as contract workers between 1842 and 1900.

Large-scale displacement is by no means an exclusively modern phenomenon. I estimate that well over 100,000 men, women, and slaves were displaced as a result of the Peloponnesian War, half of that number being residents of Attica. Many cities ceased to exist in that period, including Histiaea, Plataea, Thyrea, Torone, Scione, Cyme, Melos, Hyccara, Iasus, and Cedreiae (see appendix E). Some of them were razed to the ground; others were resettled by immigrants. Abandoned settlements were in fact a feature of the Greek landscape at all periods of history. Overall, about seventy-five cities were destroyed in the period covered by this survey, some more than once (Hansen and Nielsen 2004, index 20 [pp. 1363–64]). Plataea held the record, being destroyed three times (in 480, 426, and 373). In forty-two cases the population was massacred and/or enslaved. In twenty-two, the *polis* underwent *dioikismos*— that is to say, the survivors were dispersed among the villages out of which the *polis* had originally been an amalgam.

In addition, many prominent individuals have undergone exile, both voluntary and enforced, including Hannah Arendt, Mikhail Baryshnikov, Napoleon Bonaparte, Marc Chagall, Albert Einstein, Victor Hugo, Richard Wagner, Frédéric Chopin, Sigmund Freud, Thomas Mann, Vladimir Nabokov, Alexander Solzhenitsyn, Thich Nhat Hanh, and Elie Wiesel. The list of those who went into exile in Greek antiquity was equally distinguished (see appendix D).

My own awareness of the issues posed by immigration dates precisely to April 20, 1968, when Enoch Powell, the Conservative Member of Parliament for Wolverhampton South East, delivered his infamous "Rivers of Blood" speech, coincidentally (or not) less than three weeks after the assassination of Martin Luther King. He intended it to be an attack on the Race Relations Act that had been introduced in the same year by the Labour Party. The act had outlawed discrimination on the "grounds of colour, race, or ethnic or national origins" in public places. In so doing, it had also made discrimination in housing illegal. Previously it had been commonplace to see advertisements for rented rooms in Britain include the words "No Coloureds" (or "No Irish"). Now such notices were banned.

Britain had experienced considerable immigration from the Commonwealth countries in the postwar years, and Powell saw himself addressing a ticking time bomb. Allegedly quoting what he called "a decent ordinary fellow-Englishman," he claimed that "in fifteen or twenty years the black man will have the whip hand over the white man"—a highly insensitive and inflammatory phrase if ever there was one, particularly in light of King's recent assassination. He went on to predict that by the year 2000 there would be five to seven million Commonwealth immigrants and their descendants living in Britain, representing approximately one-tenth of the total population. Powell was a brilliant classicist—he became professor of Greek at the University of Sydney at the age of 25—and he thought fit to end his speech with a Sibylline prophecy from Vergil's *Aeneid* (6.87), from which it derived its popular title:

> As I look ahead I am filled with foreboding. Like the Roman, I seem to see "the River Tiber foaming with much blood." That tragic and intractable phenomenon, which we watch with horror on the other side of the Atlantic but which there is interwoven with the history and existence of the States itself, is coming upon us here by our own volition and our own neglect. Indeed, it has all but come.

Powell's answer to the "problem" of immigration was voluntary reemigration, which was to be facilitated by "generous grants and assistance." Though many applauded his speech, he was dismissed from the Shadow Cabinet and narrowly avoided prosecution for exacerbating racial tensions. Margaret Thatcher, though certainly not in the same camp as Powell, nonetheless used the word "swamp" to describe an influx of immigrants, and the metaphor is commonplace in what passes for political discourse on the subject. It goes without saying that the scale of permitted immigration remains an extremely contentious issue to this day, both in the United States, the UK, and throughout the world.

There is nothing new in this circumstance. Appeals by asylum-seekers, as well as petitions from would-be immigrants, were certainly debated in assemblies throughout the ancient Greek world, and it would be surprising indeed if those debates had not at times become acrimonious and heated. Plutarch in a throwaway line notes that the Athenian lawgiver Solon "observed that Athens was filled with people who were constantly streaming into Attica from elsewhere in order to find security" (*Sol.* 22.1). Though Plutarch cannot have known what Solon took note of, it is entirely conceivable that some of Solon's contemporaries did indeed fear that they were being "swamped" by immigrants. It is important to note at the beginning of this survey, however, that to our best knowledge no Greek state ever settled an identifiably "foreign" ethnic minority within its territory. Only very occasionally do we hear of groups of Phoenicians and other non-Greeks residing in cosmopolitan cities such as the Piraeus, Athens's port, or Syracuse, and they did so in very small numbers. It follows that race would not have been an issue for the Greeks in any discussion about immigration in the same way that it has in the modern world, particularly with regard to those identified as "black." Nor, so far as we know, did any Greek state implement a policy on immigration or seek to enforce a quota. It just so happened that some states, Athens *in primis*, were open to immigrants, whereas others, most conspicuously Sparta, were not.

Though the plight of migrants and refugees in the Greek-speaking world would have been similar to their plight today, absent the halting efforts of humanitarian agencies and the distracted gaze of the international community, there are some striking differences. Many people are at least somewhat sensitized to the predicament faced by displaced persons today, whereas the best minds of Greek antiquity show virtually no concern for their welfare. A rare instance of humanitarian concern for refugees on the part of a large number of people is briefly recorded by Diodorus Siculus (19.54.2). When the Macedonian general Cassander, "in his desire for glory," rebuilt Thebes in 316 following the destruction of that city some twenty years earlier by Alexander the Great, "many Greek cities participated in the *sunoikismos* [resettlement], both because of their pity for the unfortunate people and because of Thebes's renown." We are left wondering to what extent these same cities would have come to the rescue of these unfortunates if they had belonged to a city of no particular consequence. Likewise when the Athenians expelled the Samians and sent their own settlers to the island, the Greek world sympathized with the Samians and provided them with asylum, though perhaps more out of enmity toward the Athenians than sympathy for the Samians (see later, chapter 11).

Another striking difference is that migration in the Greek-speaking world, whatever its cause, often represented a far more radical upheaval in people's lives than it does today. Describing the moment when her parents became refugees, Vijay Agnew (2005, 6) writes: "The hurried nature of my parents' departure from Quetta, now part of Pakistan, meant that they carried little with them that was not necessary for physical survival. No albums or pictures of the past survived." Greek migrants invariably faced the prospect of total severance from the past, and in the absence of the practice of keeping diaries and journals, let alone photographs, the only way that memories could be kept alive was through recitation and story-telling.

The Silence of the Sources

Intensifying Peloponnesian War Sparks Refugee Crisis: Athenian Correspondent Reports That 250 Children Die of Hunger Each Day!

Even if some enterprising Greek had invented the newspaper, I seriously doubt that refugees would have made the headlines. No one to our best knowledge, including Thucydides, who occasionally took note of population movements, ever concerned himself with what we would call today the "global implications" of war, famine, and disease for the thousands of victims of such disasters. This is perhaps all the more surprising in light of the fact that Thucydides was himself exiled from Athens for many years and must have experienced some degree of discomfort, hardship, and prejudice, even though he would have continued to lead a charmed life, like most high-profile exiles. All that he tells us about his exile, however, is that it "gave him the leisure to get a better sense of events"—and thus in effect to become a better historian (5.26.5). Of course, being an exile like Thucydides with wealth and status is a very different experience from being a common refugee. From the perspective of a Greek and indeed Roman historian (a number of whom incidentally went into exile) refugees and other homeless individuals just didn't merit writing about; or to put it more accurately, they merited a brief mention at most. No historian was particularly interested in recording the sufferings of the undifferentiated masses, and none ever encouraged his readers to dwell on human suffering at length. Why would he? Greek history has provided us with a narrative that privileges the interests and concerns of intellectuals, the well-to-do, and, crucially for our focus here, the settled. It has little to tell us about the dispossessed. The historians belonged to the city élite and assumed that their readers did too. They therefore tell the story from the perspective of a small minority of politically powerful and largely stable cities, about twenty at most. To the extent that we can build up a picture of the dispossessed at all, the data must be culled primarily from the marginalia of history.

"The Athenians crossed over to Euboea again under the command of Pericles and conquered the whole island," Thucydides reports of the year 446. "While they settled the rest of the island on agreed terms, they expelled the people of Histiaea and occupied their land themselves" (1.114.3; cf. D.S. 12.22.2). And that is that. No further reference to these exiles occurs in his work. They are just one more community consigned to the ash heap of history in a brief, inconsequential statement. Given the bias of our sources, literary as well as epigraphical, it is all too easy to picture the Greek-speaking world from the perspective of the prosperous citizen of a big and thriving city-state. And yet there is an urgent

FIGURE 1 Silver *tetrôbolon* (four-obol coin) from Histiaea, Euboea, ca. 267–146. The obverse depicts the head of the nymph Histiaea with her hair rolled up and wreathed in a vine. The reverse depicts her seated on the stern of a ship, holding a standard, a trident beneath the hull. The legend reads (*HISTI)AIEÔN*. The city was destroyed by the Persians in 480 after the Battle of Artemisum. It recovered, became part of Athens's maritime confederacy, and in 446 defected, along with other Euboean *poleis*. The rebellion was quickly crushed, and the Histiaeans were deported to Macedonia. A small number remained, however, and at the end of the Peloponnesian War, the city was resettled as Oreos, probably with descendants of the original population (Hansen and Nielsen 2004, 657).

story to be told, and one that has up to now received little attention from ancient historians. Indeed its omission has replicated the silence of our sources.

That said I do not mean to pass judgment on Thucydides and the other historians who failed to pay much attention to the struggles of refugees and other migratory peoples. They simply did not see it as their business to chronicle their sufferings. That does not, however, mean that they were indifferent to their plight or inherently lacking in compassion. It goes without saying that we know nothing about their capacity for compassion. What we can say with certainty is that life for the vast majority of people in ancient Greece was extremely tough, that many more people lived on the edge than do today in the West, and that compassion was a luxury that not everyone could afford. As Herbert Butterfield (1931, 16) stated, "The study of the past with one eye, so to speak, upon the present is the source of all sins and sophistries in history, starting with the simplest of them, anachronism."

Even in the modern world it is virtually impossible to obtain accurate statistics about movements of peoples. *A fortiori* we cannot begin to estimate the proportion constituted by the migratory population in ancient Greece. Such data as we have are disjointed and piecemeal. To make matters worse, the figures in our sources are inherently unreliable, both because the Greeks could provide only rough estimates of population size and because numbers are frequently transmitted incorrectly in the manuscript tradition. It is clear, however, from what we know about overseas settlements and mercenary service that from the beginning of the historical era, and probably much earlier, Greece had what is called a large "exportable proletariat." It may have been for this reason that both Plato (*Rep.* 5.460a, *Laws* 5.740b–d) and Aristotle (*Pol.* 7.1335b 19–26) were concerned to restrict the size of the citizen body of individual *poleis*. It is not until the middle of the second century BCE that we have evidence to suggest that the prospect of a dwindling population was causing anxiety in Greece (Polyb. 36.17.5–10). The literary evidence suggests that migration reached its peak in the fourth century, when communal life itself threatened to be overwhelmed by the numbers of homeless persons. However, much of the evidence that supports this view is propagandist in nature. And though population movement is our concern, let us not forget the fact that in the seventh and sixth centuries many Greeks never traveled more than a few miles from their birthplace (Purcell 1990, 37).

"It is clear that the *polis* exists by nature and that by nature man is a being who lives in a *polis*," Aristotle famously declared (*Pol.* 1.1253a 1–3). Neither he nor any other political theorist of whom we have record thought it worthwhile either to imagine a different state of being or to focus his attention on those Greeks who faced a very different reality. Yet even for Athenians the chance of being forced by circumstance from their homes represented a very real danger. Indeed it became a reality during the Persian and Peloponnesian wars. And once we turn our attention away from the major centers of power to the periphery, the picture darkens appreciably. Given the precariousness of life in the ancient world we can well suppose that at any period of history the landscape would have provided the spectator with haunting images of refugees, forced from their homes by human conflict or natural disaster.

Nowhere is the silence of our sources more deafening than with regard to women and slaves, both those who were ejected from their homes and those who remained behind, when their husbands, fathers, or owners were exiled. Any woman who took to the high seas or to the open road unaccompanied by a man would have had little chance of survival. A striking difference between then and now was the paucity of outlets abroad for women. It is estimated that in 2005 half the world's migrants were women, many of them propelled to leave their homeland in the hope of achieving release from its restrictive traditions and social practices. By contrast, only a small number of Greek women would have been able to seek a livelihood abroad, due to the lack of career options. Virtually the only way for a woman to escape the confining lifestyle to which the vast majority conformed was by becoming a prostitute (see later, chapter 9), an anodyne term that hides the fact that many of the women who found themselves so identified would have been victims of sex trafficking. The fact, too, that women played only a minor role in overseas settlement leaves us wondering what would have been the fate of those who were left behind. Slaves disappear without trace.

Causes of Population Displacement

Modern theories of migration differentiate between a complex series of interconnecting factors on the micro-level, viz individuals and whole families who have personal reasons for wanting to migrate; meso-level, viz networks and systems that facilitate the process; and macro-level, viz demographic, political, and economic conditions that help determine the rate and size of a migration flow (Goldin et al. 2011, 97–120). Self-evidently we cannot apply this kind of sophisticated theorizing to the ancient evidence. At the macro-level, however, the Greeks certainly understood that war was a cause of population displacement. At the beginning of his history of the Peloponnesian War, Thucydides identifies the characteristic features of a life that is unpredictable, unsettled, and subject to constant upheavals. It is what he imagines to have been the life of the primitive settlers who first inhabited the Greek mainland (1.2.1–2):

> It is clear that the land that is now called Hellas did not have a settled population in ancient times, and that formerly there were many *metanastaseis* [migrations] whenever individual tribes readily abandoned their land under constant pressure from people who were more numerous than they were. Lacking commerce, having no free communications with one another either by land or by sea, cultivating only as much land as was necessary to keep alive, having no reserves to fall back on, not growing crops on the land, since they never knew when an invader might deprive them of those crops, and not having walls, all because they thought that their daily necessities were all that they needed, it hardly mattered to them if they were uprooted, and for that reason they did not acquire powerful city-states nor have any other resources [that is, either military or naval].

This is a striking passage for many reasons. Its underlying assumption is based partly on the memory of a dimly remembered past that has been passed down by oral tradition, and partly on speculative inference. Indeed by prefacing his remarks with the words "It is clear," Thucydides admits that his analysis owes little to what we would call evidence, though this does not alter the fact that his inference is of high quality. Indeed this is the first attempt by a historian to describe the living conditions of those wretches for whom survival against the odds is the essential and primary goal.

Thucydides paints a picture of backward and closed-off communities whose members lived a semi-nomadic existence, largely dependent for their survival on hunting and gathering, and incapable of consolidating and flourishing because of constant migratory movements. Though he leads us to believe that this was a lifestyle that had long ceased to be current in his day, I strongly suspect there were parts of Greece where it had not entirely been superseded. Backwardness, however, was not the only cause of migration, as he points out (1.12.2):

The fact that the Greeks returned only after many years from Troy led to revolutions. *Staseis* [political upheavals] generally occurred in the city-states, and it was the people who were driven out who founded city-states.

The example he cites in support of his important claim that war causes political upheaval, which in turn generates population displacement, is the ancestors of the Boeotians, who were allegedly driven out of Arne in Thessaly by the Thessalians sixty years after the fall of Troy and who subsequently settled in Boeotia as refugees. No doubt this was just one of many upheavals that were thought to have occurred around this time. He concludes (1.12.4):

It was only long after the war had ended that Greece finally became stable, no longer prone to upheavals and able to send out *apoikiai* [settlements] abroad.

Though Thucydides does not draw any analogy between the migratory movements that were occasioned by the Trojan War and the frequent unsettlements that were brought about by the Peloponnesian War, it is evident that he had this latter event in mind when he cast his imagination back to the past.

Stasis (political strife), as we shall see, was a routine feature of life in the Greek city-state, and it commonly resulted in the expulsion of one or other faction, either oligarchic or democratic, or, less commonly, one or other ethnic group. It was in fact one of the principal causes of mass displacement, just as it is in the modern world. Other stimuli in the modern world include demographic growth, religious conflict, environmental disaster, war, famine, and the desire for economic advantage. In ancient Greece a similar set of determinants operated, absent religious conflict, which for the most part counted for little.

The best we can do in seeking to determine the cause of population movement in the Greek world is to make some crude generalizations. Though demographic growth, famine, and an eagerness to establish markets for the sale and purchase of goods are likely to have prompted a *polis* to dispatch a group of pioneers to found a settlement, we are hardly ever in a position to prioritize these (and other) factors. We know, too, that some settlements were founded by groups that were politically disaffected. The expansion of the Greek world consequent upon the conquests of Alexander the Great in the last decades of the fourth century, which resulted in mercenary soldiers settling as far east as the Hindu Kush and beyond, was fueled in part by demographic growth. Armed conflict was as much a source of dislocation then as it is now, especially when the Greek world was in turmoil, as during both the Persian and Peloponnesian wars. Human trafficking was extremely prevalent as a result of both piracy and warfare. Those most at risk were women, children, and young adults. Large numbers of people were displaced to serve the military and political ambitions of tyrants and states. Dionysius I, for instance, ruler of Syracuse (405–367), forced tens of thousands to relocate to his capital, not only to provide a counterweight to Carthage's increasing domination of the western part of Sicily, but also to strengthen his hold over that city. In somewhat similar fashion the city of Megalopolis was established in 368 to reduce Sparta's military domination of the Peloponnese. Environmental disasters probably caused displacement, too, though the evidence is inconclusive.

As for individuals, *aeiphugia* (permanent exile) was a common punishment for those convicted of homicide and treason, since long-term imprisonment was not an option in the Greek world. We already hear of itinerants in the *Odyssey*, and they became numerous in the fifth and fourth centuries. The majority of metics who resided in Athens were probably motivated to leave their homes to improve their economic circumstances. At least some, however, must have been compelled by exigency. The topographical diversity of the Mediterranean landscape made it essential for the population of each micro-region to be highly mobile in order to capitalize on the full range of environmental opportunities (Horden and Purcell 2000, 385). An unknown number would have been either transhumance pastoralists, viz those who follow a fixed pattern of movement, or semi-nomadic, viz those who do not adhere to any fixed pattern. An example of a transhumance pastoralist is the herdsman in Sophocles' *Oedipus Tyrannus*, who spends his time "on Mount Cithaeron and places nearby" (l. 1127). A related phenomenon is that of internal migration, as for instance in the case of Athenians moving from one deme to another (Osborne 1991, 151–57).

To conclude, we tend to think of migration in negative terms, focusing on the causes, frequently catastrophic, invariably pressing, that propel individuals to abandon their homes and seek a livelihood often thousands of miles away. Alternatively, following the lead of Queen Elizabeth I and Enoch Powell, we decry the tension and disruption that refugees create in the host community and the strains that they place upon the social fabric. But it is impossible to overestimate the enormous benefits that have accrued to human society, including ancient Greek societies, from the intermingling of peoples of dissimilar ethnic identities.

2

THE WANDERER

The Centrality of Wandering to the Experience of Being Greek

From earliest times the Greeks were in restless movement, propelled from their familiar habitat either by human force or by the exigencies of their environment. And so it remained throughout antiquity. The whole earth, as Aeschylus puts it, "is forever trodden upon by wanderers" (*Eum.* 76). The fact that the Greeks had the psychological wherewithal to up-root themselves and settle elsewhere was largely due to the strength of their traditions, their powerful sense of collective identity, and last but by no means least the persistence of their religious practices, though in this regard we should not, of course, assume that they were unique among Mediterranean peoples. Rather, it was a matter of degree than of kind. For many, especially exiles and fugitives of low social status, there was a real possibility that they would remain on the move for all time.

Religion, I suspect, kept many of them from faltering. We have only to think of the central role that Apollo played in overseas settlement and of the importance of laying out sacred precincts whenever a new foundation was established to appreciate its stabilizing force. Migrants, exiles, fugitives, and their like would have continued to think of them-selves as being placed under the protection of the same gods they had worshipped all their lives—gods, we should note, who, though local to their home and community, accompanied them as fellow wanderers —as they sought to settle elsewhere. The unforgettable picture of the elderly Anchises clutching images of his household gods when Aeneas and his family are escaping from the ruins of Troy in Vergil's *Aeneid* book 2 would surely have resonated with the Greeks.

Even the stay-at-home Spartans gave importance to wandering and institutionalized it in the education of their citizens. As members of the *krupteia*, the secret commission that preceded their entry into the citizen body, at least some Spartan youths were required to live outside the *polis* for two years and "wander both day and night all over the country" (Pl. *Laws* 1.633c3–4). The experience of being a wanderer may therefore have been a precondition to becoming a Spartan citizen. As we shall note later in this chapter, moreover, the wanderer, at least from an ideological standpoint, was not seen in exclusively pejorative terms, despite the very real prejudice directed toward individuals who experienced this condition.

I use the word "wanderer" to describe the tens of thousands of men, women, and children who left their homes without a settled route or fixed destination. A wanderer in this sense was not only *apolis* (without a city-state), but also *aphrêtôr* (without a phratry), and *anestios* (without a hearth). In other words, he or she was stripped not only of civic and political identity, but also, even more fundamentally, of social and familial identity. Without attachment to a phratry, a Greek was denied membership of one of the primary divisions of Greek society, and without attachment to a hearth, he or she was estranged from that most basic unit of Greek life, namely the *oikos* or *oikia* (home, household).

In later chapters we will look at wanderers, whether their condition was temporary or permanent, in their different capacities as asylum-seekers, evacuees, economic migrants, and the like. Here, however, I offer an overview of their state of being, both psychological and physical, as it is depicted in a variety of literary genres excluding the historical, which is the primary focus elsewhere. It is all we have to compensate for the absence of qualitative data.

Homer

In the Homeric poems we encounter a variety of wanderers, including captives who have been sold into slavery, traders and pirates who have ventured far from their homelands, fugitives who are seeking to escape retribution for their crimes, and ethnic groups such as the Phaeacians who have uprooted themselves to escape a predatory neighbor. It is a world that surely reflects the reality of the eighth century.

In it the solitary wanderer was an object of suspicion and contempt. Smarting from the abusive and humiliating treatment he has received at the hands of Agamemnon, Achilles likens himself to "some kind of dishonored *metanastês* [wanderer]" (*Il.* 9.648). He does so in order to indicate that Agamemnon is treating him with the utmost scorn. He repeats the comparison when Patroclus requests that he be allowed to lead the Myrmidons into battle to halt Hector's assault upon the Achaeans (16.59). The contempt in which the wanderer was held would have been all the more unbearable in a culture that placed such a high store on honor. It was, moreover, Zeus, the father of gods and men, who was held responsible for making men homeless. "When Zeus the thunderer bestows unmitigated grief upon a man, he makes him an object of contempt and drives him over the face of the earth so that he wanders, honored neither by men nor by the gods," Achilles states at the end of the *Iliad* (24.531–33).

To wander without end in sight was the fate of Leto, when, pregnant with Apollo and Artemis and pursued by Hera, she roamed the Mediterranean in the hope of finding somewhere to give birth, before eventually the island of Delos welcomed her (*Hom. h. Ap.* 30–50). The unburied Patroclus describes himself as having to "wander pointlessly around the wide gates of Hades"—an eschatological view that retained its force in classical times (Hom. *Il.* 23.74; cf. Eur. *Suppl.* 62).

The world evoked by the *Odyssey* further testifies to the bleakness that beset persons of no fixed abode. Consider Odysseus's expression of gratitude to the swineherd Eumaeus for granting him shelter under his roof (15.341–45):

> I wish, Eumaeus, that you could be as dear to Zeus the father as you are to me for having called a halt to my *alê* [wandering] and my dreadful sorrow. No life is worse for mortals than *planktosunê* [roaming]. Even so, because of crippling hunger men have to endure grievous hardship, when wandering and pain and sorrow come upon them.

What further increased the misery of the vagrant was the fact that he aroused mistrust. In particular he was regarded as someone who was prepared to invent any rigmarole to earn a crust of bread. As Eumaeus had earlier pointed out, "*Alêtai* [wanderers] in need of provisions randomly tell lies and have no interest in telling the truth" (14.124–25). Odysseus's yearning to return home should thus be seen against the background of his despised identity as a wanderer. He resembles Menelaus, who "returned from people he could not have expected to return from, after being driven off course to a place so far across the deep that not even birds return from it in the same year" (3.319–22). Not for nothing, therefore, when he is making his way to the palace of the Phaeacian king Alcinoüs, had Athena advised him, "Don't look at anyone or ask anyone any questions. For they don't easily put up with strangers" (7.31–32). The fact that Odysseus was hospitably received by the Phaeacians despite his unprepossessing appearance and abject neediness is one among many signs that he has ventured into fairyland. In short the Greeks of Homer's age were in no doubt as to the dangers and discomforts of homelessness.*

Lyric and Elegiac Poetry

The Spartan elegiac poet Tyrtaeus (mid-seventh century), some of whose compositions are thought to have been recited during military campaigns, perhaps even in the immediate lead-up to a battle, contrasted the wretched condition of the man who has been driven from his homeland after his city has fallen with the valiant hoplite who sacrifices his life (fr. 10 *IEG*):

> It is good for a good man to fall and die fighting in the front ranks for his native land, whereas to leave one's city-state and rich fields and be a beggar is the most wretched condition of all, being a wanderer with one's

---

* Discussion of the fugitives Bellerophon, Tlepolemus, Phoenix, Patroclus, and Theoclymenus, all of whom appear in the *Iliad*, is reserved for chapter 8.

dear mother and aged father and little children and wedded wife. For he is hateful to everyone whom he approaches, being bound to neediness and hateful poverty. He disgraces his lineage and betrays his good looks. Since there is no consideration, no honor, no respect, and no pity for a man who is a wanderer, let us fight with courage for our land and die for our children and never spare our lives.

In other words, the exile is stripped of everything that makes life worthwhile. His disgrace is compounded by the fact that he is publicly deemed to be a coward. Here as elsewhere Tyrtaeus is exhorting the Spartans to risk their lives in battle, using as blackmail, so to speak, the wretchedness of a wanderer's life, which includes destitution for all his dependents.

Exile features in the work of the lyric poet Alcaeus of Mytilene, who was driven from his home on the island of Lesbos in ca. 600 as a result of political unrest. Alcaeus's comments appear in poems that were intended for delivery at a symposium or drinking party, and as such may well have had a political and/or educational function. The relevant lines appear to be autobiographical, though we cannot dismiss the possibility that he has adopted an imaginary persona. In one of them Alcaeus appeals to the triad of Zeus, Hera, and Dionysus "to save us from these labors and painful exile" (fr. 129.11–12 Campbell). In another he articulates his despair to a friend as follows (fr. 130B 1–9 Campbell):

I poor wretch live the lot of a rustic, longing to hear the assembly being summoned, Agesilaidas, and the council: the property in possession of which my father and my father's father have grown old among these mutually destructive citizens, from it I have been driven, an exile at the back of beyond ... (trans. Campbell).

The corpus that is ascribed to the elegiac poet Theognis of Megara (ca. 640–540?) also includes references to an exile's lot. Though it is possible that Theognis was forced from his homeland, the verses supporting this supposition, in which he claims that "other men possess my flourishing fields," are corrupt (ll. 1197–1202 *IEG*). Earlier in the collection he speaks with feeling about the isolation that a homeless person faces (ll. 209–210 *IEG*):

> To be sure, no-one is a friend and trustworthy companion to one who is a *pheugôn* [exile]. This fact is more painful than *phugê* [exile] itself.

Elsewhere, however, he warns his friend Cyrnus to steer clear of such people (ll. 333–34 *IEG*):

> Never be friends with a man in exile, Cyrnus, looking to the future. Once he returns home, he won't be the same man at all.

Tyrtaeus's gripe is that exiles try to ingratiate themselves to advance their own interests. But once they no longer need your services, their promises will quickly be forgotten.

Finally, these lines written by the Athenian elegiac poet and lawgiver Solon strike a decidedly and deliberately poignant note (fr. 36.8–12 *IEG*):

> I brought back many people to Athens, back to their homeland that was founded by the gods. Some of them had been sold legally, others illegally, still others had fled through compelling necessity. They no longer spoke the Attic tongue, as is the case when men wander in all directions.

We should bear in mind that Solon composed these lines in order to depict himself as an enlightened reformer who did outstanding service on behalf of his compatriots. The suggestion that the returnees had forgotten their mother tongue can only have been true of those who were children at the time of their departure.

Tragedy

The solitary wanderer features in tragedy. In Aeschylus's *Prometheus* we are told, evocatively, that Zeus has "thrown" her wanderings at Io for having rejected his advances (l. 738). When Oedipus discovers the horrific nature of the crimes he has committed, he repeatedly asks Creon to grant his request to become *apolis* (without a city) (Soph. *OT* 1381–82, 1440–41, 1518). We never discover whether Creon agrees to this, notwithstanding the fact that Apollo's oracle had previously ordered "the expulsion of the unholy one" (ll. 96–98). Euripides reverses the picture. The last scene of the *Phoenician Women* is devoted to Creon's banishment of Oedipus, which he administers in accordance with the seer Teiresias's pronouncement that the city will not prosper so long as he resides in it (ll. 1589–94). In response, Oedipus describes the awfulness of such a fate for someone like himself, who is blind, elderly, and without anyone to attend him. "If you expel me, you will kill me," he states flatly (l. 1621). Even so, his dignity prevents him from supplicating Creon to reverse his decision. His daughter Antigone, who was betrothed to Creon's son Haemon, condemns Creon for the hubris he has perpetrated against her father and then accompanies him into exile. "Banishment with a blind father is a disgrace," Oedipus warns her (l. 1691). "Miserable sufferings await you far from your homeland and the prospect of death in exile," Antigone responds, undeterred (ll. 1734–36). In Euripides' *Bacchae*, whose ending is known only from a twelfth-century Medieval adaptation titled *Christus Patiens*, Dionysus banishes Agave and her sisters from Thebes on the grounds that they have become polluted murderers through the killing of Pentheus.

Only once in tragedy does an exile describe his experiences abroad. This occurs in an exchange between Polyneices and his mother Jocasta in Euripides' *Phoenician Women*. Polyneices has just returned to Thebes after having been exiled by his brother Eteocles. Eteocles had refused to give up the throne to him after a year as had been agreed, and Polyneices returns with the intention of wresting it from him. In the interim he had been living in Argos (ll. 387–406):

JOCASTA: The first thing I want to know is what's it like to be deprived of one's city? Is it a terrible misfortune?

POLYNEICES: It's the greatest misfortune—greater than can be put into words.

FIGURE 2 Silver *statêr* (the largest coin struck by a *polis*) from Thebes, ca. 480–56. The obverse depicts a Boeotian shield, a pun on the word *bous* ("ox"), because Greek shields were covered with oxhide. The reverse depicts an amphora in an incuse (that is, recessed) square. Ill-advisedly, Thebes sided with the Persians when Xerxes invaded Greece in 480—an act of betrayal that the Greeks deeply resented. After the Battle of Plataea, the Greek coalition besieged Thebes and forced it to give up its Persian sympathizers. On the eve of the outbreak of the Peloponnesian War several unfortified Boeotian towns sent their civilians to Thebes for protection, thereby doubling the size of Thebes's population. Thebes was conquered by Philip II of Macedon in 338. In 335 it revolted unsuccessfully against Alexander the Great, who razed it to the ground. Some 30,000 men, women, and children were enslaved. The city was rebuilt in 316 but on a much smaller scale than its predecessor.

JOCASTA: What's its character? What hardship befalls exiles?

POLYNEICES: The worst is that you no longer have freedom of speech.

JOCASTA: You mean you're a slave because you can't say what you're thinking?

POLYNEICES: You have to endure the ignorance of those who have power over you.

JOCASTA: This is indeed painful, to have to suffer in silence the stupidity of others.

POLYNEICES: You have to act as a slave, against your nature, in order to make money....

JOCASTA: Didn't your father's guest-friends give you assistance?

POLYNEICES: They would if I'd have been wealthy. They don't do anything for you if you're not.

JOCASTA: Your aristocratic birth didn't advance you socially?

POLYNEICES: Not having any resources was the evil. My birth did not fill
my belly.

JOCASTA: It seems that one's fatherland is the dearest thing to mortal
man.

Polyneices' remarks are an indictment of the evils of exile. As we shall
see later, they were later used by philosophers, who refuted them point
by point to demonstrate that exile was in fact a tolerable, even desirable
condition for the man who is set on the path of enlightenment.

And yet Polyneices' fate is hardly that of the typical refugee, not
least because he had the good fortune during his sojourn abroad to
marry the daughter of Adrastus, the king of Argos. He thus speaks from
a position of immense privilege, even though, being the citizen of a
city-state that values freedom of speech, he bemoans the fact that he
had to keep a close watch on his tongue. Having to work for his living
was no less irksome to him. He says nothing, however, of the physical
hardship endured by refugees, of which he presumably knows nothing. In short, Euripides presents Polyneices' experience from a highly
privileged, Athenian perspective. This, we may note, contrasts sharply
with Sophocles's portrayal of the elderly and blind exile Oedipus, who
is almost pathologically fearful of being dishonored by anyone whom
he encounters (*OC* 49–50). Polyneices' most revealing statement is that
his Argive guest-friends refused to lend him any assistance on account
of his poverty—an interesting and no doubt realistic commentary on
the limitations of charity in the Greek world even when the two parties
were bound by ties of obligation.

Oratory

With good reason, given their personal agenda, defendants in Athenian
lawsuits commonly described exile as a fate worse than death. "If I go
into exile as a result of your verdict," says a fictitious defendant, "I shall
become a beggar in a foreign country, an old man who is *apolis*," *First*

Tetralogy 2.9). "No fate is worse than having nowhere to go, being without a city-state, enduring hardship every day, and being unable to look after one's family," says the representative of a group of Plataean exiles who are seeking to settle in Athens (Isoc. 14.55).

The most detailed account of a refugee's existence is found in Isocrates's *Aegineticus*, so-named because it was written on behalf of an unnamed political exile from Siphnus, who had been granted permanent residence in Aegina. In it the speaker describes what happened to his family when they sought to settle at Troezen (19.22–23):

> As soon as we arrived we succumbed to such severe diseases that I myself only just survived, though within thirty days I buried my young sister who was just fourteen years old, and not five days later I buried my mother as well. Previously in my life I had not known suffering, but now I had experienced both exile and having to live among foreigners as an alien. I'd lost my fortune, and in addition I'd witnessed my mother and my sister being expelled from their homeland and ending their lives among strangers in a foreign land.

Though the speaker has good reason to play on the sympathies of the jury, the tragedy he describes—that of the more vulnerable refugees, women especially, perishing from sickness or exhaustion soon after their departure—must have been all too familiar.

When he was not earning money from fee-paying exiles by writing on their behalf, however, Isocrates was far from sympathetic to the plight of migrants. In a panegyric composed in ca. 370 he heaped praise on Evagoras, king of Salamis on Cyprus, who, after fleeing from the island to avoid being assassinated, "despised the wandering existence of exiles, the way they seek help from others in order to facilitate their return, and the manner in which they ingratiate themselves with those who are inferior" (9.28). To escape such a fate Evagoras took matters into his own hands and succeeded in returning to Cyprus with the aid of some fifty companions. Commendable though it no doubt was, Evagoras's enterprise was hardly an example that the average exile could hope to emulate. In other political pamphlets Isocrates makes it clear that he has nothing but fear and loathing for the vast majority of refugees, on the grounds that they present a threat to the stability of civilized society.

Philosophy

The condition of the exile provided a fertile source of comment for philosophers of various persuasions. Democritus of Abdera (b. 460–57), who is jointly credited with Leucippus as the inventor of atomist philosophy, is said to have declared, evidently with pride, "I have wandered more extensively than anyone of my generation" (68 B 299.6–8 *DK*). Aristotle's successor Theophrastus took this to mean that Democritus considered himself to be richer than Odysseus and Menelaus combined— the two most famous wanderers of legend—on the grounds that he had become a true philosopher because of his travels, whereas they had merely acquired a heap of treasure (68 A 16 *DK* = Ael. *VH* 4.20). Pythagoras was also "a great wanderer," who visited Egypt, Babylon, Delos, and Crete, before finally establishing his philosophical school in Croton (Porph. *Vit. Pythag.* 6–21; D.L. 8.2–3).

The Cynic philosopher Diogenes of Sinope (ca. 412/403–ca. 324/21), quoting from a lost tragedy, described himself as "a man who is *apolis* [without a city], a man who is *aoikos* [without a home], a man deprived of his fatherland, a beggar, a wanderer, a man who lives from day to day" (D.L. 6.38 = *TGF, Adesp.* 284). Since the Cynics believed in the principle of living according to nature, this state of being did not, as he saw it, constitute a handicap. On the contrary, he claimed to have benefited from the change of perspective that homelessness had bestowed upon him. When someone was abusing him for being an exile, Diogenes is said to have replied, "It was my exile that turned me into a philosopher, you jerk!" (D.L. 6.49). In other words, his period in exile had liberated him not only from the constraints of the *polis* but also from dependency on the civic order, thereby enabling him to achieve his anti-political goal of self-sufficiency. Even so, the benefit to the soul has to be weighed against the inevitable wear and tear on the body. Though the testimony is of dubious authenticity, the elderly Plato is said to have declined an invitation to leave Athens and give advice about founding a colony on the grounds that the frailty of his age prevented him from "wandering about and running the kinds of risks that one encounters both on land and at sea" (*Ep.* 11.358e 6–8).

Plato's pupil Aristotle deemed the wanderer to be outside the human fold. He wrote (*Pol.* 1.1253a3–7):

> He who is without a city-state by nature and not by circumstance is either a rogue or greater than a human being. He resembles the man "without a phratry, without laws, and without a hearth" who is reviled by Homer (*Il.* 9.63–64), for he is by nature without a city-state and he yearns for bloody war. He is analogous to an isolated counter in a game of draughts.

Aristotle, it seems, was incapable of conceiving an acceptable alternative to a *polis*-centered life. And since the *polis* was a civilized and indeed civilizing force, the exile, having to fight for his survival on a daily basis, was in his view reduced to the condition of a brute animal. To make matters worse, such a person threatened the security of the *polis* to which he formerly belonged by yearning for "bloody civil war," since only as the result of an overthrow of the governing faction could he eventually hope to return to his homeland.

In his *Encomium of Helen*, probably dated 370, Isocrates chastised the sophists "for daring to assert that the life of beggars and refugees is more enviable than that of the rest of us." He continued, "They use this as proof that if they can speak to good effect on a worthless subject, then they'll have plenty to say about a subject which has real merit" (10.8). In other words, if sophists have the skill to refute what is blindingly obvious—that the life of the refugee is the most wretched condition imaginable—then there is no argument under the sun that they cannot prove or disprove. His comments make clear that the philosophical genre of consolation was already well-established by the first half of the fourth century, even though no extended example has survived from this period. It was to last for well over half a millennium.

The lot of those Greeks who were driven into exile was compounded of uncertainty, danger, hardship, and privation. All this, however, was nothing to a man of solid moral fiber. "Cheer up and get a grip of yourself. It isn't such a bad thing being an exile, especially if you put on a brave face. You might even see it as a welcome challenge to the fortitude you've developed all your life." That is because exile is primarily a state of mind, rather than a physical state of being. The evils that it visits upon an individual are therefore surmountable, partly by other attendant goods that one may possess to offset them and partly by a positive mental attitude. The first surviving treatise of this kind is by a Cynic philosopher called Teles, who flourished in ca. 235 BCE (pp. 21.2–30.1, Hense 1909). Though its composition lies outside the period covered by this survey, the arguments are likely to have been well-rehearsed, since, as we have just noted, the genre was already a century and a half old. Teles first sets up the proposition that exile, far from harming a man's soul or his body or even his possessions, actually gives him the opportunity to improve his material circumstances, as the lives of the mythical Phoenix and the historical Themistocles demonstrate. He then refutes a number of objections that might be raised to his proposition. For instance, in response to the claim that exiles are deprived of freedom of speech, Teles argues that many of them do indeed enjoy influence with foreign potentates; to the objection that exiles are not permitted to return home, he replies that no one alive has complete freedom of movement; and to the argument that exiles must suffer the disgrace of being buried abroad, he points out that this is the fate of many of the best men. He then ridicules Polyneices' request to be buried in his native Thebes, given the fact that his body will either rot or be scavenged wherever it lies (Eur. *Phoen.* 1447–50).

The longest surviving example in the genre is Plutarch's treatise *On Exile*. We do not know the addressee's identity for certain, but it is likely that his name was Menemachus, a native of Sardis in Lydia, who passed a portion of his exile in Athens at the end of the first century CE. Rather in the manner of a preacher delivering a sermon, Plutarch takes his cue from Euripides's *Phoenician Women* (l. 388–89):

What's it like to be deprived of one's city? Is it a terrible misfortune?
It's the greatest misfortune—greater than can be put into words.

He then seeks to demonstrate that exile, far from being an unbearable condition, is actually superior to any other kind of existence (*Mor.* 599f–600a):

> Suppose we assume that exile is something terrible, as the hoi polloi claim both in their conversations and in their verses ... it is still possible to blend misfortune with what is valuable and pleasant in your present circumstances, namely abundance, friends, freedom from politics, and the necessities of life. ... I bet that there are many citizens of Sardis who would prefer your situation, and be happy to exist on these terms in a foreign land, rather than be like snails that are glued to their shells and have nothing else of value or pleasure except for a home.

Urging fortitude and good cheer, Plutarch puts forth the bold proposition that "There is no such thing as one's native land by nature," on the grounds that "we are merely the occupants and users" of wherever we happen to be currently residing. Quoting Socrates' description of himself as a global citizen, Plutarch proclaims that the overarching sky, "within which no-one is an exile or an alien," constitutes the boundaries of a philosopher's real native land. He continues:

> By nature we are free and unconstrained. It is we who tie ourselves down, constrain ourselves, confine ourselves, and herd ourselves into uncomfortable and unhealthy quarters. Wherever a man has moderate means to live well, he is neither without a city nor a hearth, nor is he a foreigner.

Plutarch quotes from a certain Stratonicus, who inquired of his host on the tiny island of Seriphus what crime was punished there with exile. On learning that those guilty of fraud were exiled, he quipped, "So why don't you commit fraud and get out of this confinement." He claims that it is the exile who is truly blessed by fortune, since "the man who has one city is a stranger and a foreigner to all the rest" (600e–602b).

He then goes on to extol the advantages of the life of withdrawal, which include walking, reading and—joy of joys!—uninterrupted sleep. Few men of good sense and wisdom have died in their native lands, he claims, whether voluntarily or under compulsion. Next he lists exiles from legend and myth, including Theseus, Cadmus, and Apollo (602c–606d). Finally, moving to a higher philosophical plane, he glosses an observation by Empedocles of Acragas (ca. 492–32)—"I too am an exile from the gods and a wanderer" (31 B 115 *DK*)—as follows:

> All of us . . . are *metanastai* [migrants] and *xenoi* [strangers] and *phugades* [exiles] here . . . and it is truest to say that the soul is in exile and wanders, driven by divine ordinances and decrees.

Plutarch's treatise is a rhetorical *tour de force*, which seeks to prove what is counterintuitive in order to demonstrate the power invested in the human mind to shape its own destiny—or at least to shape its response to its own destiny. For all its speciousness it is not without the power to move by its eloquent and uplifting pleading. Dimly emerging from its paradoxical and contorted reasoning is the vision of a world stripped of boundaries that has a very modern ring to it, however far we may still be from achieving that ideal. That said, it is obvious that Plutarch, like so many others we have discussed, is analyzing exile from a position of privilege. His argument would have offered scant consolation to the vast majority of refugees, many of whom departed from their homelands with only enough food to keep them going for a few days. Even the well-heeled must have suffered some loss of status and income when they were deprived of their citizenship, as Polyneices had hinted at—a fact that Plutarch studiously ignores (Seibert 1979, 377).

Myth and Legend

From the fifth century BCE onward, and perhaps earlier, those Greeks who identified themselves as belonging to the Dorian ethnic group saw themselves as the product of a population movement that had taken place generations ago, and they fashioned a myth of exile and relocation to give that movement substance. As Herodotus wrote, "The Dorians were a people who wandered extensively" (1.56.2). He was referring to the notion that the Dorians were descended from the Heraclidae (or descendants of Heracles), whose ancestors had been driven into exile from the Peloponnese following the death of their founding father.

In light of what we have seen up to now about the status and condition of the wanderer, the belief that one's ancestors had returned to a land from which they had once been exiled or fled might seem to amount to a humiliating admission of ethnic inferiority. To have been forced to leave one's home for whatever reason conjures up notions of subservience, failure, and defeat—a hardly inspiring cultural inheritance to be burdened with. There was, however, a very different way of looking at it. From a propagandistic standpoint the claim that one's ancestors had in the dim and distant past been driven from their homeland could be turned to considerable political and ideological advantage: first, it served to exemplify their resolve and capacity for endurance, in that they had proven, over the course of several generations, their ability to survive against great odds; and second, it constituted proof that the gods had looked favorably upon their enterprise. Not for nothing the semi-divine Heracles became a god. The fact, moreover, that the Dorian Greeks thought of the migratory movement as a "return," was profoundly suggestive. It meant that their ancestors were not immigrants, far less invaders. These were exiles, returning to take possession of what was justly and indissolubly theirs.

No detailed account of the return of the Heraclidae has come down to us in literature. The legend is first alluded to by Homer, who makes an anachronistic reference to Dorians inhabiting Crete during the heroic age (Od. 19.177). The earliest author to make explicit reference to it is Tyrtaeus (fr. 2.14 IEG). Tyrtaeus is also the first to mention the three Dorian tribes—namely, the Dymanes, Hylleis, and Pamphyloi—into which those claiming descent from Heracles divided themselves (fr. 19.8 IEG). Two centuries later Herodotus briefly mentions the first unsuccessful assault of the Heraclidae on the Peloponnese following the death of Eurystheus, Heracles's tormenter (9.26). Thucydides' account, written perhaps a generation later, is more explicit (1.12.3): he claims that sixty years after the fall of Troy the Thessalians expelled the inhabitants of a town called Arne, who then migrated south and

settled in Boeotia. Then, twenty years later, the Dorians and the Heraclidae (he treats them as two separate peoples) seized the Peloponnese.
Thucydides traces the origins of the upheaval to factional squabbles
that were generated by the delayed return of the Greek army from
Troy. Irrespective of whether the Trojan War was a historical event or
not, his awareness of the consequences of an extended war in terms of
population movement is impressive. The earliest known account of the
"return," no longer extant in its original form, was written by Ephorus
in the fourth century (*FGrH* 70 F 117).

It has been convincingly suggested that the legend of the return of
the Heraclidae developed as a way of "providing the emergent states in
the Peloponnese with a respectable pedigree" (Hooker 1979, 360). As
such, it marks an important moment in the history of ideas, by illus-
trating how the experience of migration constitutes a way of affirming
and consolidating a collective sense of national identity, since a belief
in common descent contributes toward the development of group
formation. Irrespective of the degree to which the myth of the return
has any basis in fact—a subject that continues to be keenly debated by
scholars—its contribution to a sense of common purpose can hardly
be exaggerated. For the Dorians it was what Hall (1997, 185) has aptly
dubbed "a social reality," and that is what mattered in the end.

Claiming descent from a refugee movement was by no means exclusive to the Dorians. According both to Genesis and to modern paleon-
tologists, we are all descended from refugees. In fact the earliest human
encounter with reality in Genesis is symbolized by exile. The Hebrews,
too, claimed descent from wanderers, though in their case their wandering was prompted both by a yearning to escape servitude and by a
desire to worship the Lord unimpeded. It is worth noting, however, that
their "return" does not seem to have had the same emotional intensity
for the Dorians as the Exodus event did (and does) for Jews today. The
chief festival for those of Dorian identity was the Karneia, which was
celebrated in honor of Apollo Karneios. Unlike the Jewish festival of
Pesach, however, the Karneia seems not to have been a festival of lib-
eration, though the ritual of carrying model boats that formed part of
it may have commemorated the crossing into the Peloponnese from

Antirhion to Rhion. The Romans, too, saw themselves as a people descended from refugees and deportees.

From the period of the Persian Wars onward the Athenians, in contradistinction to the Dorians, maintained that they had always inhabited the same land. The earliest reference to this belief occurs in Pindar's *Second Isthmian Ode* (dated ca. 470), in which the poet asserts that the Athenians were descended from an early king called Erechtheus, who was born from the earth (2.19). Herodotus recognized the force of the claim by having the Athenian envoy to the Sicilian tyrant Gelon boast (7.161.3; cf. 1.56.2): "We, the Athenians, are the most ancient *ethnos* [people, ethnic group] and the only Greeks who are not *metanastai* [refugees]." Thucydides, speaking in his own voice, declared that Attica "was occupied by its original inhabitants" (1.2.5). He went on to explain that this was due to the poverty of its soil, which had failed to attract migrants from abroad and thereby (blessedly) eliminated the possibility of internal strife. In the Funeral Speech, too, he has Pericles remind his audience that they were descended from ancestors "who always inhabited the land without interruption in a succession of generations" (2.36.1). The belief features in Euripidean tragedy. Praxithea in Euripides' lost play *Erechtheus* proudly declares (fr. 50.7–10 Austin): "We are not a people brought together from elsewhere by the fall of dice like the inhabitants of all other cities, but we are *autochthones* [seeded or born from the ground]." Elsewhere, however, Euripides pointed out the absurdity of autochthony as literally understood, notably when he has Xuthus in the *Ion* assert categorically, "The earth does not bear children" (l. 542). Its absurdity notwithstanding, it became commonplace in the fourth century, notably in what Cohen (2000, 83) calls "the platitudinous banalities of encomia delivered at public funerals . . . [which] produced a genre that strung together formulaic tales to reify state ideology and mythological tradition." The following is an example, written no doubt to order, by the metic Lysias (*Epitaph.* 17):

The origin of the Athenian way of life is lawful. Most people derive from a mixture of groups and have taken possession of foreign soil by expelling others, whereas the Athenians are autochthonous and their fatherland is their true mother.

To conclude, no people chooses a myth of origin in order to feel bad about themselves, though it may be that the Athenians had an ideological edge over the rest in boasting of autochthony. In so doing, as Lysias indicates, they were making a case for ethnic purity. In analyzing ancient beliefs about autochthony, Detienne (2001, 55) trenchantly observes, "We provide ourselves with the means of better understanding those murderous throbbings of identity which pulse in the human societies of yesterday, today, and tomorrow."

3

THE SETTLER

Why the Greeks Settled Abroad

The Greek diaspora is most conventionally understood primarily in terms of what I shall call settlement abroad.* From the twelfth century BCE onward there is no evidence of any significant influx of population into mainland Greece. However, that period did witness a considerable migration from the mainland into areas previously uninhabited by Greeks. The details are hazy, but it seems that what scholars call the Ionian migration took place in the early Dark Age, around the eleventh and tenth centuries, and was in the nature of a mass exodus. It led principally to the settlement of the Aegean islands and the (now Turkish) Western Anatolian coastline in the region between Smyrna and Miletus. Some time later Aeolian Greeks living in Thessaly settled in the region north of Smyrna, while Dorians from the Peloponnese settled to the south of Miletus.

A second wave of settlement occurred in the archaic period and lasted from around the middle of the eighth century to the end of the sixth, though, as Hall (2002, 92) and others have noted, archaeology has now brought to light "a far more continuous sequence of contact and

---

* I have taken to heart Robin Osborne's observation (1998, 269): "A proper understanding of archaic Greek history can only come when chapters on 'Colonization' are eradicated from books on early Greece." See, too, Purcell (1990, 56), who complains of "the ethnic presumptuousness and false sense of purpose in the term" that had no bearing on the phenomenon. It was Finley (1976, 174), who first drew attention to the inappropriateness of the term "colony" as a description of early Greek settlements. I am grateful to one of the readers for Princeton University Press for directing me to the origins of the debate.

FIGURE 3 Silver *drachma* from Larissa, the chief city in Thessaly, ca. 365–44. The obverse depicts the head of the nymph Larissa, for whom the city was named. The reverse depicts a horse. An inland city surrounded by mountains and rich in pastureland, it was famous for its horses. The legend in the exergue reads (*LARIS*)*AIÔN*. Larissa was the first Thessalian city to strike coins. Polyperchon II, *tagos* (federal commander) of Thessaly, exiled many of its citizens in 370/69.

encounters between Greeks and non-Greeks." To the extent that we can measure difference between the two "movements," the one that began in the eighth century was more concentrated, at least in the number of settlements. First Sicily and southern Italy were settled, then the coast of Macedon and Thrace, followed by the Black Sea region, and then Cyrenaica in Libya, southern coastal France, and southeast Spain. The *mêtropoleis* (mother-cities) that sent out the largest number of pioneering ventures in the archaic period include Miletus (36 settlements), Corinth (13), Eretria (8), Chalcis (7), Megara (5), Thasos (5), Phocaea (4), Sybaris (4), and Syracuse (4).*

In the course of the archaic and classical periods, 279 settlements known commonly as *apoikiai* (literally "homes away from home") were founded in what today are Albania, Bulgaria, Egypt, France, Georgia, Italy, Libya, Romania, Russia, Sicily, Spain, Turkey, and Ukraine. Some 88 of them were secondary foundations—that is, founded by a mother-city that had itself been settled by a mother-city—notably those in Sicily and

---

* My count is from Hansen and Nielsen (2004, index 27 [pp. 1390–96]). It includes both foundations and refoundations. The numbers are necessarily approximate.

southern Italy. The movement took the form it did because the Mediterranean constituted "a milieu of interlocking routes onto which the coastlands and harbours faced" (Horden and Purcell 2000, 11). Though most settlements were founded overseas, some were established in adjoining territory, such as Acrae, Camarina, Casmenae, and Tyndaris, which Syracuse founded. The scale of migration to southern Italy was such that later historians referred to the region as *Megalê Hellas* (*Magna Graecia* in Latin), meaning Great Greece.

The later movement came to an end only when all the best coastal sites had been occupied. It would hardly have succeeded were it not for the fact that Greek traders were on the lookout for mercantile profit. This in itself, however, hardly explains why so many Greeks came to settle permanently abroad. One theory, less popular than it used to be, is that many settlements were founded in response to overpopulation and land hunger. This, too, is what some later Greeks believed. Plato spoke of "the masses having grown too numerous for the country's food supply" in relation to Crete (*Laws* 4.707e), and of "an excessive abundance of population" in general, viz a population that exceeded his recommended maximum of 5,040 citizens—that is, some 20,000 persons in all (5.740de). Archaeological evidence indicates that a handful of settlements, including Pithecusae and Syracuse, expanded very rapidly, partly perhaps in response to a demographic crisis. Paradoxically, however, there is no conclusive evidence of overpopulation in those parts of Greece that dispatched settlements in greatest numbers, viz the Megarid, Corinthia, Achaea, and Euboea, whereas those regions where it is inferred that substantial demographic growth did occur, notably Attica and the Argolid, did not send out any colonies (Whitley 2001, 125–26). Another explanation is resource fluctuations. The crisis on Thera that led to the settlement of Cyrene, for instance, was prompted by seven years of drought (see later). Political motives should not be ruled out either, notably in the case of settlements sponsored by tyrants. Nicolaus of Damascus (*fl.* first century BCE) claims that Cypselus, tyrant of Corinth, dispatched his political enemies as settlers to Leucas and Anactorium in ca. 630, "so that he could rule those who remained more easily" (*FGrH* 90 F 57.7). In conclusion, though overpopulation

FIGURE 4 Silver *statêr* from Anactorium, a coastal city in Acarnania, ca. 300–250. The obverse depicts the winged horse Pegasus, which was caught by Bellerophon while it was drinking at the fountain of Peirene in Corinth. The reverse depicts the head of Athena (or less likely Aphrodite) wearing a Corinthian helmet, probably because it was Athena who gave Bellerophon the magic bridle used to capture the winged horse Pegasus. Anactorium was founded by settlers from Corinth in ca. 630, and the coin type imitates that minted by Corinth. The Corinthians captured the city in 432 and sent out new settlers. In 425 the Athenians and their Acarnanian allies seized Anactorium after it had been betrayed from within (Thuc. 4.49). The site has yet to be excavated.

and land hunger may have been prominent factors, each community had its own specific mix of reasons for sending pioneers abroad.

It is commonly alleged that a specific group of settlements was established primarily as trading posts or, to define this group in a more limited sense, as ports-of-trade. A settlement of this sort is generally referred to as an *emporion*, viz "an *ad hoc* community [comprising] a mixed and possibly shifting population of traders" (*OCD⁴ s.v.*). The earliest and most northerly Greek settlement in the west, Pithecusae, modern-day Ischia in the Bay of Naples, is generally assigned to this category, though the exact nature and purpose of this foundation are still contested and there is evidence at the site for mixed marriages in the later period (Hansen and Nielsen 2004, 285–87). A major problem is that the word *emporion* is rarely used in ancient sources and it remains unclear whether the Greeks themselves actually employed it in the sense in which modern historians have interpreted it. We should be wary, therefore, of making a neat distinction between an *apoikia*, the usual word to describe a settlement, and an *emporion*. It is also important to take into account that an *apoikia*, like an *emporion*, would have had a number of temporary inhabitants, especially in its early days before its population became settled.

Not all ventures were state-supported and state-led. Ancient sources tend to emphasize the compulsory and organized nature of emigration, but some were private undertakings for personal gain. Examples include the settlement of Rhodes by the fugitive Tlepolemus (Hom. *Il.* 2.653–70; see later, chapter 8) and the abortive attempts by the Spartan prince Dorieus to settle first in North Africa and later in Sicily (Hdt. 5.42–45). Another private venture was that of the Athenian general Miltiades, son of Cypselus, to whom the Thracians living in the Chersonese appealed for military assistance in dealing with their neighbors. After receiving Delphi's approval, Miltiades accepted the invitation "because he was unhappy with Pisistratus's rule and wanted to leave." He sailed off with other Athenians of similar political persuasion and became a tyrant in the Chersonese (Hdt. 6.34–36). Though we only rarely hear of private ventures of this sort, the phenomenon may well have been more common than its infrequency in our sources suggests.

The Role of Apollo

We can hardly overestimate the courage, spirit, and enterprise of the pioneers. They succeeded, so the belief went, because they placed themselves under the protection and patronage of Apollo of Delphi, who in Callimachus's arresting phrase "weaves the foundations of settlements" (*Ap.* 57). Without Apollo's support those who ventured forth would have been as rudderless as the boat people who set sail from Vietnam, Haiti, Cuba, and elsewhere. With Apollo's patronage the crew of hopefuls was assured, in theory at least, an ultimate end to the wanderings, however riddling the description of the geographical location that he had given them. That at least is the picture we receive from our literary sources.

Indeed it is impossible to investigate settlement abroad without confronting the issue of Delphi's centrality to the whole enterprise.

Graham (1982a, 159) observed, "Believing in their gods and hence in themselves, [the Greeks] had the morale required to create permanent new communities far from home." More recently Malkin (1987, 112–17) described Delphi as "the hub" around which all aspects of the movement operated. Even so, it is by no means certain that all ventures were preceded by a consultation with the Delphic oracle. It is conceivable that the consultations were a fifth-century fiction, as Osborne (1998, 267) and others have pointed out.

Nonetheless we can be certain that every settlement had a unique and sometimes inspirational story to tell about its foundation and that it would have taken pride in handing that story down from one generation to the next. The uses of a foundation story were immense: it could forge a sense of common identity and it could justify a contemporary political agenda. Both Herodotus and Thucydides have preserved a number of such narratives, though to what extent they are grounded in historical fact is questionable. Regrettably no first-person account has survived, unless we count a short fragmentary poem in the first-person plural by the elegiac poet Mimnermus of Smyrna, which alludes with tantalizing brevity to the hubris and violence of the settlers who founded Colophon (fr. 9 *IEG* = Str. *Geog.* 14.1.4 C634). In addition, the natural philosopher and theologian Xenophanes, who was a native of that city, wrote an epic poem on the *ktisis* (foundation) of Colophon and another on the *apoikismos* (settlement) of Elea by Colophonians in flight from the Persians. His poems on the subject amounted to 2,000 lines in all (D.L. 9.20).

The Size and Composition of a Settlement

There is little evidence as to the typical number of pioneers who initially set sail in search of a new home. We have figures of 200 for Apollonia in Illyria (Steph. Byz. *s.v. Apollonia*) and 1,000 for Leucas (Ps.-Scylax 34 in *GGM* I.36). If we suppose that each of the 279 settlements required at least 200 to be a going concern, then the number of first-wave pioneers must have been roughly 56,000. However, some enterprises, like the one dispatched to found Leucas, are likely to have been considerably larger. If we include secondary and even tertiary influxes, and make allowance as well for ventures that came to grief with perhaps total loss of life, then the number of Greeks who sought to settle abroad is likely to have been several times that number.

Whereas the original nucleus would usually have been drawn from a single city-state, the next generation was frequently recruited from a variety of different city-states. Archilochus of Paros's characterization of those who founded Thasos as "wretches from all over Greece," for instance, is probably a pejorative reference to late-comers (fr. 102 *IEG*). Some three generations after Cyrene was founded from Thera in ca. 630, Delphi issued a pronouncement inviting "all Greeks to become *sunoikêsontai* [permanent settlers]." The oracle backed up its offer of land distribution to all-comers with the menacing prophecy that any-one who failed to take advantage of the invitation would come to regret it in the future (Hdt. 4.159.2–3). Since the god of Delphi seems often to have provided a somewhat imprecise description of an intended foundation's site, before setting out the pioneers would be advised to consult with traders who knew likely places in the designated region in which to settle. That they did so is suggested by the fact that all the chief cities that dispatched settlers—Chalcis, Corinth, Eretria, and so on—were very active in trade (Murray 1993, 107).

Designating the Oikist

We do not know how the leader of the pioneering group, termed *oiki-stês* (oikist, founder of an *apoikia*), was identified or appointed, unless we accept the "official" explanation—namely, that he was often desig-nated as such by the Delphic oracle. The typical oikist is likely to have been of aristocratic background but marginalized perhaps because of a physical defect or because he nursed a grudge against his peers. In other words, he may have been motivated as much by adverse circumstances as he was by ambition and greed. Before announcing his candidacy, he would probably seek Delphic approval. It may have helped not to

FIGURE 5 Silver *triêmiôbolon* (obol and a half) from Thasos, ca. 411–350. The obverse depicts a kneeling satyr holding a *cantharus* (drinking vessel). The reverse, which bears the legend *THA(SI)ÔN*, depicts an amphora. Thasos was settled by Parians in ca. 710–680 (Thuc. 4.104.4). The island experienced some eight instances of *stasis* from 411 to 340/39 (Gehrke 1985, 159–64).

appear too eager. Battus of Thera, for instance, who became the oikist of Cyrene, reportedly went to Delphi in order to request the god's assistance in overcoming his speech impediment only to be informed that the oracle had nominated him to be the leader of an overseas settlement (Hdt. 4.155).

The set of qualities that an oikist needed was indeed formidable. They included charisma, self-confidence, shrewdness, self-reliance, and resourcefulness. No less importantly, he had to be a seasoned mariner, ideally equipped with a first-rate knowledge of the principal sea routes and some experience of the region in which he hoped to establish a settlement. The eventual success of the enterprise would have depended very largely on his unwavering determination, given the challenges that he faced both from the elements and from the indigenous population. He might also be presented with a challenge to his leadership whenever the enterprise faltered or faced a setback, as indeed Aeneas did on more than one occasion. The fact that the job description included the ability to demonstrate superhuman strength of will in the face of overwhelming odds is suggested by the fact that the oikist may occasionally have been worshipped as a hero after his death in the belief that his posthumous presence would continue to protect the settlement.

Identifying the Site

When Odysseus arrives at the land of the Cyclopes, the poet describes the amenities of the uninhabited island that lay close to the mainland as follows (Hom. *Od.* 9.131–36, trans. Lattimore (1965)):

> Not a bad place at all; it could bear all crops in season, and there are meadow lands near the shores of the gray sea, well-watered and soft; there could be grapes grown there endlessly, and there is smooth land for plowing; men reap a full harvest always in season, since there is very rich soil. Also there is an easy harbor.

Homer is wearing the cap of a potential oikist. It was evidently an instinctive habit of mind, and no doubt many of his contemporaries would have evaluated a site's potential in similar terms. Describing the island as "not a bad place at all" is a striking example of litotes. It is a mark of the Cyclopes' isolation, self-centeredness, and uniquely favored circumstances that they have never seen fit to turn their favored location to their own advantage. Though settlements varied considerably in geographical configuration, regular features include an offshore island (or islands) like this one, a peninsula, and a river on one or both sides of the settlement. Many sites, too, especially those in southern Italy, were situated at the end of a trade route that had been in existence long before the settlement was founded.

Presettlement contacts between Greeks and indigenous peoples must have been commonplace, as Graham (1990, 45) pointed out, and they may well have been a factor in determining the choice of a site, as our literary sources occasionally indicate. Arganthonius, the wealthy Iberian king of Tartessus in southern Spain, invited the Phocaeans "to settle wherever they wished" in his kingdom (Hdt. 1.163.3). Though the Phocaeans rejected his offer, some settlements are known to have been founded at the invitation of the local population, or at any rate with their consent, such as Megara Hyblaea in Sicily (see later, chapter 4). Even so, we cannot assume that the oikist would have decided on a precise location before setting sail. And even if he had, unforeseen circumstances might well have forced him to change his plans and seek an alternative elsewhere.

Choosing the Pioneers

Though many pioneers, lured by the promise of a better life, joined on a volunteer basis, others were conscripted (*katalegesthai*). A fourth-century inscription relating to the establishment of the settlement at Cyrene in North Africa, which allegedly preserves the original wording of an original decree of the seventh century, required one of every two brothers to relocate from Thera to the new foundation, the intention being that no *oikos* would be without an heir (*ML* 5.28–29 = Fornara 18; cf. Hdt. 4.153). The decree also contains the following proviso, which testifies to the severity of the situation that prompted the undertaking in the first place (ll. 37–40):

> Anyone who refuses to sail if he is sent out by the city shall be liable to the death penalty and his property will be taken from him. Anyone who receives him or harbors him, whether he be the father aiding the son or a brother his brother, shall suffer the same punishment as the man who refuses to sail.

I know of no other example of pioneers being threatened with death should they attempt to return home, but the Therans are unlikely to have been exceptional in passing such a measure. The 279 settlements that flourished (not to mention the unknown number that failed) would have included many pioneers who, even if not compelled by the state to abandon their homes, did so only with grave misgivings. Irrespective of whether the fourth-century copy replicates the language of the seventh-century original or not, the proviso strikes a highly plausible note, since "no-one leaves homes and embarks on colonization for fun" (Graham 1982a, 157).

Imagine for a moment the plight of an impoverished farmer, living in a city-state in which famine is beginning to take its toll. The harvest has failed for two or three years in a row and all his supplies are exhausted. An emergency assembly is held to discuss the crisis and at the end a vote is called. The majority decision is that some of the population will be required to emigrate. The farmer has no alternative. Starvation is staring him in the face. Volunteers are called for. Unless enough people step forward, the state will introduce conscription, at which point the terms under which pioneers depart may be far less favorable. He considers his options. As if the threat of starvation is not enough to motivate him, those advocating emigration hold out the enticing prospect of a better life that will elevate his social status overnight.

The fact that the pioneers often went out "on equal and fair terms," as inscriptions state, indicates that in theory all social distinctions were abolished as soon as the expedition departed. It also suggests that the majority of volunteers came from the lower classes, like the "wretches from all over Greece," whom Archilochus mentions. After all, it was they who had the least to lose and the most to gain. Physical fitness was the primary qualification in the selection process. Those who were feeble or past their prime would have been a distinct liability. Mental resilience was also essential. It goes without saying that pioneers are more likely to be focused and committed if they are single. For all these reasons raw youths, particularly younger brothers, and widowers who were still in the prime of life, not destitute but hoping to improve their economic circumstances, were probably selected or conscripted in greatest numbers.

We almost never hear of women accompanying settlers abroad, and, even if this was occasionally the practice, they would have been few in number, given the fact that the success of the enterprise was dependent upon able-bodied men. Women represented an encumbrance, added to which their chances of survival would have been much lower than that of men. Of 27,000 emigrants from France to Canada between 1608 and 1763 only 1,767 were women, and a comparable imbalance between the sexes may have existed in antiquity (Poussou 1994, 27; cited in Horden and Purcell 2000, 385). One exception to the rule is priestesses, who may have been included in the first wave of settlers because female deities were served by women (for example, Str. *Geog.* 4.1.4 C179: cult of Artemis in Massilia). Another is prostitutes. Though female Greek names occur on gravestones in some cemeteries, it is possible that they belonged to indigenous women who had adopted these names once they married.

Departing

Probably on the eve of departure both those setting sail and those remaining at home took a solemn oath binding one another to the terms of their agreement in perpetuity. The decree relating to the foundation of Cyrene indicates that the entire population attended the ceremony, including "men, women, boys, and girls." It also alludes to wax images being burnt when the oath was taken, with a curse upon anyone who breaks the oath to the effect that "he shall melt and dissolve like the images, both himself, his descendants, and his property . . . whereas those who abide by the oath, both those sailing to Libya and those remaining in Thera, will enjoy an abundance of good things, both they and their descendants" (*ML* 5.44–51 = Fornara 18).

According to late sources the pioneers were provided with fire from the city's sacred hearth, with which to kindle a fire in the sacred hearth of their new settlement. The purpose of this ritual is thought to have been to symbolize the indissoluble tie that existed between mother-city and settlement, but it may have had other meanings as well, such as to guarantee the continuity of the life force in their new homeland (Graham 1982a, 148–49). Possibly some rite of exclusion revoked the pioneers' ties with their compatriots, though we do not hear of any. Having performed a sacrifice to secure a favorable omen, they embarked on pentecontors, viz warships capable of being rowed by 50 oarsmen that had a capacity of perhaps 80. If, as seems likely, a minimum of 200 settlers had been identified, a flotilla of four ships set sail. Who funded the flotilla goes unrecorded, but it is likely that the oikist was at least partially responsible.

From this moment on the oikist was in complete charge, no longer bound to the authorities in the mother-city and invested with the power of life and death over his companions both during the voyage and in the settlement's foundation period. This is indicated by the word *autokratôr* (one possessing full powers), which is used in the fifth-century decree that lays down the terms for the establishment of the Athenian colony at Brea (*ML* 49.8–9 = Fornara 100). Under his leadership, the pioneers had now assumed the status of homeless persons, even in the eyes of their compatriots. They were in effect *xenoi* (foreigners), if not out-and-out *phugades* (exiles). Their condition as outsiders is graphically illustrated by Herodotus's account of the fate of the pioneers who departed from Thera (4.156). Having failed to establish a settlement on the coast of Libya, they decided to return home. When they tried to land on the island, however, their former compatriots pelted them with missiles to prevent them from disembarking. They had no alternative but to set sail for Libya again, knowing this time there was no turning back. Eventually they established a settlement on an island called Platea that lay off the Libyan coast.

Only under extreme conditions did settlers have the right of return. The inscription relating to the settlement of Cyrene states that they will be permitted to reclaim their citizenship and property on Thera only if they are still experiencing "unavoidable hardship" after five years have elapsed following their departure (*ML* 5.33–37 = Fornara 18). Since "unavoidable hardship" meant suffering loss of life, it was highly unlikely that many of them would ever have seen their homes again, and had they done so they would no doubt have been treated as much with contempt as with compassion (cf. also *ML* 20.6–10 for terms on which pioneers can return to their homeland).

Laying the Foundations

From the moment they finally disembarked on dry land and decided to call it home the settlers had numerous tasks to fulfill. In many cases they would have been taking possession of virgin land. So they would have had to fell trees, prepare the ground, and sow the grain. Their first task was to construct palisade defenses to make sure that their settlement was secure against attack. They also had to establish it on a religious footing. This meant erecting a temporary wooden altar to Apollo *Archêgetês* (Founder-Leader), who, as we have seen earlier in this chapter, had overall responsibility for the success of their venture. It was the oikist's responsibility to provide the settlement with a name (Thuc. 4.102.3). He also had to lay out precincts for the gods and designate a place to bury the dead. Early on, too, he had to identify land for cultivation, probably allocating it through a process of allotment (Hom. *Od.* 6.6–10). The likelihood of factious disagreement breaking out at this juncture must have been considerable, particularly since the allotments could hardly have been identical in quality, even if they were identical in size. From the middle of the fifth century it was customary to lay out the streets according to a regular grid plan, as was the case at Thurii (D.S. 12.10.7). Some seventy *poleis* in all were divided up in this way (see Hansen and Nielsen 2004, 1367).

The oikist was assisted in his undertakings by a *mantis* (professional seer), who was credited with having divined the precise location of the settlement and who conducted rites consecrating it to the gods. Over the course of time the *mantis* also had to help draw up *nomima* (regulations, customs, traditions) that would form the basis for the settlement's social, political, and legal institutions. This included the division of the citizen body into tribes, the appointment of magistrates, the introduction of a lawcode, the establishment of a pantheon, the arrangement of the festival calendar, and much more besides. Overall *nomima* constituted "a powerful assimilative force when settlers of varied origins would join a nucleus of founders and coopt their identity by being absorbed in the social order" (Malkin 2012, 189–97).

It would no doubt have taken many years, perhaps as much as a generation, before a settlement was fully up and running. It is unclear how long the oikist would have retained the status and powers of an *autokratôr* or by what process those powers would have been handed over to a properly constituted government. Once the *apoikia* had been established on a secure footing, however, its inhabitants would typically dispatch a pentecontor back to the mother-city to report on its progress and invite additional settlers to join them (Schaefer 1960, 87).

Experiencing Nostalgia

The burden of leaving one's homeland was both physical and psychological, involving as it did separation from parents, siblings, grandparents, and friends, and in some cases from wives and children as well. The image of Odysseus "longing for his wife and his homecoming" at the beginning of the *Odyssey* no doubt captures perfectly the emotional state of many Greek settlers, since very few of them could expect to set eyes on their relatives again (1.13). In *Aeneid* book 3 Priam's son Helenus has reproduced Troy in miniature, with all the features of the former city (ll. 349–51). Being reminded constantly of his former life, he is wedded to the past, incapable of embracing the present—unlike Aeneas, who looks forward, no matter how dimly, to what lies ahead. Though some mother-cities—most notably, Corinth, Miletus, Syracuse, and Sinope—retained close political links with their offshoots, sometimes keeping them in a state of dependence, there is no evidence that any of them sought to facilitate emotional ties. How could they, given the constraints of communication in the ancient world? Besides which, it would have been highly counterproductive. The new settlement had to assert its own independent identity and validity from the start or else it would calamitously fail.

Leaving the Greek-inhabited world would have been like leaving planet earth. Even though in many cases there would have been pre-settlement trading contacts between the local people and the mother-city, there was no knowing what alien forms of life existed out there nor whether the group would survive its many ordeals. To comprehend the mindset required, we have only to reflect upon Homer's portrait of Odysseus, regardless of the fact that Odysseus is seeking to return to his homeland rather than establish a new homeland elsewhere. He exhibits exactly the kind of craft, guile, and instinct for survival that would put him head and shoulders above his fellow-competitors in any reality TV show. They are, moreover, precisely the qualities that have distinguished anyone who sets out for an unknown destination in any period of history. His encounters with bizarre peoples evoke both the worst-case and best-case scenarios of what lay beyond the edge of the Greek-inhabited world. It is no surprise that the *Odyssey* was composed at a time when the expanding and hard-pressed population was seeking a new home-land in Sicily and southern Italy—the region where Odysseus's fanciful adventures are likely to be situated.

Relations between Settlers and Indigenous Populations

Our focus up to now has been on those bands of plucky Greeks who demonstrated such courage and enterprise in sailing out into the unknown. But that is only half the story of any diaspora. We should not ignore those who were on the receiving end of their courage and enterprise. The subject is one that is fraught with complication. As Tsetskhladze (1998, 44) has said of the Black Sea region, "Not many things are clear in the study of Greco-native relations," and the same can be said of Greek-native relations in general. What is axiomatic, however, is that in many cases the settlers would have had to displace the local population, and that to achieve this they resorted to violence.

There are no accounts seen through the eyes of non-Greeks and only brief references to non-Greeks in Greek sources. Thucydides tells us that the Sicels, the native inhabitants of Sicily, were repeatedly driven out of their territory, first by the Corinthians who settled in Syracuse, then by the Chalcidians who settled in Leontini, and later by other Chalcidians who settled in Catania (6.3.2–3; cf. D.S. 11.76.3). Archaeology confirms Thucydides' testimony at least in the case of Syracuse, where the neighboring Sicel site at Pantalica was abandoned shortly after the original Corinthian foundation was established (Vallet 1968, 110f.). It remains unclear, however, whether relations between Sicels and Greeks were antagonistic from the start or whether they became so only when the Greeks began to multiply and represented a threat to Sicel survival. There was a tradition that Androclus, a legendary king of Athens and one of the leaders of the Ionian migration, expelled the non-Greek inhabitants of Ephesus before establishing it as a Greek settlement (Str.

Geog. 14.1.21 C640). There is also evidence that the indigenous population that occupied the territory around Sybaris and Taras in southern Italy fled as a result of Greek migration.

Though violent encounters between indigenous peoples and Greeks are likely to have been commonplace, there were occasions, too, where the settlers and the local inhabitants lived amicably together. A case in point is Emporium, modern Ampurias, on the coast of northeast Spain, where the local people, known as the Indicetans, chose to share the same circuit wall with the Greeks in the interests of security and so cordoned off their residential area by a cross-wall. In time they created a unified state with combined Greek and non-Greek institutions (Str. *Geog.* 3.4.8 C160; cf. Demetriou 2012, 45–46). At Incoronata and Policoro (probable site of Siris), cities in the instep of Italy, burials dating to the seventh century suggest, too, that Greeks and natives coexisted peacefully. The Phocaeans, who began founding settlements in the western Mediterranean in the sixth century, seem to have made a point of cultivating close relations with the local inhabitants (Domínguez 2006, 448). We have already seen that the Iberian king Arganthonius invited Phocaeans to settle in his territory, and it may be that the Phocaeans circulated the story to demonstrate the high esteem in which local peoples held them. There is also evidence that, from the late-fifth century onward, indigenous Oscans living in Neapolis were granted citizenship and even allowed to hold magistracies (Lomas 2000, 177).

We should also bear in mind that 129 of the 279 settlements were indigenous from the start and became hellenized only as the result of a long period of acculturation (Hansen and Nielsen 2004, index 27 [pp. 1390–96]). In such cases we should probably be thinking not of a sizable contingent arriving in one burst, so to speak, but of a steady but constant trickle of individuals over time.

At times what had begun as a fruitful and symbiotic relationship eventually became hostile and exploitative. In some cases the settlers became reliant on local labor and enslaved the indigenous population. This is what happened at Syracuse, where the land that belonged to wealthy Greek aristocrats known as *gamoroi* came to be worked by an underclass of locals who were "slaves called the *Kullurioi*," possibly a pejorative term meaning "donkey men" (Hdt. 7.155.2; cf. Arist. fr. 586 Rose). At Heraclea Pontica on the shores of the Black Sea a tribe called the Mariandynoi, nicknamed "the gift-bearers," placed themselves under the control of Greek settlers, for whom they worked as laborers in return for military protection (Pl. *Laws* 6.776cd; Ath. *Deipn.* 6.263e). Last, the Byzantines are said to have treated the indigenous Bithynians as the Spartans did the helots (Phylarchus *FGrH* 81 F 8). As Fisher (1993, 33) put it, these three instances may be "only a few tips of a large number of nasty icebergs."

Conversely the Greeks themselves sometimes underwent subjugation. At Posidonia, for instance, according to the fourth-century historian and musical theorist Aristoxenus, the indigenous Lucanian population enslaved the Greeks and suppressed their culture. The immigrants were left with one festival "where they gather together and remember their old language and customs, and after weeping and wailing with one another, they depart" (*ap.* Ath. *Deipn.* 14.632ab; see Lomas 2000, 178). Most striking is the case of Greeks inhabiting the Black Sea region and the western coast of Turkey, who from the late sixth century onward fell under the control of the Scythians, Lydians, and Persians, though as Graham (1982a, 156) notes this was not accompanied by barbarization of the Greek communtites.

Women Settlers

Though a few women from the mother-city probably joined a settlement once it had been securely established, it is by no means certain that they would have settled in sufficient numbers to enable it to reproduce itself. There would often, therefore, have been a compelling need to recruit local women. "Recruiting" could take various forms, viz intermarriage, abduction, rape, or any other type of carnal heterosexual union. The Greeks preserved the belief that they occasionally resorted to violence to resolve the shortage of women. Herodotus tells us that the Athenian settlers who participated in the foundation of Miletus abducted a number of Carian women (1.146.2–3). They later added to this outrage by massacring the women's fathers, husbands, and sons. This incidentally had the consequence of depriving the women of any legal status, since without a male relative to give them away, they could not marry their abductors. The women thus took a solemn oath "neither to eat with the men [viz their abductors] nor to mention them by name." Though Herodotus enjoyed cordial relations with the Athenians, he originated from Halicarnassus in Caria, and it is perhaps for this reason that he dwells on the plight of the indigenous population. The story is indicative of the tense (to say the least) domestic relations that abduction would have generated, though not surprisingly perhaps there is no record of a similar instance in our sources.

The Greeks did not in principle disapprove of intermarriage, and it is likely to have occurred frequently when a settlement was in its infancy. Sicel names found on gravestones in Greek cemeteries at Syracuse have been plausibly interpreted as evidence of intermarriage. As the *apoikia*'s population stabilized, intermarriage may well have decreased. However, there is evidence that it was still being practiced in the late fifth century, notably between the Elymians, a local Sicilian people, and the Greeks who inhabited western Sicily (cf. Thuc. 6.6.2). Very occasionally, too, we hear of dynastic marriages between Greeks and neighboring non-Greeks, no doubt intended to cement good relations between the two (see Hall 2002, 102–3, for examples).

Intermarriage has profound consequences both for the individuals concerned and for society as a whole. The offspring of such unions often experience cultural and social isolation, as well as political disenfranchisement. Was the experience of the children of ethnically mixed unions living in a Greek settlement broadly similar? Some at least are likely to have grown up bilingual and may well have felt a stronger attachment to the indigenous culture. Thucydides (4.109.3–4) tells us that the indigenous populations of many of the cities on Athos were bilingual, and this may well have been the case, too, on the island of Lemnos, which was inhabited by several non-Greek peoples before it was settled by the Greeks (*IG* XII.8, pp. 2–3; Boardman 1999, 85–86).

Setbacks, Failures, and Eventual Successes

Pioneers could never predict the outcome of their voyage. Violent tempests are a frequent occurrence in the Mediterranean, and once their ships had been driven off course, they would be exposed to all manner of dangers, as the tortuous wanderings of Odysseus and Aeneas make abundantly clear. As their ships could hold only limited supplies of food, they would frequently have to stop to replenish their stock, often taking enormous risks to do so. Starvation, both along the way and on arrival at their destination, was an ever-present danger. One cannot but sympathize with a Corinthian pioneer called Aithiops, who, en route to found a settlement at Syracuse, became so hungry that "he sold his mess-mate the *klêros* [allotment of land] which he had drawn by lot for the price of a honey cake" (Archilochus fr. 293 *IEG* = Ath. *Deipn.* 4.167d).*

The dangers that attended even the best-prepared undertaking can hardly be exaggerated. The Greeks have for the most part recorded their successes, not their failures. An exception is Ennea Hodoi, which the Athenians made nine attempts to settle before they finally established a viable foundation nearby at Amphipolis (see appendix B). Some ventures no doubt ended calamitously and with total loss of life. Others faltered because the settlers simply lost their resolve. Some settlements dissolved because they succumbed to internal strife. Yet other expeditions will have succeeded only after many twists of fortune. Often pioneers settled in what they believed to be an ideal location, only to be ejected after a few months or even a year—the situation that Vergil explores with profound insight in the *Aeneid*, in which the hero makes many missteps and is forced to relocate several times before reaching his final destination, only to face concerted opposition once he does.

Sometimes the original Greek pioneers quarreled with the newcomers. This is what happened at Thurii, where those who originally

---

* Recent bone analysis conducted by anthropologists at the Smithsonian Museum of Natural History has revealed that the English settlers at Jamestown, Virginia, had to resort to cannibalism to survive the harsh winter of 1609–10, and we need hardly doubt that Greek settlers would have been equally hard pressed.

established Sybaris treated *hoi prosgraphentes* (those who signed up later) as second-class citizens (D.S. 12.11.1–2). Among other injustices, the Sybarites claimed the land that was nearest to the urban center and allocated to the newcomers land that was far away. In response, *hoi prosgraphentes*, who greatly outnumbered the Sybarites, rose up and massacred the latter. They then summoned pioneers from all over Greece and apportioned land on equal terms. Even in cases where the original inhabitants and the later settlers managed to coexist peaceably, some resentment may well have simmered beneath the surface, ready to flare up at a moment's notice.

Thucydides' account of the wanderings and travails of some enterprising settlers from Megara perfectly exemplifies the complex trajectory that many pioneers had to undergo (6.4.1–2). These Megarians first settled at Trotilus on the east coast of Sicily. Their foundation did not prosper, however, so they threw in their lot with some Chalcidian pioneers, who had settled at Leontini. In time, however, the Megarians fell out with the Chalcidians and were expelled from Leontini. They went on to found Thapsus, situated a short distance away along the coast. When their leader died, they again became refugees. At the invitation of a Sicel king called Hyblon, they founded Megara Hyblaea a few miles to the north of Thapsus, naming the city in his honor (see later, map 2). There they lived peaceably for 245 years until Gelon, the tyrant of Syracuse, expelled their descendants. A face-saving device to explain the failure of a pioneering venture was to tell tall tales about encounters with monstrous races. Although Herodotus did not himself believe in the reports of a goat-footed people who lived in the mountains nor in men who sleep for six months at a stretch, as related by the bald-headed Argippaioi (4.25.1), even the ultra-rationalist Thucydides did not deny outright the existence of the Laestrygonians or Cyclopes. In fact he concludes his excursus on the peoples of Sicily with the comment, "We have to satisfy ourselves with what the poets said and with what anyone else knows" (6.2.1). Given their level of ignorance of the world around them, many Greeks probably set out from home with the fear of encountering monstrous races never wholly absent from their minds (Garland 2010, 162–66).

The Athenian Postscriptum

The great age of sending out settlers came to a close in the early sixth century. The movement did not, however, cease altogether. At least seventy-two settlements were founded in the fifth and fourth centuries. The most active city-state in the fifth century was Athens, which from 478–404 sent out some thirty bands of settlers, many to existing sites whose populations they had banished for this purpose (see appendix B). We read of two types of Athenian settlements, *apoikiai* and *klêrouchiai*, though ancient authors do not invariably differentiate between the two. The number of settlers varied considerably—from as few as 250 at Andros to as many as 4,000 at Chalcis. Whereas membership of a cleruchy was restricted to Athenian citizens, noncitizens were also permitted to settle in *apoikiai*. In some *apoikiai* in fact the noncitizens greatly outnumbered the citizens. It goes without saying that the non-Athenian settlers would have been required to be supportive of Athens's foreign policy and political system, since the institutions of the settlement would be modeled closely on those of Athens.

Though some settlements had a clear military and strategic importance, notable examples being Amphipolis on the northern coast of Thrace and Thurii in Lucania, this was not true of all, so other motives for founding them must have been in play. One we can detect was to increase the number of hoplites in Athens's army. The majority of cleruchs and colonists probably belonged to the lowest property-owning class—namely, the *thêtes*—though those in the next-to-lowest class, known as the *zeugitae*, also participated. Cleruchs received a *klêros* (allotment), from which their name *klêrouchos* (allotment holder), derives. As such they became automatically liable to military service as hoplites.

The Alexandrian Post-Postscriptum

At the end of the period covered by this survey Alexander the Great founded settlements in places as far away as eastern Iran, where urban entities had previously been rare. Plutarch (*Mor.* 328e) puts their total number at "over 70," but this is greatly exaggerated, and the number of actual *poleis* may have been as few as six. They were founded for a variety of purposes. Though the majority was military, some were primarily commercial. This was certainly true of the greatest of them all, Alexandria on the Nile Delta, which was founded in the spring of 331.

With the possible exception of Alexandria on the Nile Delta, the populations of most of the foundations comprised Greeks and Macedonians on the one hand and indigenous peoples from the surrounding neighborhood, especially nomads, on the other. Griffith (1935, 23) calculated that in total Alexander settled 36,000 Greeks and Macedonians abroad. Most were mercenaries, who would have had little say in the matter. Not surprisingly, some, "longing for Greek customs and the Greek way of life," and "submitting only out of fear of Alexander," resented having to settle so far away from their homelands (D.S. 18.7.1). So when Alexander died, they abandoned their settlement and headed back to Greece. We do not know how many remained, and we learn little about how they fared.

4

THE PORTABLE *POLIS*

Uprooting the City

An overseas settlement constituted a select number of pioneers who agreed to found a new *polis* in the hope of preserving or bettering their lives. In the face of an overwhelming threat to their livelihood, however, perhaps due to pressure from hostile neighbors or as the result of an environmental catastrophe, all the inhabitants of an existing *polis* might take the radical step of abandoning their homes and relocating elsewhere, a process that is generally known as *metoikêsis* or *anachorêsis*.

It is easily overlooked that the *polis* was inherently portable, since our literary sources emphasize the predilection for permanence and continuity. As we shall see, however, permanence and stability were not invariably the norm. We know for a fact that the Phocaeans, the Teians, the Clazomenians, the Ephesians, the Milesians, the Samians, and the Athenians, as well as the inhabitants of many Sicilian cities, either underwent relocation or at least seriously considered the option, and that is aside from the various peoples who were deported, whom we shall discuss in the next chapter.

The Greek *polis* did not relocate only as a single unit, reconstituting itself in a form similar to its previous instantiation. It did so also in association with other *poleis* by a process known as synoecism, though we should note that the word *sunoikismos* (literally "the joining together of households") does not occur until the hellenistic period. A synoecism took place when two or more neighboring *poleis* or, alternatively, two or more neighboring villages consolidated their inhabitants in a single entity, either by incorporating them into an existing *polis* (or *poleis*) or by combining to build an entirely new *megalopolis* (literally "big *polis*"). Such a process had two quite separate aspects, one political, requiring the assimilation of citizens from different states into a single community, and the other physical, geographical, and architectural (Hornblower 1982, 83).

There must have been many occasions, however, when vested interests prevented the inhabitants of a city-state that was facing assault and possible destruction from reaching an agreement about what course of action to adopt, with the result that a stand-off between two factions occurred. A case in point involves the Cimmerians, a people who originally lived to the north of the Caucasus. When the Scythians were about to invade their territory, the Cimmerians held a debate about what action to take. The *dêmos* advocated flight, whereas the aristocracy voted to stay put. Eventually, the aristocracy were forced to commit collective suicide in order to avoid a worse fate at the hands of the invaders (Hdt. 4.11). Though it seems highly unlikely that the Cimmerians argued the merits of relocation in the manner indicated, debates of this sort may well have taken place when a Greek city-state was threatened with subjugation.

Likewise when a *polis* fell to an invader, those who could do so would escape in the *mêlée* and attempt to relocate elsewhere, which is what Aeneas and his companions did when Troy fell to the Greeks. Vergil's description of the flight of Aeneas with his family at the end of *Aeneid* book 2 is the most graphic account we possess from antiquity of the consequences of such a catastrophic event. The prospect of escaping in such circumstances would have been extremely bleak, especially if the refugees included a cumbrous assortment of noncombatants, including women, children, and the elderly. At sea, the refugees would have been vulnerable to pirates and tempests, whereas on land they could easily fall prey to bandits and wild animals.

The portability of the *polis* is indicated by the fact that those seeking to relocate continued to identify themselves as citizens of their original *polis* until they had succeeded in establishing new roots elsewhere, at which point they would usually assume a new name. Aeneas and his companions describe themselves as Trojans until they make peace with the indigenous population of Italy and agree to be called Latins. In other words, a *polis* remained intact so long as there were citizens to identify themselves with it, irrespective of whether it existed in a fixed location. This practice—sense of ownership, we might call it—tells us much about the nature of Greek citizenship and Greek identity.

It goes without saying that relocation would have been extremely traumatic, especially when it was forced upon a population virtually overnight. This was equally true whether it came about as the result of a collective decision reached after considerable debate and self-searching or whether it was imposed from the outside. Inevitably, some of the refugees would be forced to abandon a family member before they departed, while others would become separated from a loved one along the road, just as Aeneas loses his wife, Creusa, in his haste to escape. And once a family member was left behind, there was little chance of him or her being found again. It should come as no surprise that a persistent theme running through accounts of resettlement is the reluctance of a sizable percentage of the population to participate in the venture, rather than to await the arrival of the enemy, on the grounds that life was no longer worth living. That is precisely the mental state of Aeneas's father, Anchises, when Troy is being burned to the ground—before the occurrence of portents that induce him to see a future beyond Troy. His is a mental state drawn from life.

Instances of Relocation in Early Greek History

Relocation was known to Homer, who reports that the Phaeacians under the leadership of King Nausithoüs chose to abandon their original foundation and settle in Scheria, "far away from men who eat bread." They took this decision because they were being harried by the Cyclopes, a people who were "greater in strength" than they were (*Od.* 6.4–10). Nausithoüs's decision paid off—at least in the short term. The Phaeacians led an idyllic, if cloistered, existence. That was until the shipwrecked Odysseus fetched up on their shores and inadvertently destroyed the island's ecology, since his hosts had angered Poseidon by harboring the accursed refugee. Surrounded by an impenetrable wall after his departure, they will suffer the fate of never being able to seek a homeland elsewhere—a nightmare scenario for a community now denied a "home from home."

Homer's brief reference to the relocation of the Phaeacians to Scheria, although imaginary, reflects a contemporary reality. Similarly, "barbaric" neighbors were threatening the East Greeks at the time when the poems were taking shape (Demand 1990, 28–33). It was pressure from the Scythians that initially drove the Cimmerians to abandon their ancestral lands and plunder the land the Greeks were inhabiting (Hdt. 1.6.3). Their departure produced a power vacuum that was filled by the Lydians, who, unlike the Cimmerians, were bent on systematic conquest and domination of the territory they entered. It was to escape the Lydian advance that shortly before 650 some of the inhabitants of Colophon decided to relocate to Siris, a city in the instep of southern Italy—one of the earliest instances of long-distance relocation on record (Arist. fr. 584 Rose; Ath. *Deipn.* 12.523c).

The Persians, too, if we are to believe Herodotus, contemplated relocating to a more abundant and agreeable land in the early days of the reign of Cyrus the Great, founder of the Achaemenid dynasty (9.122). Cyrus, however, rejected the suggestion on the grounds that rugged terrain produces brave men, whereas terrain that is easier to work produces weaklings. In consequence, the Persians "chose to rule while inhabiting a poor land, rather than be enslaved to others while cultivating the plains." And that, incidentally, is how Herodotus chooses to end his *History*, which indicates the importance he attached to the theme of relocation. Likewise, as we shall see next, when the Persians began advancing against the Ionians, two city-states chose to relocate rather than submit to their rule.

The Relocation of the Phocaeans

The first to do so were the Phocaeans, whose lengthy and convoluted migration Herodotus reports in detail (1.164–65). Phocaea, modern Foça, was an Ionian city on the western coast of Anatolia that lay to the north of the Gulf of Smyrna. Some ten or fifteen years before the Persians had begun encroaching on the region, the Phocaeans had received an offer from Arganthonius, king of wealthy Tartessus, to relocate (see earlier, chapter 3). They declined, seemingly because the prospect of an easy life outside their homeland held no appeal for them. So instead, and with Arganthonius's help, they erected a wall around their city, intending initially to resist the Persians at all costs.

When the Persians began to advance to the coast around the middle of the sixth century, Phocaea became one of the first Ionian *poleis* on their hit-list. It soon became evident that resistance was hopeless. Just as the Persians were poised to capture the city, however, their Median general Harpagus promised to leave the Phocaeans alone on condition that they agreed to destroy one wall tower and one house—a symbolic token of their submission to Persian rule. Playing for time, the Phocaeans requested a day to debate his proposal. Harpagus agreed, and in the meantime they hastily put on board ship all their women, children, and movable property (including, we are told, their gold and silver statues), and set sail. The result was that the Persians gained possession "of a city that was emptied of people," as Herodotus (1.164.3) evocatively put it.

This was not the end of the matter. For many years the Phocaeans were a people without a homeland, compelled to suffer a string of disappointments. They first offered to buy the nearby Oenoussae Islands from the Chians, evidently because they wished to resettle close to their original homeland. The Chians turned down their offer, however, fearing that the Phocaeans, who were a highly successful mercantile community, would eventually pose a threat to their own commercial interests. So with considerable daring the refugees returned to Phocaea, slew the Persian garrison that had been left in charge of their city, and laid a solemn curse on all those who refused to accompany them in search of a new homeland. This they did by sinking a mass of iron into the sea and making everyone take a solemn oath not to return to Phocaea "until the iron rose to the surface again,"—that is, never. They now saw themselves as a people without a homeland, though they continued to identify themselves as Phocaeans, which, as we have seen, was commonly the case when a *polis* became portable.

We learn much about the psychological toll of relocation from the fact that neither their oath nor fear of the Persians was sufficient to make all the Phocaeans keep their word. Soon after they set sail for Alalia, a *polis* on the west coast of Corsica that had been founded some twenty years beforehand by their former compatriots, half of the refugees were overcome by "a pitiful longing for their city and the customs of their country" (1.165.3). In consequence, the homesick half detached itself from the main fleet and sailed back to Phocaea. Though we do not know what became of them, it is highly doubtful they escaped the clutches of the Persians. Yet such was their longing—pitiful indeed—that they preferred servitude or even death to the hazards and travails of relocation.

The more enterprising half sailed on and established themselves in Alalia, as they had planned to do from the start. Though their legal status in Alalia is unclear, the enlarged settlement seems to have constituted a synoecism of sorts. The fact, moreover, that the new settlers were permitted to establish sanctuaries to their gods provides evidence of their integration. For five years or so the combined population made a livelihood by plundering and raiding. In time, however, their actions provoked the anger of both the Etruscans and the Carthaginians, who joined forces against them. A naval battle ensued, in which the Phocaeans got the better of their enemies. It was, however, a Pyrrhic victory, since 40 of their pentecontors were seized and the remaining 20 were rendered unfit for battle. These ships now returned to Alalia, where, after picking up all the women and children, the majority sailed to Rhegium on the toe of Italy. Since a pentecontor could accommodate about 80 persons at most, the maximum possible number of refugees would have been 1,600. At least some of those who failed to get on board were stoned to death by the Etruscans. The Delphic oracle later ordered the Etruscans to atone for their crime by establishing a hero cult in the victims' honor.

On arrival at Rhegium, they encountered a man from Posidonia, who helpfully informed them that Delphi had not intended them to establish a settlement but only a hero cult on Corsica. At his suggestion they set sail once again and succeeded in taking possession of the de-

MAP 1 The western migration of the Phocaeans.

serted city of Elea, which lay a few miles to the south of Posidonia. No doubt it was in Posidonia's interest to have allies who could help them in their struggle against the neighboring Italic peoples.

Herodotus obviously admired the Phocaeans for their courage and tenacity—he explicitly states that they had refused the relatively generous offer of the Median commander Harpagus to accept submission because they wanted to remain free (1.164.2)—and the main point of his lengthy digression, which comes relatively early on in his narrative, seems to be that their hard efforts paid off in the end. Their story thus celebrates the lengths to which the Greeks (or at least some Greeks) were prepared to go to maintain their Greekness rather than become the slaves of the Persians. Greekness, he suggests, had less to do with walls and houses than it did with a state of mind.

He ends his account by referring briefly to the evacuation of the inhabitants of the island of Teos, who, like the Phocaeans, managed to escape from Harpagus in the nick of time (1.168). The Teans sailed to Thrace, where they founded the city of Abdera, perhaps by purchasing land from the local inhabitants. Previously a certain Timesias of Clazomenae had acquired the site, but he had been driven out by the Thracians. As a result the site was unoccupied at the time of their arrival, just as Elea had been at the time of the arrival of the Phocaeans.

Plans to Relocate "All the Ionians" in the West

The mass migration of the Phocaeans and the Teans before the Persian advance into Asia Minor in the 540s speaks eloquently of the fear and hatred that the Persians instilled in the Greeks. According to Herodotus there was more than one occasion when the Ionians en masse thought the unthinkable, viz the wholesale evacuation of their homeland. The sixth-century sage Bias of Priene, anticipating Persia's increasing domination in the region, had allegedly recommended that they should undertake a mass exodus to Sardinia and "found a single city of all the Ionians." In this way, he declared, they would "free themselves from slavery, become prosperous by taking possession of the largest of all the islands, and rule over others" (1.170.2). Herodotus judged the plan to be "eminently practical" and observed that, if the Ionians had adopted it, they "would have prospered more than any other Greeks." Bias, if we are to lend the story any credence, evidently understood what are referred to today as the human development gains that derive from relocation.

Following the failure of the Ionian Revolt five years later, the inhabitants of Zancle invited the Ionians to found a new city in northeast Sicily at a place called Kale Akte (Fair Promontory). The only Greeks to take up the offer, however, were the Milesians and the Samians, and in both cases it was only a fraction of their populations that did so. The majority of the Milesians who had survived the fall of their city to the Persians in 494 had already been deported, while the only Samians who were attracted by the offer were the oligarchs who had been driven into exile as a result of civil strife, following their decision to abandon the Ionians in their revolt shortly before the Battle of Lade (Hdt. 6.13, 19.3, 22–23).

Their story has several twists. On its way to Sicily, the flotilla was intercepted by Anaxilaus, tyrant of Rhegium, who urged the Ionians to take possession of Zancle, which happened to be undefended at the time of their arrival. Before the Ionians could act upon this suggestion, however, the Zancleans learnt of Anaxilaus's plot and rushed home, having first elicited military support from Hippocrates, the tyrant of Gela. Hippocrates, however, proved to be duplicitous. He took possession of Zancle, imprisoned its king, and gave the city to the Ionians. He did so on condition that the Ionians hand over half of all the urban slaves who were living in the city and all the agricultural slaves. In addition, he enslaved and deported most of the citizen population. However, when he transferred 300 of the most prominent Zancleans to the Ionians and urged them to slit their throats, the latter refused to do so. Herodotus clearly admired the Samians both for their resourcefulness and their compassion—he fails to mention the Milesians for some reason—and he ends by saying, "So this is how the Samians, having escaped from the Persians, acquired Zancle, the most beautiful city of all" (6.24.2).

One other attempt at relocating all the Ionians occurred. After their victory over the Persians at the Battle of Mycale in 479 the Greeks held a conference to weigh the merits of permitting them to settle in the west. Evidently there was a strongly held opinion that it would be impossible to protect the Ionians in the long term and that one day the Persians would exact savage reprisals for their defeat. The Spartans and others recommended that the Ionians should be relocated in those port cities on the mainland that belonged to Greeks who had "medized," viz sided with the Persians. The Athenians, however, vehemently opposed the plan on the grounds that the Peloponnesians had no right to determine the fate of the Athenian settlers who resided in Ionia. One of the consequences of the debate was to strengthen Athens's hand by drawing attention to the Ionians' need for naval protection (Hdt. 9.106.2–4).

Themistocles' Threat to Relocate the Athenians

On the eve of the naval battle that was fought in the straits off Salamis in 480, the commanders of the Greek fleet heatedly debated whether to hold the line or withdraw south. When the Athenian general Themistocles strongly advocated holding the forward position, a Corinthian named Adeimantus taunted him with being "a man without a fatherland" and objected to any proposal being put forward "on the recommendation of a man who is a mere *apolis* [without a city]" (Hdt. 8.61). His point was that Athens, following the evacuation of its women and children, no longer enjoyed the status of an independent polity.

Themistocles angrily retorted that his city-state and its land were greater than that of the Corinthians, and that if the allies withdrew and made no attempt to defend the straits, the Athenians with their fleet of 200 triremes would set sail for Siris in southern Italy, "which has long been ours and which an oracle prophesied we would settle"(8.62.2). As the Athenians had already evacuated their civilian population to Salamis, Aegina, and Troezen in advance of the Persian invasion of Attica (see later, chapter 6), Themistocles' threat had to be taken seriously. His advice carried the day, and the Greeks won a spectacular victory.

Did Themistocles seriously contemplate the permanent resettlement of the entire citizen body? Was he in fact telling the truth about the oracle? Was Herodotus inventing? Scholars have generally been skeptical. True, months earlier Apollo had recommended that the Athenians should "flee to the ends of the earth." Even so, the difficulties in implementing an operation of this magnitude on the eve of a battle are mind-boggling, particularly since the civilian population had already been dispersed to three separate locations. Only a fraction of the evacuees could have been transported to Italy, and many thousands would have been abandoned to their fate. It is also uncertain what reception the Athenians could have expected from the people of Siris, particularly since the latter would have had little if any advance warning of their arrival. In light of the fact that the refugees would have been under armed escort, however, they would have had little option but to receive them. An alternative possibility is that Siris was unoccupied at the time, though the problem with that hypothesis is that it was certainly occupied by ca. 440 (Hansen and Nielsen 2004, 294).

Even if Themistocles' threat seems like a desperate stratagem and a not entirely plausible one at that, there were, as we have seen, precedents for an overnight evacuation. A naval victory in the straits off Salamis was, moreover, anything but a foregone conclusion, and, if the Greeks had lost, the Athenians would have had no alternative but to relocate instantly with what ships they had remaining. It is not unlikely, therefore, that Themistocles did have such a plan in mind, though there is no evidence that he ever put it to the Athenian Assembly. It might have seemed too defeatist.

The Synoecism of Olynthus

In 433/2 the people of Chalcis in Thracian Chalcidice, fearing that war with Athens was imminent, tore down the walls of their coastal towns and relocated to Olynthus "in order to form one strong city." They did so with the help of Perdiccas, the local king of Macedon (Thuc. 1.58.2). Not all the people in the region participated, however. Resettlement almost invariably met with stout resistance among some of the population.

The Chalcidian settlers did not build an entirely new city. Instead they expanded an existing one. But though there is archaeological evidence for an increase in the population of Olynthus at this date, it is highly unlikely that everyone moved to the new city at once. It is interesting to note that the walls of the expanded city were made of mudbrick and erected with haste, which suggests that the settlers were eager to preempt Athenian aggression. Those who joined in the merger now identified themselves as a new political unit known as the Chalcidian League.

The Athenian Fleet as the *Dêmos* in Exile

A particularly interesting instance of *polis*-relocation is recorded in the case of the Athenian fleet. When the oligarchy known as the Four Hundred seized power in Athens in 411, it "slew a handful of men whom it considered useful to get rid of, imprisoned others, and exiled others still" (Thuc. 8.70.2). Learning of its actions, the sailors in the Athenian fleet that was stationed at the island of Samos revolted against the Four Hundred, claimed that it and it alone represented the *dêmos*, and formed itself into a self-determining political entity. It did so on the grounds that "the *polis* had revolted from them" (8.76.3). The sailors in the fleet thus came to resemble other *poleis* in exile. They held meetings of the Assembly, in which they voted to replace all the generals and trierarchs whom they suspected of treason by others who were favorable to their cause; heard an appeal from Alcibiades that led to his election as general; and received ambassadors from the Four Hundred and from Argos (Thuc. 8.76.2, 77, 81.2–82.1, 86). It was largely as a result of the opposition of the fleet that a more moderate form of government, known as the Five Thousand, ousted the Four Hundred, after the latter had ruled Athens for about four months. The Five Thousand were in turn replaced by a full democracy when the fleet won a significant naval battle over the Spartans at Cyzicus, an event that signaled the dissolution of the fleet's separatist status in exile.

Dionysius I of Syracuse's Program of Mass Resettlement

Nowhere was the *polis* more portable than in Sicily. In the debate that took place in the Athenian Assembly in 416 about whether to dispatch an expedition to conquer Sicily, Alcibiades contemptuously observed,

FIGURE 6 Bronze coin from Syracuse, time of the tyrant Agathocles, 319–289. The obverse depicts the head of Persephone. The reverse depicts a butting bull. In the exergue is the legend *SURA-KOSIŌN*. Gelon, tyrant of Gela, transferred his capital to Syracuse in ca. 485 and by mass deportation caused it to double in size. By the middle of the fourth century, however, Syracuse's population had declined appreciably. It was resettled in ca. 340 by Timoleon under an oligarchic constitution. Syracuse experienced nineteen instances of *stasis*—the highest number of any *polis*.

"Its cities are populated by mixed hordes of people and they have easy *metabolai* [transfers of people] and additions of citizens. No one feels he has his own homeland. . . . Everyone thinks that either by specious words or by party strife he can get hold of someone else's land and settle there, if things don't turn out for the best" (Thuc. 6.17.2).

Alcibiades' words must be taken with a grain of salt: he wanted to persuade the Athenians that the conquest of Sicily would not present them with a major challenge. Even so, his observation was not wide of the mark. Seven years previously the aristocracy of Leontini had deported the commoners and relocated them to Syracuse, where they were granted citizenship (Thuc. 5.4.2–3). And though the Greek cities of Sicily had been relatively stable over the past few decades, in the first half of the fifth century the Deinomenid tyrants had resettled the populations of Catania, Camarina, Euboea, Megara Hyblaea, and Naxos (see later, chapter 5). The earliest mass resettlement, though not in this case a deportation, had taken place in ca. 485 under Gelon, tyrant of Gela, who had permitted 10,000 mercenaries to settle in Syracuse. Not surprisingly the Syracusan citizens regarded the mercenaries as interlopers, particularly those who were Sicels and Campanians, and for this reason they had denied them full political rights (D.S. 11.72.3).

Dionysius I, who became tyrant of Syracuse in 405, knew better than anyone that mercenary settlements could be usefully turned to political as well as military advantage. They served not only as payment for services rendered, but also as a stronghold of loyal support. It is also the case that a mercenary army is a portable *polis* in waiting, so to speak, since mercenaries look to their commander for settlement when their period of service draws to an end. The earliest one to be founded in Dionysius's reign, however, owed nothing to his initiative. A year after he took control of Syracuse, some Campanian mercenaries, whom he had recently ejected from Aetna because of their untrustworthiness, marched to Entella, where, "having persuaded the citizens to receive them as *sunoikoi* [fellow-inhabitants], they attacked them by night, slew those of military age, married the wives of the men they had deceived, and took possession of the city" (D.S. 14.9.9). How Dionysius responded to this flagrant act of rebellion is not recorded. Henceforth, however, he took personal responsibility for settling his mercenaries.

Accordingly in 403, after seizing Catania and enslaving its population, Dionysius resettled it with a contingent of Campanian mercenaries. In the same year he enslaved the population of Naxos. Naxos (not to be confused with the Aegean island of the same name) was the oldest Greek settlement on Sicily. He now destroyed it, leaving perhaps only its temples intact, and handed over its territory to the neighboring Sicels in the hope of gaining their support (D.S. 14.15.2). He also took Leontini and removed its population to Syracuse, this time leaving the city intact. Two or three years later he founded a colony at Adranum, about ten miles to the northwest of Mount Aetna. After defeating Carthage in 396 he resettled Leontini with his mercenaries (14.78.2–3). Last in 392 he expelled "most of the Sicels who were living in Tauromenium" and "selected and settled in their place the most suitable of his mercenaries" (14.96.4).

By the time of his death in 367 Dionysius had relocated the inhabitants of no fewer than fourteen *poleis*, five of which were intended for his mercenaries. With the exception of Messina (formerly Zancle), all the cities on the east coast of the island were now either abandoned or

MAP 2 Sicily.

had been resettled. Much of southern Italy was also within his sphere of influence. But though he had confined the Carthaginians to the northwest part of Sicily, he had not succeeded in his larger aim, which was to expel them from the island altogether. Moreover his resettlements, particularly those involving mercenaries, were a failure. Mercenaries almost by definition lack the skills and mindset that are needed to create a stable urban entity and promote civic virtues. Nor should we forget the horrendous consequences that his program of self-aggrandisement had for the tens of thousands of indigenous peoples who became displaced, of whom we learn virtually nothing.

Timoleon's Revival of Syracuse

Some twenty years after the death of Dionysius I, the Corinthian general Timoleon undertook one of the most ambitious ancient urban relocation programs on record. In ca. 365 Timoleon had been implicated in the killing of his brother and had been living under a cloud ever since. When he was approached by Syracusan exiles living in Corinth, he decided to throw in his lot with them. He arrived in Sicily in ca. 346/5 at the head of a small army to challenge Dionysius's successor and eldest son, Dionysius II. After successfully besieging Syracuse, Timoleon drove Dionysius into exile. He then defeated the Carthaginians and went on to "uproot all the tyrants throughout the island" (D.S. 16.82.4). He too, however, never succeeded in driving the Carthaginians out of Sicily.

Even so, it was extremely fortuitous for the Sicilian Greeks that Timoleon arrived at the exact moment he did. By all the evidence, archaeological as well as literary, Dionysius I's policy of mass resettlement had been a failure, and at the time of his death the Sicilian *polis* could fairly be described as a failing enterprise. Writing of the period immediately prior to Timoleon's arrival, Plutarch describes the island as "*anastatos* [uprooted] and *apolis* [bereft of cities] because of wars, added to which most of the cities were occupied by barbarians of mixed ethnicity and by unemployed mercenaries" (*Tim.* 1.1). Horses, he goes on to say, were grazing in the Syracusan agora, other cities were inhabited by deer and wild pigs, and their citizens were neglecting the summons to fulfill their civic duties (22.4–5; cf. D.S. 16.83.1). One estimate is that the population of Syracuse, which at its peak exceeded 100,000, had now sunk to below 10,000, doubtless as a result of "casualties in war and strife, executions and banishments, voluntary withdrawals of citizens unable to make a livelihood in conditions of insecurity" (Westlake 1969, 284). Though Plutarch's description of Sicily as *anastatos* and *apolis* may be something of an exaggeration, the picture he paints of long-term devastation is amply supported by archaeological data.

Now that he had dealt with the Carthaginian threat to Syracusan independence, in ca. 340 Timoleon appealed to Corinth for help in increasing the city's population. The Corinthians responded by inviting the Syracusans and Sicels who were living outside Sicily to return to their ancestral home "on equal and fair terms," much as if Syracuse were a new foundation (Plu. *Tim.* 23.6). Initially only a few of them answered the call. It is fair to assume that many of those who had left their homelands long ago had done very well for themselves and were reluctant to exchange their current prosperity for an uncertain future in what many of them no longer thought of as home. So the Corinthians extended the offer of Syracusan citizenship to all Greeks, irrespective of ethnicity. Once again the response was disappointing. Eventually, however, when peace was formally concluded with Carthage, some 60,000 Greeks volunteered, including 10,000 mercenaries (Plu. *Tim*. 23.6 = Athanis, *FGrH* 562 F 2; cf. D.S. 16.82.5).

Many of the Sicilian Greeks who migrated to Syracuse had been living in Carthaginian territory. They did so in part to escape the tithe that the Carthaginians exacted from all subject peoples domiciled within their territories. Indigenous people who had long been hellenized probably contributed to the ranks of the immigrants as well. Another group comprised deportees from Leontini, whom Timoleon forcibly relocated to Syracuse. The Leontines had earned his resentment because their tyrant Hicetas had opposed him when he first arrived in Sicily (D.S. 16.82.7). It may be that an exchange of populations took place between the deportees arriving from Leontini and some of the colonists who had settled in Syracuse (Westlake 1969, 290).

It probably took several years before Syracuse's fortunes finally revived. No population transplantation ever runs entirely smoothly, and there was considerable opportunity for disagreement even within the ranks of the newcomers. Those who arrived first would obviously have received preferential treatment, including, most conspicuously, larger allotments of land, and this is likely to have built in resentment from the beginning, especially if there was only a relatively short lapse of time between the arrival of other groups of settlers. We learn, too, that Syracusan exiles returning from abroad were permitted to repurchase their former homes, which meant that the current owners had to be bought out and in effect evicted (Plu. *Tim*. 23.6–7). We do not know how they were compensated. It is also unclear how the original owners would have provided proof of ownership. Probably many bogus claims were lodged by those falsely claiming to have been exiled. Timoleon also resettled the town of Aetna, after first slaughtering its mercenary population (D.S. 16.82.4).

Timoleon's goal seems in large part to have been to rehellenize Sicily, both by increasing the size of its Greek population and by reducing the numbers of foreign mercenaries. As the author of the *Eighth Epistle* attributed to Plato had noted several years earlier, there had been a real possibility "may the god prevent it—that the Greek language would be eliminated from the whole of Sicily, either by the Carthaginians or by the Italians" (353e). It was largely due to Timoleon that this danger had finally been averted, and for that he deserves much credit. He excelled, we might say, in what Purcell (1990, 47) described in a masterly phrase as "the creative politics of management of the human resource." He also seems to have been an accomplished self-publicizer. He could not have succeeded without convincing thousands of Siceliots that they would benefit by supporting his cause, as he arrived in Sicily with inadequate forces to win by military might alone.

Writing of the year in which he established a new constitution for Syracuse (339/8), Diodorus states: "An abundance of new settlers now flooded into Sicily and thanks to a long period of uninterrupted peace the land was again cultivated, producing crops in all their variety" (16.83.1). Plutarch is equally congratulatory of Timoleon's efforts, ending his biography with the following eulogy (39.7): "Using the constitution and the laws which he introduced, the Syracusans lived happily for a long time." Timoleon was buried in the agora at Syracuse—a fitting honor for a man who had earned his status as the city's second founder and a strong indication of the depth of gratitude he had earned from its people.

Mass Resettlement in the Peloponnese

Mainland Greece also experienced mass resettlement in the fourth century. The decisive defeat of the Spartans by the Boeotians and their allies at the Battle of Leuctra in 371 resulted in the establishment of three cities in the Peloponnese. The initiative was aimed at containing Spartan influence and reducing its people to a second-rate power. The first of the three was Mantinea in eastern Arcadia (371/370), actually a

MAP 3 The containment of Sparta.

refoundation. This was followed by Messene in the southwest Peloponnese (369) and Megalopolis in southwest Arcadia (368). I will reserve discussion of Messene for chapter 11, since it was promoted as the refoundation of a settlement whose people had continued to exist in exile for hundreds of years.

Mantinea. Largely at the prompting of the Argives, Mantinea had been refounded as a synoecism of four or five Arcadian villages some time between 464 and 459. In 385, however, the Spartans had carried out a *dioikismos* (the division of a *polis* into its original communities or villages) (D.S. 15.12; cf. Str. *Geog.* 8.3.2 C337). Very likely the villages out of which Mantinea had been constituted as a *polis* had never been completely abandoned. Though the wealthy seem to have been happy with this arrangement, since it enabled them to live closer to their estates, the majority of the population resented the Spartan move deeply. Their resentment rankled and, following Sparta's defeat at Leuctra, they voted "to make Mantinea a single city and to surround it with a wall" (Xen. *Hell.* 6.5.3). They then proceeded to put the decision into effect, despite efforts from Sparta to dissuade them. A number of Arcadian towns participated in the building project, while the Eleans contributed three talents. The alliance between the Mantineans and the other Arcadians proved to be short-lived, however. At the Battle of Mantinea, fought less than a decade after the synoecism, the Mantineans betrayed the Arcadian cause and sided with the Spartans (Paus. 8.8.10).

Megalopolis. The synoecism of Megalopolis in ca. 368/7 was on a much larger scale than that of Mantinea and involved at least twenty communities (D.S. 15.72.4). Though Pausanias was of the opinion that the Theban general Epaminondas "might with justification be regarded as its *oikistês*," this claim remains unproven (8.27.2, cf. 9.14.4). The synoecism was not named "Big City" for nothing. Megalopolis's fortification walls had a circumference of 5 miles, which means that the city could have accommodated a population of about 30,000. Scholars differ as to whether the enclosed area was fully inhabited, however. One attractive theory is that it was intended to provide shelter for the army, poised to attack the Spartans should they attempt to pass the road that ran close to the city. If that is the case, its population may have been no more than 10,000.

Pausanias tells us that the Arcadians agreed to abandon their former homes and settle in Megalopolis "out of zeal and because of their fear of the Spartans" (8.27.3). From its inception, however, the synoecism ran into difficulties, no doubt because many of its inhabitants had been conscripted. We hear of three groups of peoples who "changed their minds and, being no longer willing to abandon their former cities, were forcibly brought to Megalopolis," while a fourth group—namely, the inhabitants of Trapezous—left the Peloponnese for good in preference to being resettled (8.27.5). Then six years later a number of those who had been transplanted to Megalopolis, finding that they were unable to adjust to life in the new city, abandoned the new settlement and returned to their former homes. The rebellion, if that is the right word, was put

FIGURE 7 Silver *triôbolon* (three obols) from Megalopolis in Arcadia, ca. 175–68. The obverse depicts the laureate head of either Zeus Lykaios, tutelary deity of Megalopolis, or Zeus Amarios, principal deity of the Achaean League, to which Megalopolis belonged (Polyb. 5.93.10; see Malkin 1987, 132). The reverse depicts Pan seated on a rock, holding a staff in his left hand. An eagle is to his left. Arcadia was a favorite haunt of Pan and one of his principal centers of worship. Allegedly founded by Epaminondas in ca. 368/7, Megalopolis was sacked by the Spartans in 223 and refounded by Philopoemen a few years later. This coin dates to the period of its second foundation.

down by the Thebans, who, in Diodorus's words, "by sacking some of the cities and terrifying others, compelled their peoples to change their residence to Megalopolis." Diodorus concludes his account of Megalopolis not without a pinch of irony: "So the *sunoikismos* of the cities, having reached such a pitch of disorder, was moderately successful in the end" (15.94.3).

The Synoecism of Halicarnassus

At some point in the decade from 377 to 367 the Persian satrap of Caria named Mausolus began moving his capital from inland (Carian) Mylasa to coastal (Greek) Halicarnassus. He did so by relocating the inhabitants of six (less plausibly five) towns that were close to Halicarnassus (Callisthenes, *FGrH* 124 F 25 = Str. *Geog.* 13.1.59 C611; Pln. *NH* 5.107). As a result of this move, Halicarnassus became a predominantly Carian or, more specifically, Lelegian city. The Carian immigrants, dubbed, perhaps prejudicially, *neopolitai* (new citizens) by the existing citizens, eventually became at least partly hellenized, since they were required to participate in the Greek governmental system. Epigraphical evidence indicates that the ethnically mixed citizen body made decisions—no doubt of a somewhat routine nature—in the name of the *dêmos* and the *boulê* (council). This seems to have been in accordance with Mausolus's own predilection, since he not only promoted the institutions of the Greek *polis* but also borrowed the language of Greek democracy (cf. Hornblower 1982, 105).

Predilection apart, there was also a compelling strategic reason why Mausolus moved his capital to Halicarnassus—namely, to gain access to the sea. In 378 Athens had founded its second naval confederacy. Mausolus wanted to build up a navy to counter the threat from an increasingly belligerent Athens. A further motive lay in the fact that a populous center would enable him to strengthen his control over the region and, in so doing, weaken the power of the Carian League. He made this control palpable by undertaking an extremely ambitious building program in his capital. Its most enduring architectural legacy turned out to be the project undertaken by his sister-wife, Artemisia—namely, the famous Mausoleum, one of the Seven Wonders of the Ancient World, which occupied pride of place and may have determined the overall layout. The city also acquired extensive new walls and an imposing mudbrick palace faced with marble.

The synoecism of Halicarnassus represents a largely successful experiment in relocation, not least because there are few signs of destruction at the Lelegian towns whose populations were transferred. To judge from the Athenian tribute lists of the fifth century, moreover, some of these towns had been quite substantial in size. Indeed it has been suggested that the population of Halicarnassus now increased four or five times (Bean 1980, 81). Even so, archaeological evidence indicates that life went on amid the rubble of the towns whose populations were supposedly evacuated (Hornblower 1994, 225). By the hellenistic period the Carian element living in Halicarnassus seems to have become thoroughly assimilated, holding out the tantalizing possibility of inter-ethnic integration.

5

THE DEPORTEE

Political *Stasis* as a Cause of Deportation

Deportation in the archaic and classical Greek world commonly took the form of the forced removal either of a large group by their political opponents or of the entirety of the population by a foreign enemy or tyrant—a phenomenon not unlike that of ethnic cleansing today (see appendix C). A frequent cause was factional squabbling between supporters of democracy and those of an oligarchic persuasion. Antagonism between the oligarchic "few" and the democratic "many" was never far beneath the political surface. This state of affairs, once it became acute, was described as *stasis*, a polysemous term that covered a multitude of political exigencies, including partisanship, sedition, and, at the extreme end of the spectrum, revolution and civil war. Typically when factionalism became rife, oligarchs sought to deprive democrats of their basic rights, including citizenship, and to establish a "moderate aristocracy," while democrats sought to deprive oligarchs of their privileges, including land-ownership, and to establish *isonomia* (equality under the law). In the Peloponnesian War, as Thucydides states, oligarchs brought in the Spartans to strengthen their power base within the city, whereas the democrats brought in the Athenians (3.82.1). *Stasis* also occurred when different ethnic groups within the same city divided into factions.

If relations between the two factions broke down completely, those in the ascendant would deport their opponents, a practice attested by the middle of the sixth century. Though deportation may strike us as a radical solution to a political impasse, in the absence of a party political system that provided for the orderly transfer of power through the device of an election, it was often the only option available. It was certainly better than the executions that took place under Greece's early tyrants (for example, Hdt. 5.92 epsilon 2). It was better than the massacre of their oligarchic opponents by the Corcyrean democrats, which the latter used to settle private scores, so that "practically nothing was left of the oligarchs" (Thuc. 3.81, 4.48). And it was better, too, than the slaughter of 1,000 to 1,200 oligarchs by democrats during a particularly vicious bout of *stasis* in Argos (D.S. 15.58; Gehrke 1985, 251). The city most subject to *stasis* was Syracuse, whereas Sparta was exemplary in not being subject to its attendant ills for centuries.

Mass deportation, albeit cruel and inhuman, functioned as a valuable safety valve in that it relieved political pressure. Indeed it is hardly an exaggeration to state that the survival of the *polis* at times of crisis depended upon the expulsion of one of the two warring parties, since if conditions deteriorated further, it would become ungovernable and civil slaughter would result. But usual though the recourse to deportation was as a temporary expedient when *stasis* threatened to erupt in bloodshed, it was hardly a long-term solution. Indeed in many cases it merely prolonged the agony, since if the deportees gained the support of a neighboring community they would agitate to be reinstated and then almost certainly exact vengeance on their ousters. Diodorus Siculus (11.76.4), for instance, writes of the year 461, "The peoples who had been expelled from Himera, Gela, and Camarina . . . returned to their homelands and drove out those who had illegally seized the dwellings of others." It follows from this that attachment to one's social group often signified more than attachment to one's *polis* (Hansen and Nielsen 2004, 125).

Since the Greeks did not have a word for "deportation" and since, too, *phugê*, its nearest equivalent, can mean either "flight" or "exile," we rarely know whether a group of people who abandoned their *polis* at a moment of crisis did so voluntarily or under compulsion. Whichever was the case, however, we need hardly doubt that their departure constituted in effect a deportation. We rarely hear how many were driven into exile. Those of a moderate persuasion would presumably have chosen to remain, even though they might have been subject to prejudice under the newly constituted governmental system.

Though deportation may be viewed as a relatively mild expedient compared with the indiscriminate slaughter of one's political opponents, it was hardly humane. Not for nothing the author of the *Seventh Epistle* that is attributed to Plato repudiated it as a way of resolving a constitutional crisis. Instead he recommended patience, prayer, and keeping a low profile (331d):

> The man of good sense . . . should not resort to violence to his fatherland to bring about a change in the constitution, whenever it is impossible to make it the best of its kind, by sentencing men either to exile or to death. Rather he should remain inactive and pray for what is good both for himself and for his city.

Another type of deportation involved the transfer of an entire population either by a state that had recently conquered the region or by a tyrant who was seeking to expand his power. The purpose was to increase the military and political authority of those who were instrumental in effecting it. It was Sicily in the first half of the fifth century and again in the fourth century that experienced mass population transfer most often, due primarily to the policies of its so-called tyrants. As Rhodes and Osborne (2003, 377) have pointed out, however, the word "tyrant" in the fourth century may sometimes have been used in a pejorative sense to describe a factional leader to whom the user of the term was politically hostile.

One of the most famous instances of deportation by a foreign power in antiquity involved the removal of the Jews to Babylon by King Nebuchadnezzar following the destruction of Jerusalem in 597 BCE, though we have no way of knowing how many Jews were involved in the transfer. No comparable example is recorded in the Greek case, though Ptolemy I Soter, after his conquest of Palestine in ca. 320, is said to have deported many thousands of Jews and settled them in Egypt. Where deportation is mentioned in our sources, we rarely receive any indication of the numbers involved.

Surviving as a Deportee

Deportation is a severe test of endurance, both physical and psychological, aggravated by the fact that in many cases the deportees are forced to leave all their possessions behind them. When the Athenians took Potidaea in 429 after a three-year siege and expelled the entire population, they "permitted the men to leave with only one cloak, the women with two, and a fixed sum of money for the journey" (Thuc. 2.70.3). Likewise when Philip II of Macedon took Methone in Messenia a century later, he permitted the inhabitants of that city to depart with "only a single cloak" (D.S. 16.34.4–5). Deportees would rarely have been allowed to take their baggage animals and carts with them, so it is unclear how they would have been able to transport the elderly, the infirm, the sick, and the pregnant women. Many of those who were incapable of walking must have been left behind, to face either starvation or slaughter. In cases where the primary objective was to increase the population of a neighboring city, however, deportees are likely to have received better treatment. Even then, however, their plight would have been unenviable, for they had to abandon not only their homes, but also their household shrines and family tombs.

Deportees often faced jeers and insults as they were hustled through the city gates into a frighteningly exposed world. Lacking weapons and armor, they were extremely vulnerable to predators. All too frequently they had to look on helplessly as the weakest fell by the wayside, from either exhaustion, exposure to the elements, or hostile attack. So if the trek was long and arduous, as would commonly have been the case, the column would have been constantly diminishing in length, as more and more stragglers fell by the wayside. Some deportees may in effect have undertaken a death march, with most if not all dying along the way—the fate of hundreds of thousands of Armenians at the hands of the Ottoman Turks in 1915. However, we never actually hear of this barbaric practice being enforced in the ancient world. Equal risks attended those who sought to escape by sea.

Probably the best option for deportees was to find accommodation in the countryside surrounding the *polis* from which they had been evicted—in other words, to become what we would call today "internally displaced"—as many Athenians did to escape the rule of the Thirty Tyrants, though whether this was a common ploy at other times is impossible to gauge. The next best option was to seek refuge with others of the same political persuasion in a neighboring *polis*. This would have been feasible, however, only if their political allies were sufficiently powerful and secure to admit them. The decision to provide refuge to a group of exiles, perhaps numbering in the hundreds, would hardly have been uncontroversial, so the deportees needed to make a powerful appeal to the self-interest of their hosts. Aristocrats presumably had the best chance of finding refuge abroad by claiming guest-friendship, an institution that was still very much alive in the classical period (see later, chapter 7).

How the deportees were accommodated inside the receiving *polis* is unclear. It might have been possible to distribute a small group of individuals in existing dwellings, but a large group would have had to live in tents or their equivalent, perhaps outside the city walls. If numerous, they posed a serious threat to the political and social stability of the *polis*, not least because they would have imposed a heavy burden on the city's infrastructure. And the longer the deportees remained, the more likely they were to incur resentment—a phenomenon known today, somewhat euphemistically, as "compassion fatigue."*

Unless a preexisting tie existed or unless they could demonstrate their usefulness to the receiving community, their chances of survival were slim. When *stasis* broke out in Arcadia in 370/69, more than 1,400 fled, some to Pallantium, others to Sparta. Those who fled to Pallantium were slaughtered, whereas those who sought refuge in Sparta prevailed upon their hosts to come to their assistance (D.S. 15.59). Another striking example involves a Gallic tribe called the Mandubii, who, after being deported from Alesia, tearfully appealed to Julius Caesar to receive them inside his fortifications, even offering to become slaves

---

* "They once received us as guests and brothers," commented a Syrian refugee living in Jordan. "Now they see us as a curse" (cited in the *Guardian* [April 23, 2013] in an article subtitled "Solidarity with Northern Neighbours Wanes as Jordanian Government Says Cost of Hosting Refugees Could Reach $1 Billion.")

in perpetuity in return for food (*Gal.* 7.78). Caesar responded by set-ting guards on the ramparts to prevent the Alesians from entering—an example of *refoulement*—namely, the expulsion of a refugee "to the frontiers of territories where his life or freedom would be threatened" (Article 33, paragraph 1, of the 1951 Refugee Convention). In conse-quence of their rejection, they probably starved to death, and the fact that Caesar does not refrain from mentioning the incident indicates that he expected his readers to accept it as routine.

Whether or not deportees stayed together in one group depended on circumstances. A large group is more able to defend itself, but its size be-comes a risk when food is in short supply. At times it would have been in the best interests of deportees to break up into small groups. When the Athenians deported the Samians in ca. 365, some settled on the mainland opposite, some took refuge in cities along the coast of Asia Minor, and others probably served as mercenaries under the Persian king, since Philip II of Macedon had recognized the Athenian claim to their island (D.S. 18.56.7). The few Samian deportees who survived—probably no more than a handful—returned to their homeland a gen-eration later (see chapter 11).

Deportees were vulnerable not only to predators, but also to any un-scrupulous individual who might want to exploit them. A case in point involves "the thick" as they are called literally, or "men of substance" as we might translate the term, who were expelled from the island of Naxos by their democratic opponents in ca. 500 (Hdt. 5.30). The deportees ap-pealed to Aristagoras, deputy tyrant of Miletus, in the hope that he would support their bid to return home. Sensing an opportunity to advance his own agenda, Aristagoras agreed. He then requested military backing from Persia. The Persian king Darius likewise agreed, and with a similarly self-serving agenda. He calculated that by seizing Naxos he would be able to conquer all the Cyclades and thereby acquire a vital stepping-stone for an invasion of Greece. The Milesians and Persians laid siege to the island, but to no avail, and after four months they departed. The sole benefit that the deportees derived from the expedition was the construction of a wall that their supposed allies built to give them protection.

Conversely, deportees might sometimes exploit those whom they petitioned for help. One such instance of double-dealing on the part of deportees involves the Colophonians, who, after they had been granted asylum by the Smyrnaeans, plotted to seize control of their city (Hdt. 1.150). When their hosts left the city to celebrate a festival in honor of Dionysus, the Colophonians barred the gates to prevent them from reentering. Luckily for the Smyrnaeans, their neighbors came to their rescue, and eventually an agreement was struck by which the Colophonians were permitted to retain control of the city on condition that they restored their property to the Smyrnaeans. The ousted Smyrnaeans were subsequently dispersed among eleven neighboring cities, where they were accorded full citizen rights.

Deportees who found accommodation abroad were viewed with suspicion in wartime. The fourth-century military tactician Aeneas Tacticus recommended that every effort should be made to prevent them from communicating with traitors living within the city, viz from becoming what we would call a "fifth column." He wrote (10.6):

> If there are exiles, issue a pronouncement about what to do in the case of any citizen or foreigner or slave who absconds to them. In addition, anyone who makes contact with any of the exiles or with anyone they send, or who sends a letter to them or who receives a letter from them, should face either danger or a penalty. Both outgoing and incoming letters must be submitted to a board of inspectors before they are delivered (trans. Whitehead 1990, 53).

Aeneas further advised that the state should "draw up a register of everyone who owns more than one set of arms and armor, and not allow anyone to remove arms [that is from the city] or accept them as security" (10.7). Foreign vagrants, styled *talapeirioi* (much-suffering ones), were to be expelled at regular intervals (10.10). To thwart any attempt by exiles to repossess the city, a price should be put on the head of any monarch or general or ruler in exile, with the further incentive that if the assassin died in the attempt the money should be paid to his children or next of kin (10.16). Similar suspicions in wartime were directed toward economic migrants who lived permanently abroad, as they have been throughout history.

Deportations by the Sicilian Tyrants Gelon, Hieron, and Theron

Mass deportation was a tactic employed by a number of Sicilian tyrants to gain control over territory that they considered vital for their national interests. The Deinomenid tyrant Gelon (r. ca. 491–478/7), who ruled Gela, seized control of Syracuse in 485 at the invitation of some exiles. He then deported the inhabitants of Gela, Camarina, Megara Hyblaea, and Euboea (again not the island but an unlocated town in Sicily) to Syracuse, which even before this development was the greatest city in Sicily. He did so both to consolidate his power base and to counter the rising power of the Carthaginians, who were posing a threat to Greeks in the eastern part of the island.

The first of these deportations involved "more than half" the population of Gela. Our sources do not tell us which half was deported—it may have been either the rich or the poor, since there are arguments for proposing both. The rich half would have helped Gelon to consolidate his political support, whereas the poor half would have provided him with military assistance. The next to be relocated were the inhabitants of Camarina, who had unsuccessfully tried to rebel against his rule. Instead of massacring the prisoners whom he had captured, as was common practice after a siege (see later in this chapter), however, he gave them Syracusan citizenship. After quelling a revolt by the oligarchs of Megara Hyblaea, he again spared the survivors. On this occasion, however, he awarded Syracusan citizenship only to the oligarchs, even though they had led the revolt, whereas the poor were enslaved, even though they were innocent. He followed the same course with regard to the population of Euboea, granting citizenship to the wealthy but enslaving the poor. In each of these four cases we should probably be thinking of deportation rather than transfer, despite the liberal grants of Syracuse citizenship. Gelon also settled over 10,000 mercenaries in Syracuse (D.S. 11.72.3). As a result of all these relocations the population of Syracuse doubled

FIGURE 8 Silver *litra* from Gela, after ca. 425. The obverse depicts a bearded naked horseman carrying a spear and wearing a Phrygian helmet. The reverse, which bears the legend *GELAS*, depicts the forepart of a man-headed bull, intended to personify the River Gela, for which the city was named. According to tradition settlers from Lindus in Rhodes founded Gela in 689/8 (Thuc. 6.4.3; Hdt. 7.153.1). In 485 Gelon transferred "more than half" its population to Syracuse. It was repopulated in ca. 461 and again became prosperous. The Carthaginians sacked the city in 405, and the survivors took refuge in Syracuse. Gela was resettled by Timoleon (Plu. *Tim.* 35.1–2; cf. Talbert 1974, 153–55).

in size. How he tackled the many problems involved in enlarging the city is unrecorded. Clearly he must have initiated a massive building program to provide housing for the new residents. In addition, he had to introduce measures to increase the food and water supply. All in all, it was an extremely ambitious program. And yet it seems to have succeeded. Herodotus, who was his contemporary, states that Syracuse "immediately grew and flourished" (7.156.2).

Gelon died in 478 and was succeeded as tyrant of Syracuse by his brother Hieron, who likewise used mass deportation to consolidate his power. Unlike Gelon, however, his primary objective was to settle his mercenaries. To this end he deported the populations of Naxos and Catania to Leontini and then some four years later resettled Catania with 10,000 mercenaries. Half of these were drawn from the Peloponnese and half from Syracuse. (Naxos seems to have remained abandoned.) Hieron then renamed the city Aetna in honor of the eponymous volcano that had erupted the year he had come to the throne. He even pressed into service court poets such as Pindar (*Pyth.* 1.60–62) and

Bacchylides (fr. 20C Campbell) to commemorate the city's refoundation, and he commissioned Aeschylus to write a play titled the *Women of Aetna*, which the Athenian playwright duly performed in Sicily (*Vit. Aes.* 8–11). The unpalatable fact remains that the resettlement of Catania involved the displacement of a large number of the indigenous population, for whom it was little short of a catastrophe. According to Diodorus Siculus, Hieron's primary motivation was self-interest: he wanted a loyal base of supporters available in an emergency and to be heroized as Aetna's oikist after his death (11.49.1–3).

In 466 Hieron was succeeded by his brother Thrasybulus, who was soon forced into exile owing to his unpopularity and ineptitude. Democracy was now restored to all the Greek cities that had been ruled by tyrants. Furthermore an agreement was reached whereby the mercenaries who had taken up residence in these cities should depart with their possessions and settle in Messenia. As Diodorus Siculus (11.76.6) reports, "*Stasis* and disorder among the cities in Sicily was brought to an end, and the cities, having ejected the forms of government that had been introduced by foreigners, apportioned out their lands in allotments among all their citizens."

Gelon's contemporary Theron of Acragas (r. 489–73) also employed mass deportation. Discovering in 483 that a number of conspirators in Himera were plotting against him, he slaughtered the guilty ones and replaced them with settlers from abroad. Diodorus reports that these new settlers henceforth lived amicably with those among the Himerans who had not joined the conspiracy (11.48.6–8, 49.3–4)—aptly characterized as "a remarkable example of peaceful coexistence in a century marked by cruel episodes of ethnic antagonism" (Asheri 1992,151).

Deportations during the Peloponnesian War

Several deportations are known to have taken place during the Peloponnesian War and no doubt many others occurred of which we have no report, since hostilities necessarily intensified the political divisions within individual *poleis*. On the positive side of the equation, wartime deportees would have had little difficulty in putting their services to good use, so long as they were prepared to take up arms against their homeland, since virtually the entire Greek world was divided into two opposing factions.

Epidamnus. The deportation of oligarchs from Epidamnus by their democratic opponents that occurred shortly before the outbreak of the Peloponnesian War is a classic demonstration of how a localized instance of *stasis* could spark a major conflagration. Thucydides writes (1.24.3–5; cf. D.S. 12.30.2–5):

> As time went by Epidamnus became a powerful and populous city. Having, however, succumbed for a good number of years to *stasis*, allegedly as the result of war with the neighboring barbarians, the city became weakened and was deprived of much of its power. Immediately before the outbreak of the Peloponnesian War, the *dêmos* drove the oligarchs into exile. The deportees joined forces with the barbarians and proceeded to harry those in the city by land and by sea.

Thucydides omits to tell us how the *dêmos* gained control of Epidamnus, other than to indicate that it was a consequence of the external pressures of war. Nor does he tell us what tactics the *dêmos* employed to expel their opponents, though it is a reasonable assumption that the latter must have feared for their lives. Quite possibly some took to their heels before any deportation order was given, whereas others did so only after the order was promulgated. That, of course, is assuming that an order was issued. It may be that the oligarchs voluntarily fled following a riot orchestrated by the most violent elements of the *dêmos*. It is worth noting that no historian has provided us with a detailed explanation of how any instance of *stasis* resulted in deportation.

Fearing the coalition of oligarchs and barbarians that now formed, the democrats sent ambassadors requesting help in resolving the conflict to Corcyra, which, jointly with Corinth, was Epidamnus's mother-city. The Corcyraeans were loath to become involved, however, so they consulted Delphi as to whether they should hand their city over to Corinth for protection. Having received Delphi's support for this plan,

MAP 4 *Stasis* in Epidamnus.

they now sent an embassy to their other mother-city. The Corinthians agreed to assist and issued an announcement that "anyone who wished" should depart as an *oikêtôr* (settler) to Epidamnus to supplement the citizen body, which had been depleted by the removal of the oligarchs. They also dispatched some mercenaries to help defend the city against its enemies.

In the meantime, the oligarchs who had been driven into exile made an emotive appeal to the Corcyraeans for help, "pointing out the tombs of their ancestors" to emphasize their common ancestry. Their appeal also succeeded, and the Corcyraeans launched an attack on Epidamnus with the intention of restoring the oligarchs. Corinth then issued a second appeal for volunteer settlers to depart for Epidamnus, promising that they would enjoy political equality (1.24.6–27.1). The conflict between Corcyra and Corinth was a major contributor to the outbreak of the Peloponnesian War, since Athens took the side of Corcyra, whereas Corinth was a member of the Peloponnesian League. We hear nothing further of the exiles, who, we are bound to note, have ceased to be of any interest to the historian.

Aegina. Shortly after the outbreak of war the Athenians deported the Aeginetans, along with their wives and children, from their island "on the grounds that they were chiefly responsible for the conflict that had come upon them" (Thuc. 2.27.1). The Spartans permitted the Aeginetans to settle in Thyrea, a region between Laconia and the Argolid, "because the Aeginetans had always sided with Sparta" (4.56.2). The number of deportees who took up the Spartan offer was evidently sufficient to pose a threat to the Athenians, who seized Thyrea in 424 and slaughtered most of its inhabitants. They then deported the survivors to Athens and executed them. Aegina now became an Athenian *apoikia*, inhabited by Athenians. Meanwhile the Aeginetans who had declined the Spartan offer to settle in Thyrea and thus escaped the massacre were "scattered throughout the Greek world" (2.27.2). At the end of the war they were permitted to return home (Plu. *Lys.* 14.3).

Plataea. It was the preemptive attack on Plataea, an ally of Athens, by the Thebans in 431 that directly prompted the outbreak of war. In 429 the Spartans and their Peloponnesian allies began besieging the city (Thuc. 2.71–78, 3.20–24, 3.52–68). About 212 Plataeans managed to break out and found refuge in Athens. The rest put up a spirited resistance, but eventually, weakened by hunger, were forced to surrender. Though they appealed to their captors for leniency, the Thebans accused them of war crimes, and the Spartan judges, after asking each of their prisoners in turn if they had done any service to Sparta, determined that all the men, numbering about 200, should be slaughtered and all the women, numbering about 110, should be sold into slavery. All other noncombatants, including slaves and the elderly, had previously been evacuated (Thuc. 2.78.3–4; 3.66 and 68.2; Dem. 59.103). For a year or so, the Spartans permitted some Megarian oligarchs and a few Plataeans who had supported their cause to inhabit the vacant site. In 426, however, they destroyed its walls and no doubt other parts of the city. They used the salvaged wood to build a *katagôgeion* (hostel) for dignitaries visiting the adjoining sanctuary of Hera, the city's tutelary goddess (Thuc. 3.68.3).

In recognition of their long-standing alliance with the Plataeans, the Athenians granted citizenship to all those who had managed to escape (Dem. 59.103–4; Isoc. 12.94). Then, when they captured Scione in Chalcidice in 421, after they had slaughtered the men and enslaved the women—in other words, after they had meted out to the Scionians exactly the same punishment that the Peloponnesians had meted out to the Plataeans—they permitted the Plataeans residing in Athens to settle on the abandoned site (Thuc. 5.32.1). Many of them declined the offer and stayed put, however, evidently because they had become acculturated to Athens (Lys. 23.5–7). Incidentally, Plataea's walls were rebuilt in 386, this time with the help of the Spartans (Paus. 9.1.6), but they were again destroyed by the Thebans in 373 (Arr. *Anab.* 1.9.9–10).

Megara. Some time after the outbreak of the Peloponnesian War a democratic coup in Megara led to the deportation of the oligarchs (Thuc. 4.66–74). Initially the oligarchs fled north to Plataea where, as we just saw, they were allowed to reside temporarily (3.68.3). When the Spartans destroyed it a year later, however, the oligarchs returned to the Megarid. They took possession of Pegae, a port on the Corinthian Gulf, from which they made raids into Megarian territory. Since the Athenians were also invading the Megarid twice a year to destroy the crops, conditions inside the city soon became dire. In fact they became so dire that the democratic faction started to wonder aloud whether to reinstate the deportees in order to eliminate at least one of their problems. Seizing the moment, a group whom Thucydides identified as "the friends of the exiles" sought to introduce a proposal permitting the oligarchs to return.

Alarmed at the prospect of their enemies returning, the democrats hastily entered into negotiations with the Athenians with the intention of betraying their city to them, since this was now seen as the lesser of two evils. Before the Athenians had time to respond, however, a Peloponnesian army appeared in the Megarid. The "friends of the exiles" now seized the initiative and handed over their city to the Pelopon-

FIGURE 9 Bronze *obolos* (coin equivalent to one-sixth of a *drachma*) from Megara, ca. 307–243. The obverse depicts the prow of a warship. The reverse depicts two dolphins circling the legend *MEG(ARE)*. Megara established a number of overseas settlements in the eighth and seventh centuries. Its territory was repeatedly invaded and ravaged during the Peloponnesian War. The rural population had to provision the Peloponnesian army on its way to and from Attica, and then deal with Athens's vengeance afterward for supporting her enemies. It is unlikely that the entire population of Megara was able to shelter within the city walls, so thousands may well have perished in this period. In ca. 427 a democratic faction exiled the leading oligarchs. In ca. 424, however, the oligarchs returned, executing some democrats and exiling others.

nesians, whereupon the democratic faction fled to Athens. Those who remained permitted the deported oligarchs to return on condition that they would not exact revenge. Once reinstated, however, the oligarchs broke their oath and executed about a hundred democrats, along with the pro-Athenian democrats who had not managed to escape.

Leontini. After the Congress of Gela (424), which brought about the departure of the Athenians from Sicily following a vote by the Sicilian Greeks to respect the autonomy of all the cities on the island, the *dunatoi* (powerful aristocrats) in Leontini, with the help of the Syracusans, deported their democratic opponents just as the latter were about to undertake land redistribution on behalf of newly enrolled citizens (Thuc. 5.4.2–4). Evidently unable to find refuge as a single group, the democrats dispersed "in various directions," some to Euboea in mainland Greece. Even so, they maintained their collective identity over the years as Leontines in exile, in the hope that they would one day be repatriated.

Meanwhile the oligarchs had destroyed most of Leontini and migrated to Syracuse, where they received citizenship. After a while, however, they fell out with their hosts. So they returned to what was still standing of their old city and seized an outpost in a nearby region called Bricinniae. In 422 the Athenians sent a representative to Sicily, warning the islanders of Syracuse's imperialistic designs and urging them to join a coalition in order to "save the people of Leontini." Realizing that the mission was fuelled by Athens's own imperialistic designs, however, the Sicilians declined. A curious irony lies in the fact that the oligarchs who had taken refuge in the ruins of Leontini were now joined by "most of the deported democrats." For once attachment to *polis* seems to have trumped political affiliation.

We next hear of Leontini when the Athenians were debating whether to undertake the Sicilian Expedition in 415. Some of the *phugades* had allied themselves with a native Sicilian people called the Elymnians and were requesting that the Syracusans be punished for depopulating their city (Thuc. 6.6.2 and 19.1). The Athenians agreed, and made it one of their principal objectives to rebuild Leontini after their victory. Since the expedition failed, however, the city was not rebuilt until 405/4 by citizens of Gela and Camarina (D.S. 13.114.1; cf. Berger 1991, 137).

Deportation by the Thirty Tyrants

One of the terms of peace that was imposed on Athens by the victors at the end of the Peloponnesian War was the return of all exiles. This included many members of the oligarchic government known as the Four Hundred, who, after being expelled from Athens in 411, had fled to Decelea, occupied at the time by a Spartan garrison (Thuc. 8.98.1). Their recall was evidently intended to intimidate the democrats because of their pro-Spartan sympathies. The exiles probably began returning in March or April 404 (And. 3.11–12; Xen. *Hell.* 2.2.23; Plu. *Lys.* 14.3–4). Some six months later the Spartan-backed Thirty Tyrants came to power. According to Xenophon, "more than half the population," including most of those who were well-to-do, fled from Athens to escape being massacred (*Mem.* 2.7.2; cf. D.S. 14.5.6–7). Though "more than half the population" is an exaggeration, the fear engendered by the policies of the Thirty no doubt did indeed occasion a mass exodus.

More dislocation was to follow. In December the Thirty drew up a roster of 3,000 citizens who henceforth constituted the restricted *dêmos*. They followed this up three months later by banning those who were excluded from the roll from entering Athens and depriving them of their land (Xen. *Hell.* 2.4.1). As Krentz (1982, 64–66) has suggested, it may be that they intended the 3,000 to replicate the Spartan citizen body known as the *homoioi* (peers), which also comprised about 3,000 at this date, and further that the excluded should take on the same status as the Spartan *perioikoi* (dwellers round about), in a move to increase the size of Athens's agrarian population. How the Thirty would have redistributed the land they intended to seize, however, is unclear. Whatever the intention behind these measures, they were ill-conceived because the deportees could now more easily make common cause with the opponents of the Thirty. Under the leadership of Thrasybulus, the latter gained control of the strategic outpost of Phyle, situated on the southern slope of Mount Parnes on Athens's northern border. Thrasybulus's force would eventually include many deportees.

The scale of the disruption caused by the deportation must have been enormous. Probably most of those who were forced to leave Athens found refuge in the Piraeus as internally displaced persons, as we would call them. Others left Attica entirely, seeking refuge in Argos, Boeotia, Chalcis, Corinth, Megara, and Oropus (Krentz, 1982, 69 with refs.). We catch a revealing glimpse of the plight of those who remained in Attica from Xenophon's unflattering portrait of Aristarchus, a resident of the Piraeus, who complained to Socrates of having to give shelter to his sisters, nieces, and cousins. "It's hard to see one's relatives die," he observed wearily, "but impossible to look after so many people in times like these" (*Mem.* 2.7.2). We do not learn what his thoughts were about having to accommodate his dependent male relatives, assuming he had any.

What would Xenophon's readers have made of Aristarchus? His text gives no indication. The portrait may well be drawn from real life, however. And if a well-to-do individual like Aristarchus felt resentment at providing refuge for his closest female relatives when the alternative was to leave them to fend for themselves, what was the fate of those with no family members to turn to?

Diodorus Siculus tells us that to prevent the Athenian deportees from obtaining support abroad, the Spartans passed a decree requiring "that *phugades* be brought back from all over Greece and that anyone who obstructed this should be liable to a fine of five talents." He continues: "Although the decree was harsh, all the states obeyed with the exception of the Argives, who hated Spartan cruelty and pitied the misfortunes of the *aklêrountes* (displaced persons) and therefore provided shelter for the exiles out of humanity." The fact that the Argives are portrayed as partly motivated by pity is impressive since we rarely hear of Greeks responding to refugees in this way. Even so, we should not discount the possibility that an unflinching adherence to democratic principles was partly responsible for the Argive response. Diodorus also tells us that the Thebans passed a decree that "anyone who witnessed a refugee being led off and failed to render assistance to the best of his ability should be fined" (14.6.1–3).

We do not know how many Athenians were forced back to Athens at this time as a result of the Spartan decree, nor what fate awaited them at the hands of the Thirty once they were returned to Attic soil. Their discomfiture would have been short-lived, however, since the government of the Thirty fell soon afterward. In accordance with the settlement of 403 that followed, partisans of the Thirty were permitted to withdraw (*exoikein*) to Eleusis, while retaining their rights as Athenian citizens ([Arist.] *Ath. Pol.* 39). They were given ten days to signal their intention to do so and ten more to take up residence in Eleusis. Those abroad at the time of the amnesty were granted the same number of days after their return. Our sources do not indicate how many took up the offer. Eleusis now became in effect a semi-independent state for oligarchs who refused to live under the restored democracy. In other words, the Athenian state underwent a *dioikismos*, viz the separation of a formally unified *polis*. The two communities were reunited in 401.

Laws Ordering the Expulsion of Foreigners

In wartime some Greek states introduced an emergency measure known as *xenêlasiai* (a plural noun meaning "expulsion of foreigners"). They did so because they suspected that foreigners were likely to reveal important military secrets to the enemy or undermine the morale of their citizenry. The Athenians claimed that the Spartans passed a law to this effect on the eve of the outbreak of the Peloponnesian War (Thuc. 1.144.2; cf. Xen. *Lac.* 14.4). Since the Spartans only rarely permitted foreigners to settle permanently within their borders, however, its principal target, assuming the charge is authentic, must have been temporary visitors.

The Athenians responded by declaring that they would lift their controversial ban excluding the Megarians "from the harbors of the Athenian empire and the Attic agora" (Thuc. 1.67.4, 139.1) only if the Spartans revoked their decree in turn. In his Funeral Speech delivered the same year Pericles made much of the fact that the Athenians permitted foreigners to remain within their borders in wartime, stating, "We make our city common to all men and never by the expulsion of foreigners prevent anyone from learning or seeing anything" (Thuc. 2.39.1). Pericles' claim amounts to propaganda. It certainly served the interests of the Athenians to promulgate the belief that they promoted openness and tolerance toward strangers and that the Spartans exhibited the opposite tendency. But though the Athenians did not expel Peloponnesians residing within their borders at the outbreak of war, they may well have subjected them to prejudice, thereby prompting them to take flight.

The Massacre and Enslavement of Prisoners of War

According to the conventions of Greek warfare, the inhabitants of a conquered city were treated very differently from prisoners of war. Before a siege began, they were free to depart with their belongings. Once a city had fallen, however, it was customary to carry out *andrapodismos*. Typically this meant massacring all the men of military age and enslaving the survivors, though occasionally the men would be spared (see appendix E). The enslaved were either given to the soldiers who had taken the city or sold off at a public auction. The city was then either razed to the ground or given over to new settlers. *Andrapodismos* was the fate meted out by the Spartans to the Plataeans in 427, and the fate, too, that the Athenians almost meted out to the Mytilenaeans later that year. It is what the Athenians did to the citizens of Torone and Scione, and later to those of Melos.

Very possibly the women would have been raped before they were sent off into slavery, though our sources, perhaps self-servingly, suggest that the perpetrators of this atrocity were for the most part non-Greeks (for example, Hdt. 8.33; D.S. 13.58.1). But why should we believe that women would have been protected from the lust of Greek soldiers? There is some evidence to indicate that a more humane attitude evolved over time, at least among the Macedonians. Philip II is not known to have massacred the population of any town he conquered. When, for instance, he took Amphipolis by siege in 358/7, he "exiled those who were disaffected but treated the rest humanely"(D.S. 16.8.2).

Soldiers captured on the battlefield were either ransomed, exchanged for prisoners on the other side, or kept in captivity to exert political pressure. In this last category were the 292 Spartan hoplites captured on Sphacteria and the 700 male survivors from the siege of Torone, who were kept in Athens as hostages before being released at the end of the Archidamian War (Thuc. 4.38.5, 5.3.4). Humane standards did not always apply, however. On the eve of the departure of the Sicilian Expedition the Athenian generals took the decision that in the event of victory they would enslave both the Syracusans and the Selinuntians and impose an annual tribute upon the rest of Sicily (D.S. 13.2.6). More egregious yet was the slaughter of all their Athenian prisoners by Sparta's allies after their naval victory at Aegospotami in 405 (Xen. *Hell.* 2.1.31–32). The allies took this drastic step because the Athenians had voted before the battle to chop off the right hands of all their prisoners and had drowned the crews of two triremes they had taken.

6

THE EVACUEE

The Logistics of Evacuation

In time of war civilian populations become a handicap, especially if they happen to be living outside the city walls. Vulnerable to the enemy, they are also a distraction since they are liable to prevent the military from pursuing a coherent plan of action. They must be protected, but how? Two options are available: either they can be conveyed to a friendly community nearby or brought inside the walls, although the latter course is feasible only if there is enough space to accommodate them. Whichever option is adopted, the logistics of evacuating thousands of people in the lead-up to the outbreak of hostilities was one of the most challenging exercises a *polis* could undertake. Very often the decision would have been taken only in the teeth of great resistance by the inhabitants, many of whom, like Aeneas's father Anchises, would have found it impossible, at least initially, to conceive of a life elsewhere. "You who still have your youthful vigor and strength, take flight," he advises. "If the heavenly powers had wanted to prolong my life they would have preserved my home" (Verg. *Aen.* 2.638–42). Many families, faced with the need to make an immediate decision, must have found themselves similarly riven by discord. Rarely, too, would an entire population have made it to safety. In 409 the Syracusan commander Diocles decided to evacuate half the population of Himera on board his fleet of triremes and transport it outside the borders of their territory to escape the Carthaginians. The remainder was forced to trek to Syracuse—a distance of about 120 miles (D.S. 13.61.4–6). Many no doubt perished along the way or else fell into the hands of the Carthaginians.

Greek historians give little attention to wartime evacuations, even though they must have been commonplace. Indeed it may well be because they were so frequent that they provide only the briefest commentary.

The Evacuation of Attica before the Battle of Salamis

As soon as they heard of Xerxes' invasion of Greece in 480, the Athenians were thrown into panic. They knew they could expect no mercy from the Persians. Ten years previously they had defeated Darius's army, sent to punish them for supporting the Ionians in their abortive revolt. The Peloponnesians had agreed to make a stand in Boeotia if they were forced to retreat from the pass at Thermopylae but they had reneged on their promise and retreated to the Isthmus of Corinth, some 40 miles to the southwest of Athens. So now the Athenians had to evacuate their entire population, about 150,000 in total. This was in accordance with the advice that Delphi had given them in the form of two separate oracles (Hdt. 7.140.2, 141.4):

"Leave your homes and the high peaks of your wheel-like city and flee to the ends of the earth."

"Don't wait for the cavalry and the huge army that is coming from the mainland, but withdraw and turn your backs on them."

In other words, Apollo left them no choice. Or had he? Though the first oracle urged the abandonment of Attica, the second refrained from recommending such a drastic course.

In actual fact the Athenians had probably decided to evacuate as soon as they caught wind of the fact that Xerxes was marching on Athens. After the battles of Thermopylae and Artemisium, fought on the same day in late August, however, they knew there was no alternative. All the women, children, and resident aliens were to be transported

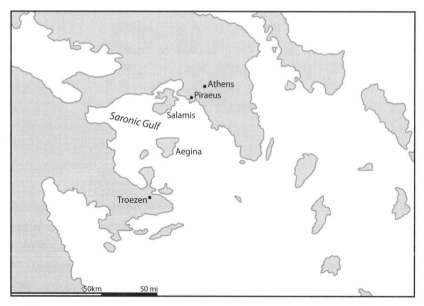

MAP 5 The evacuation of Attica before the Battle of Salamis.

either to Troezen, a *polis* on the northeast coast of the Peloponnese, or to Aegina, an island in the Saronic Gulf. Both destinations were about a day's sailing from Athens. The men of fighting age and the elderly were transported to Salamis, an island that lies only a mile from the Attic coast. Salamis and Troezen were obvious destinations (see later). Aegina was not. Indeed part of the reason why Athens, in Thucydides' memorable phrase (1.93.4), had decided to "attach itself to the sea" was her hostile relations with Aegina (Hdt. 7.144.1). Perhaps, as Strauss (2004, 60) has suggested, the island now "wished to make amends for its past," though why remains a mystery.

An inscription found at Troezen, whose lettering is of early third-century date, purports to reproduce the text of the decree that was passed by the Council and the Assembly regarding provisions for the evacuation. Though the authenticity of the document, sometimes known as the Themistocles Decree after its prime mover, has been questioned, it is nonetheless thought to contain a "historical kernel" (*ML* p. 50). Either way it sheds an important light on the manner in which the evacuation was envisaged to have taken place in retrospect. The relevant portion reads as follows (*ML* 23.4–12 = Fornara 55):

> The city is to be entrusted to Athena, the protector of Athens, and to all the other gods for them to guard and defend it against the barbarian on the country's behalf. All Athenians and *xenoi* [foreigners] living in Athens are to settle their wives and children in Troezen. . . . [Elderly people and] possessions are to be deposited on Salamis. The treasurers and the priestesses [are to remain guarding the possessions] of the gods on the Acropolis.

If the decree was passed as soon as the Athenians learned of the Persian advance in late June, there would have been time for a relatively orderly evacuation—if indeed any evacuation can ever be described as orderly. What remains problematic is whether the decision to evacuate was taken well in advance of the arrival of the Persians but only put into effect much later; or whether two separate evacuations took place, one in late June and relatively orderly, the other in early September and more frantic. Whichever was the case, it would have been a very difficult and time-consuming operation. Indeed nothing comparable had ever been attempted before. The *metoikêsis* of the Phocaeans, which we considered earlier, had been a much smaller operation.

For several weeks families of refugees made their slow and halting way through the Attic countryside to the port of Piraeus, currently undergoing fortification, and to the open bay of Phaleron to the east, where they waited to be conveyed to safety. They had abandoned not only their homes but also everything that was precious to them. All the valuables that they could not take with them—their pottery, their glass bowls, and the images of their gods—they had hastily buried in the ground. They knew the Persians, bent on revenge, would spare nothing—and so it proved. When the invaders advanced through Attica, they smashed all the funerary monuments that lay in their path and destroyed all the temples on the Acropolis (D.S. 11.14.5 and 16.2). The Athenians who had been conveyed to Salamis would have had a ringside view of the conflagration.

FIGURE 10 Attic silver *tetradrachma* (coin worth four *drachmae*), second half of fifth century. The obverse depicts the head of Athena, wearing a helmet adorned with three olive leaves, perhaps commemorating Athens's victory at the Battle of Salamis in 480. On the reverse is an owl and an olive twig with a waning moon of uncertain significance to the left. The Attic *tetradrachma* became ubiquitous in the fifth century due to Athens's political and economic hegemony. The population of Attica was evacuated during both the Persian and the Peloponnesian wars. A sizable proportion of her citizens was also deported by the Thirty Tyrants in 404.

Many of the refugees must have slept rough on the shoreline, clutching a few valuables, before a berth on board ship could be assigned to them. Priority was presumably given to the women and children, though how some semblance of order was maintained among the *mêlée* is unclear. We know little of what became of the tens of thousands of slaves. Some must have been left behind, others fled of their own accord, while those who were able-bodied were conscripted into the navy. A minority, seen as essential to the welfare of their owners, may have been evacuated. Could an Athenian live without a slave?

Plutarch evocatively describes the scene on the day of the departure to Salamis (*Them.* 10.5):

As the *polis* set sail, the spectacle filled some with pity, others with admiration at the daring of the move, as the Athenians dispatched their dependents in one direction and themselves crossed over to Salamis, oblivious to the shrieks, tears, and embraces of their nearest and dearest. The many elderly, who had to be left behind, aroused compassion. Tame and domesticated animals added to the commotion by displaying heartrending affection for their owners, running along beside them and howling as they embarked.

To add to the poignancy, Plutarch tells us that a dog belonging to Xanthippus, the father of Pericles, swam alongside the trireme that was transporting his master to Salamis, only to expire as soon as it reached dry land (10.6). A revered spot on the island known as the Dog's Tomb allegedly marked the grave centuries after.

No historian tells us how precisely the population was conveyed from Attica. A trireme's complement consisted of about 200, of whom 170 were rowers, so there would have been hardly any room for passengers. Even if it had been possible to reduce the number of rowers, conveying passengers in a vessel of this sort would have been cumbersome and hazardous. As in a canoe, even a small movement could unbalance the ship and throw the rowers into confusion. Added to which, there was no deck rail. We hear of Darius ordering the manufacture of what are called "ships for transporting horses" in advance of his expedition to Greece in 490 (Hdt. 6.48 and 95). It is not improbable that the Athenians had ships of this sort at their disposal by 480 and that they used them for transporting people. Another possibility is that they commandeered merchant ships belonging to foreigners that were docking in the Piraeus or Phaleron Bay, as well as all those that belonged to Athenian traders.

Plutarch (*Them*. 10.3) tells us that the women and children who were dispatched to Troezen were warmly welcomed by the inhabitants. The Troezenians had previously passed a law to the effect that they would "support them at public expense, give two obols to each family each day, permit the boys to pluck ripe fruit everywhere, and hire teachers to educate them." These measures suggest that they expected the refugees to be with them for some considerable time. The warmth of the reception sounds almost too good to be true and perhaps we should take it with a pinch of salt, despite the fact that Plutarch supplies the name of the man who introduced the bill—an otherwise unknown Nicagoras.

Hardly surprisingly there were a number of Athenians who were reluctant to abandon their homes, hearths, temples, and tombs, and who elected instead to wait upon events. When the threat of invasion became real following the breaking of the defense line at Artemisium-Thermopylae, however, panic probably set in, even among the most hardened. The only ones who were undeterred were those who chose to interpret the oracle urging the Athenians to "trust in the wooden wall" as a reference to the wooden palisade surrounding the Acropolis. They took refuge on that rock, determined to defend it to the last.

At this point the Athenians may have appealed to the combined Greek fleet to put in at Salamis to assist them in a secondary, viz emergency, evacuation of those still remaining. It is probably this last-minute evacuation that Herodotus describes, having omitted to mention the more orderly withdrawal (8.40–41). The allies no doubt obliged, and the Athenian fleet, which now comprised and spoke for the *dêmos*, issued a proclamation to the effect that "every Athenian should do what he could to save his children and other family members"—a clear indication that the state had limited means to assist the remaining evacuees. Convinced that Athena had abandoned the Acropolis since her sacred snake was no longer taking food, "they now made haste to remove all they had." Soon afterward, as we saw in chapter 4, Themistocles threatened to relocate the city permanently, should the Greek coalition decide to abandon Attica and retreat to the Isthmus of Corinth. No surviving source tells us anything about the evacuees after the Battle of Salamis, and we do not know when they actually returned to their homes.

The Athenians were not the only ones to evacuate their city in advance of the Persians. So, too, did the Plataeans and Thespians, who fled south en masse to the Peloponnese (D.S. 11.14.5). No doubt many other Greek peoples who inhabited cities in the direct line of fire, so to speak, between the Hellespont and Attica also took to their heels. Herodotus tells us that as the Persians advanced south they "destroyed everything," sanctuaries included. They also gang-raped Phocian women, many of whom died as a result (8.33, 35, 50.2). It was these actions and others like them that earned them the name "barbarian."

The Evacuation of Attica at the
Outbreak of the Peloponnesian War

At the beginning of Aristophanes' *Acharnians*, produced in 425, Dicaeopolis, the protagonist, is standing in the Assembly awaiting the arrival of the *prytaneis* (presidents), who will declare the meeting open. He characterizes himself as "looking away in the direction of my farm, longing for peace, hating the city, and longing for my village" (ll. 32–33). In view of these sentiments, there is a strong likelihood that Dicaeopolis is one of the tens of thousands of Athenians residing in rural demes who evacuated the countryside when the Peloponnesians announced their intention to ravage Attica.

Thucydides tells us that the country-dwellers were "dispirited and did not bear the change easily" (2.14; cf. 2.16.2). That is an understatement, if ever there was one, and one to which Dicaeopolis's nostalgia for the countryside gives strident utterance. Indeed the *Acharnians* might plausibly be interpreted as a commentary on the nostalgic longings of evacuees for the rural life that they have had to renounce. Their unhappiness would have been all the more acute because, as Thucydides points out, many of them had only recently rebuilt their dwellings after the destruction caused by the Persians half a century earlier.

The scale of the evacuation and the disruption it caused are scarcely imaginable. Since the majority of Athenians were living in the countryside at the time the war broke out, the population of the city would have virtually doubled overnight, increasing by between 50,000 and 100,000 (Thuc. 2.16.1).

Pericles, who was the architect of the strategy that now converted Athens, the Long Walls, and the Piraeus to a fortified island enclave, probably envisaged that the war would be over in a few months and that the refugees would be able to return to their homes at the end of the first year's fighting season. How wrong he was. They would remain cooped up for weeks on end for at least five years in the most insanitary conditions imaginable. The waste disposal system was nowhere near sufficient to deal with the huge influx of people and animals. A horrific plague soon broke out and morale was seriously undermined. Meanwhile the Peloponnesians destroyed their homes and ravaged their crops, completely unchecked and unimpeded.

Thucydides provides few details about the evacuation. He simply notes that the refugees took from their homes not only their furniture but also whatever else was made of wood, including doors, frames, shutters, and the like, wood being in very short supply and therefore valuable (2.14). He also tells us that the Athenians "conveyed their flocks and beasts of burden to Euboea and other neighboring islands." The fate of their pigs, goats, and chickens, as well as of their household pets, is not stated but many were presumably conveyed within the walls.

We do not know how long the evacuation took to implement, though it seems that the exercise was still going on when the Peloponnesians first invaded Attica in late May or early June 431 (2.18). Families living in the outlying demes probably had to spend at least two nights on the road, since some were located thirty miles or more from Athens. It is unclear how the flow of refugees was handled or what facilities were available either en route or on arrival. We should presumably imagine a long line queuing outside the city gates when the migration was at its height—assuming that the evacuees knew how to queue. And once inside the city, how and where were they fed? Who took responsibility for their welfare? How were they assigned a place to bed down? Many of the refugees must have arrived footsore, exhausted, and demoralized, particularly the pregnant women, the elderly, and the infirm.

It is also unclear what percentage of country dwellers actually obeyed the summons that the *dêmos* had issued. After all, it would have been extremely difficult to enforce. Inevitably, some must have been too sick or too frail to make the journey, while others of an independent mindset may have calculated that their farms were so remote that they would be safe against depredation from the enemy. They were right. The Peloponnesians invaded Attica five times, but never ravaged Decelea, Marathon, or even the Academy just outside the city walls, destined to be the future site of Plato's philosophical school (Hansen 2005, 54).

Inevitably disaffection ran high among segments of the population once the Peloponnesians, some 30,000 in all, invaded Attica. We know this to have been the case at the outlying deme of Acharnae, whose

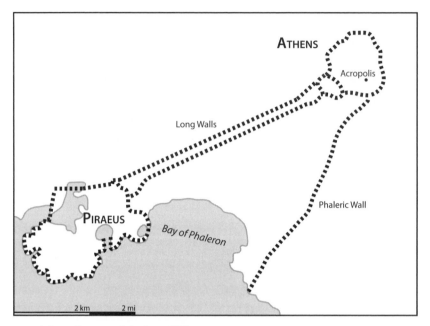

MAP 6 Athens, Piraeus, and the Long Walls.

inhabitants were among the first to see their farms being ravaged and who constituted a sizable percentage of Athens's army. Later, exasperated, weakened, and demoralized, the citizen body as a whole took vengeance on Pericles for causing such hardship by ousting him from the board of ten generals, though it later relented and reinstated him.

Though a handful of wealthy families owned a second home in the city while other Athenians had relatives or friends whose homes served as a *kataphugê* (place of refuge) (2.17.1), the vast majority had to settle either where they happened upon a vacant space or else where the authorities directed them—that is to say, in sanctuaries and hero shrines, beside the fortification walls, and on land that had previously been unoccupied (see map 6). Even land that lay under a curse was eventually settled, including an unidentified plot below the Acropolis called the Pelargicum. Only sanctuaries that could be locked up, notably the Acropolis and the temple of Eleusinian Demeter, remained out of bounds. At first all the refugees were crammed into Athens. As the pressure on space increased, however, they were permitted to settle along the unoccupied strips inside the Long Walls, as well as in the Piraeus (2.17.3). It was the dense concentration of evacuees in the Piraeus that was probably responsible for the outbreak of plague, since the port was largely dependent for its drinking water on cisterns that caught rainwater, and these quickly became polluted (Thuc. 2.48.2).

Perhaps the wood that had been salvaged was used to fashion the temporary homes that Thucydides refers to as "stifling shacks" (2.52.2). Those who lacked this resource would have had to live in makeshift tents. The entire urban area now became the ancient equivalent of a modern day refugee camp, divided probably along demotic or tribal lines. Perhaps the Athenians derived some small comfort from the inspirational speech that Pericles gave in late September or early October over those who had fallen in the first year of the war (2.34–46). Conceivably the full horror of their circumstances had yet to sink in. It would do so a few months later, when the plague broke out.

Thucydides says nothing further about the evacuees, other than to note that it was they who suffered most from the plague (2.52.1). Though he describes the symptoms of the disease in painstaking detail, he says nothing of the toll it took on family life, other than to deplore the lawlessness that it engendered. It is estimated that infant mortality commonly ran at least as high as 25 percent in the ancient world. Given the many debilitating diseases that would have afflicted the refugees, it may well have doubled in this period.

The maximum number of days that the invasion lasted each year was forty (2.57.2), and after the Peloponnesians had departed, perhaps in June, the evacuees would have been free to return to their homes. Since the Peloponnesians presumably targeted a fresh area each year, as the war continued more and more Athenians would have returned to find their farms laid waste. The annual cycle was repeated until 425, when the Spartans who had been holed up on the island of Sphacteria surrendered to the Athenians. And yet this momentous event receives no mention in Thucydides. It is possible that some evacuees, out of either preference or inertia, may have chosen to remain in the city. If so, one of the most significant social consequences of the war was to cause a shift from the countryside to the city, though the evidence for such a migration is tantalizingly inconclusive.

Several other cities had evacuated their rural populations on the outbreak of the Peloponnesian War. When the Athenians invaded Boeotia, for instance, the inhabitants of several townships in Boeotia had migrated to Thebes, thereby doubling the size of its population (*Hell. Oxy.* 12.3). Likewise, before the Thebans began investing Plataea, the Athenians had escorted all the women, children, and other noncombatants to Athens, where they remained for the duration of the war (Thuc. 2.6.3; see earlier, chapter 5). Though these are the only examples that we hear of, other communities may well have responded similarly. One of the largest evacuations must have been that of the Syracusans in 414, in advance of the Athenian attempt to invest their city by land and by sea (cf. Thuc. 6.102).

Evacuations during the Punic Wars in Sicily

A number of Greek cities in Sicily were forced to evacuate their populations during the First and Second Punic Wars that were fought between Dionysius I of Syracuse and the Carthaginians. In 406, the year of the outbreak of the first of these wars, the Carthaginians began besieging Acragas, whose people had refused their offer of an alliance. As the siege dragged on, the city began to run out of food. Eventually, when the Carthaginians intercepted a consignment of grain that the Syracusans had sent for their relief, their generals ordered an immediate evacuation (see map 2). So one night in mid-December the entire population departed under military escort for Gela, a coastal city that lay some 40 miles to the east. Diodorus graphically describes the scene as follows (13.89.1–3):

> Because there was such a mass of men, women and children leaving the city, a sudden outburst of tears and lamentation filled people's homes. Fear of the enemy gripped them, while at the same time, because of the haste with which they had to act, they were compelled to abandon to the barbarians all

the things that had given them so much joy. . . . It was not only the wealth of this great city that was being left behind but also a great multitude of human beings. For the sick were neglected by their relatives, since everyone looked after his own interests. Those, too, who were elderly, were abandoned because of their infirmity. Many who reckoned that separation from their homeland was equal to death laid violent hands upon themselves so that they might expire in the family home. The multitude that left the city, however, was at least under military escort as far as Gela. The highway and all the parts of the countryside leading to Gela was thronged with women, children, and young girls, who, exchanging the pampered lifestyle to which they had been accustomed for a strenuous march and extreme hardship, held out to the bitter end, their spirits toughened by fear.

The Carthaginians took control of Acragas the next day. Almost all of those who had remained in the city were massacred. Acragas—a very rich city—was sacked and all its treasures were shipped to Carthage.

There is no knowing how the evacuees survived the long march. Though it is inspiring to read of "spirits toughened by fear," many surely collapsed along the way. A trek of 40 miles undertaken by night is a challenge even for the most vigorous spirits, as Diodorus concedes. He indicates that the evacuees did not walk in a column but spread themselves out over the countryside, which was inevitable given the fact that the "road" would have been little better than a dirt track, so they would also have been extremely vulnerable to predators. We learn nothing about their reception by the Geloans. How much advance warning had they received? In the event Gela proved to be only a temporary stop for the refugees, who "some time later" were permitted by the Syracusans to settle in Leontini (13.89.4).

A year later they were uprooted again. Following his defeat at the Battle of Gela, Dionysius negotiated a temporary truce with the Carthaginians to recover his dead. Under cover of darkness he then evacuated the population of Gela (including presumably the Acragantine refugees), by leaving fires that burned all night to deceive the enemy. No doubt the mood of the evacuees would have been made more miserable by the fact that they had to leave their dead unburied.

FIGURE 11 Bronze *onkia* (a coin used by the Sicilian Greeks equivalent to one-sixtieth of an Attic *drachma*) from Camarina, ca. 420–405. The obverse depicts the head of a gorgon. The reverse depicts an owl with a lizard in its left claw. The legend reads *KAM(ARINAIŌN)*. According to tradition Camarina was founded in ca. 598 by settlers from Syracuse. It was destroyed by Gelon in 484 and its population transferred to Syracuse. It remained practically deserted until its refoundation by settlers from Gela in 461. In 405 Dionysius I forcibly evacuated the population to Syracuse, whereupon the Carthaginians destroyed the abandoned city. This coin is dated to the years shortly before that destruction. Not long afterward the refugees left Syracuse for Leontini. Camarina was repopulated by Timoleon (D.S. 16.82.7; cf. Talbert 1974, 149–50).

A few days later, as Diodorus reports, Dionysius ordered the evacuation of Camarina, a coastal city that lay 20 miles to the east of Gela, calculating that it would have been unable to withstand a siege once winter advanced (13.111.3–6):

> Their fear did not permit the people of Camarina to delay. Some of them grabbed the silver and gold they possessed and anything else that they could easily transport. Others, however, fled only with their parents and infant children, paying no thought to their valuables. A number of elderly and sick people who had no friends or relatives were abandoned, since the Carthaginians were expected to arrive any minute.... Now that the inhabitants of two cities had been uprooted, the countryside was awash with women and children and every manner of riff-raff. When the troops saw this, they were incensed at Dionysius and pitied the lot of those who were his luckless victims. For they saw freeborn boys and young girls of marriageable age hurrying along the road in a manner that was quite indecent for persons

of their years. In similar fashion they felt sympathy for the elderly, as they saw them being compelled beyond their natural resources to keep up with those still in the prime of life.

It remains questionable whether the resettlement of the populations of Gela and Camarina should be thought of as evacuations or as deportations. In both cases the decision to evacuate was the only option available, though this did not make the event any the less traumatic for those involved. Their resentment was no doubt intense and there were probably many who departed under extreme pressure. It is hardly surprising, therefore, that the contemporary perception was that Dionysius had exploited people's dread of the Carthaginians "to become lord of the remaining cities without exposing himself to risk" (D.S. 13.112.1). Soon afterward a revolt against Dionysius broke out and the refugees from Gela and Camarina fled once more—this time to the abandoned city of Leontini (13.113.4).

7

THE ASYLUM-SEEKER

Asylum as a Sacred Obligation

The international community first assumed protection for refugees as a result of the rise of nationalism in the late nineteenth and early twentieth centuries, and later from massive population displacement caused by World War I. The belief that refugees should be treated with respect was widely endorsed in antiquity and is enshrined in several sacred texts. In the so-called Covenant Code the Lord of the Hebrews declares that he will establish a place to which those guilty of unpremeditated homicide may take refuge so that their cases can be properly adjudicated before the deceased's nearest relative has an opportunity to undertake a revenge killing (Exodus 21:13). In later books of the Hebrew Bible, He instructs the Israelites to establish "cities of refuge" for the same purpose (Numbers 35:9–15; Deuteronomy 4:41–43 and 19:1–13; Joshua 20:1–9). The Roman historian Livy attributed to Romulus the founding of an asylum on the Capitoline Hill, where, during his reign, "An indiscriminate mass of people, some free, some servile, fled from neighboring peoples, eager for a new start in life, with the consequence that the population of Rome increased for the first time" (1.8.6). The Romans also established the reciprocal right for exiles to take refuge in neighboring cities in Latium and they later extended it to include other cities. In its definition of *birr*, the Arabic word sometimes translated as "piety," the Qur'an includes giving money to *ibn as sabil*, literally "a son of the road," meaning anyone who has no means to survive, including refugees and exiles (Second Surah v. 177). The Qur'an also requires the faithful to provide *aman* (refuge) to non-Muslims.

The Greeks, too, observed the principle of asylum, and there are many examples in their literature of the gods taking vengeance on those who mistreat suppliants. One of the explanations that Herodotus puts forward as to why Cleomenes I of Sparta went mad is divine retribution for having executed some Argive suppliants who had taken refuge in his sacred grove (6.75.3). Similarly, Thucydides reports the widely held belief that the great earthquake at Sparta in 464 was divine retribution for the fact that the Spartans had ejected helot suppliants from the sanctuary of Poseidon at Taenarum and then slaughtered them (1.128.1). Pausanias interpreted the destruction of Helice by earthquake on the north coast of the Peloponnese in 373 as proof that "the wrath of the god of suppliants is inexorable," since its inhabitants had killed some suppliants who had taken refuge in the sanctuary of Poseidon, the god thought to cause earthquakes (7.25.1). We should note, however, that it was left to the gods to exact redress against those who violated the right of asylum. There were no provisions in Greek lawcodes to punish violators.

Qualifying for Asylum

The Greek word *asulia*, which we somewhat misleadingly translate as "asylum" and which is sometimes better translated as "inviolability," literally means "not plundering" or in the case of an individual "the condition of not being plundered or abducted [viz from a sanctuary]." In theory at least *asulia* offered refuge for all, irrespective of a person's political affiliation, socioeconomic status, ethnicity, or any other qualifying condition. What complicates our understanding of the term is the fact that it is closely related to, but distinct from, *hikesia* or *hiketeia* (supplication), though the exact difference is difficult to determine. One distinction is that *asulia* might be a long-term arrangement, whereas *hikesia* was only ever a temporary expedient.

Because any long-distance traveler was usually at some risk in ancient Greece, anyone with a legitimate reason to be on the road or at sea was entitled to apply for *asulia* inside a sanctuary. This would have included athletes and spectators traveling to and from the various panhellenic festivals and games, ambassadors and state delegates en route from one city-state to another, the sick and their attendants visiting sanctuaries that belonged to the healing god Asclepius, plus tourists, merchants, and so on. At times of crisis, too, entire populations might seek refuge in a local sanctuary (see below).

In addition, orphans, adolescent girls escaping from an arranged marriage, runaway slaves, and other kinds of needy individuals could claim *asulia*. Abandoned children were sometimes deposited in sanctuaries in the hope that they would be properly cared for, perhaps by the temple authorities themselves. Fugitives and criminals were also eligible to apply, though the decision whether to grant them asylum would no doubt have been controversial. Traitors, too, could seek sanctuary, like the Argive general Thrasylus, who narrowly escaped being stoned to death by his fellow-citizens when he sought refuge at an altar (Thuc. 5.59.5, 60.6). Pursued by his army, the Spartan admiral Astyochus avoided being lynched only by taking refuge at an altar after he had threatened to thrash one of their number (Thuc. 8.84.1–3).

As Chaniotis (1996, 67) remarks, "Considerations of sin, guilt, right, and justice have no bearing on the claim of a suppliant to remain in the sanctuary"—no doubt to the disconsolation of many. Ion in Euripides' play of that name not only rails against malefactors who seek asylum, but even attacks the gods for supporting the institution (ll. 1312–20):

> It is shameful that a god ordained bad laws for mortals—statutes that were not framed wisely. Unrighteous persons should not be allowed to squat beside the altar but be driven out by force. It is not proper that hands that are soiled with sin should touch the gods. Righteous people, if they are wronged, should claim sanctuary. Good and bad people should not indiscriminately claim the same boon of the gods.

Ion's observation that the institution lent itself to abuse was doubtless correct, though it comes oddly from the mouth of a temple servant who had himself been abandoned inside a sacred precinct. We should also note that in some city-states communal law overrode the universal entitlement to supplication. In Athens, for instance, murderers and *kakourgoi* (felons), were prohibited from supplicating. This included kidnappers, thieves, male prostitutes, and deserters (Naiden 2006, 178). In addition, those who were polluted through birth, marriage, or death and those who had been deprived of their civic rights (known collectively as *atimoi*) were automatically prohibited from entering a sanctuary and thus denied the right of *asulia* (Chaniotis 1996, 72–75).

We also hear of a large number of civilians seeking refuge in a sanctuary in wartime, though it did them little good. In ca. 390, when the Spartan king Agesilaus invaded Perachora, "a multitude of men and women, both servile and nonservile, together with a large number of cattle" took refuge in the Heraeum. Not long afterward, the asylum-seekers voluntarily came out of the sanctuary, perhaps because Agesilaus threatened to slay them anyway. Those deemed hostile to Sparta were murdered, whereas the others were sold into slavery (Xen. *Hell.* 4.5.5; Sinn 1996, 67–69).

In theory at least asylum might be granted to an enemy in wartime. Claiming to be the son of a Cretan called Castor, Odysseus tells Eumaeus that he and his men once invaded Egypt with the purpose of stealing food and abducting both the women and children. The Egyptians turned the tables on the raiding party, however, "slaughtering some and capturing others." At this the Cretan stranger threw away his arms and supplicated the Egyptian king, who answered his appeal by defending him from attack from his own subjects (*Od.* 14.257–84).

Though many helpless people must have had their appeal for asylum rejected, especially if it meant angering a powerful state or person, occasionally compassion prevailed. When 300 Corcyrean boys who were being escorted to Sardis under military escort in order to undergo castration escaped from their guards and took refuge in the sanctuary of Artemis on Samos, the islanders hit on the imaginative plan of instituting a festival that required celebrants to bring cakes to the sanctuary. By this means the guards were prevented from starving the boys into submission (Hdt. 3.48).

Supplication

The current working definition of an asylum-seeker is "an individual who arrives in another state seeking protection in that state, but who has yet to be granted refugee status" (Gibney 2009, 315). The same definition works well enough for the ancient world, though we should note that many asylum-seekers would have been internally displaced as opposed to being refugees from abroad. One could petition for asylum by supplicating an individual, a god, or a community. Supplication not only took the form of a formal verbal appeal but also necessitated ritual action involving gestures and movements, the intent being to establish a religious bond between the two parties through self-abasement (Gould 1973, 94). It could occur in all sorts of situations: gods supplicated other gods, humans supplicated gods, women supplicated men, and slaves supplicated their owners (Herman 1987, 56). Scenes of supplication occur in both the Homeric poems and Greek tragedy, but rarely elsewhere in Greek literature, though defendants in lawsuits occasionally present themselves as suppliants. The act is also depicted occasionally in art (Naiden 2006, figures 2.1–9).

Though suppliants were under the protection of Zeus *Hikesios*, there was no moral or religious obligation for the supplicandus to accede to a particular request (Freyburger 1988, 512). The extent to which Zeus *Hikesios* might be expected to intervene on a suppliant's behalf is therefore questionable. Possibly his role was limited to insuring that the suppliant's vulnerability was not exploited.

It was customary to grasp either an altar or a statue within a sanctuary, as Orestes does to escape his pursuers (Aes. *Eum.* 258; cf. Hom. *Od.* 22.334–36). The most detailed description occurs at the beginning of Aeschylus's *Suppliants* (ca. 463), where the daughters of Danaüs, after fleeing from Egypt under the protection of their father to escape forced marriage with their cousins, take refuge in a sanctuary in Argos near their point of disembarkation. Soon they attract the attention of the local inhabitants and a menacing crowd begins to surround them. To placate the crowd, Danaüs urges his daughters to adopt the formal guise of suppliants. This they do by holding branches in their left hands wound around with white woolen fillets. The branches, which could be made of either laurel or olive, identify the group as suppliants. He also advises his daughters to call upon the Greek gods, specifically Apollo, Poseidon, and Hermes, who were presumably worshipped in the sanctuary (ll. 176–233).

When supplicating an individual, it was customary to touch the chin, grasp the knees, or seize the hands as a demonstration of submission. When Priam comes to supplicate Achilles for the return of Hector's body, he grasps both his knees and his hands—"the hands that killed so many of his sons," as Homer reminds his audience (*Il.* 24.478–80). However, when Odysseus is washed up on the shores of Scheria, naked and begrimed, he decides to "stand well away and supplicate Nausicaä in flattering terms, for fear that if he grasped her knees, she might become angry" (*Od.* 6.146–47). It is, of course, deeply ironic that a seasoned warrior like Odysseus should be reduced to supplicating an adolescent and defenseless virgin. But it is also one of life's ironies, and that is where the joke lies. Similarly, when the fugitive seer Theoclymenus, who has slain a fellow-tribesman, entreats Telemachus to be taken on board ship, the two refrain from physical contact, perhaps because the seer is guilty of manslaughter (see later, chapter 8).

Another instructive instance of *hikesia* is reported by Thucydides in the case of the fugitive Themistocles, who found temporary asylum with Admetus, king of the Molossians, even though the two had previously not been on good terms (1.136.1–137.1). As luck would have it, Admetus was away from his palace when Themistocles arrived. Otherwise the suppliant would surely have been sent packing. Instead he was greeted by Admetus's wife. Well-schooled in the niceties of supplication, she urged her visitor to pick up her child and squat by the hearth to await her husband's return, this being "the most solemn form of supplication." A hearth, like a sanctuary, had powerful religious significance, since it was sacred to the goddess Hestia. Her advice proved effective. Admetus overcame his animosity and granted Themistocles asylum. When Themistocles' pursuers arrived to demand that he hand over the fugitive, Admetus sent them on their way. His behavior was in sharp contrast with that of the Corcyraeans, who had previously rejected Themistocles' appeal for asylum, even though, as Thucydides notes, he had shown them favor in the past.

The Politics of Offering Asylum

There is no way of knowing what percentage of appeals for *asulia* met with success. I strongly suspect, however, that the vast majority was granted only after those being petitioned had asked the question, "What's in it for me?" The Corcyraeans rejected Themistocles' appeal because they were fearful of offending his pursuers. Soon after the Peloponnesian War ended, the Thebans, Corinthians, and Megarians, alarmed at Sparta's ascendancy, provided refuge for exiled Athenian democrats. Not for nothing Oedipus promises the chorus of Athenian citizens that he will "bring profit to those who receive him by settling in their land." The "profit," as he later explains, will take the form of assistance in their wars against the Thebans, when his corpse, as he ominously predicts, will drink their enemies' blood (Soph. *OC* 92, cf. 287–88; 616–23).

It obviously helped if suppliants had rendered some service to their hosts in the past. A speech written by Isocrates, which purports to have been delivered before the Athenian Assembly when Plataean refugees appealed for immigrant status after the destruction of their city by the Thebans probably in 373, provides insight into the kind of arguments that asylum-seekers might use. After praising the Athenians for their exemplary record toward refugees in general, the speaker reminds the Assembly of Plataea's past services. He acknowledges that he faces an uphill battle since the Thebans have secured the assistance of Athens's ablest orators. After an extended piece of Theban-bashing, he describes the pitiful plight of his compatriots in the event that the Athenians reject their appeal. "We will become the unhappiest of men," he declares. "We will have been deprived of our city-state, our land, and our possessions in the space of a single day, and, lacking all the necessities of life, will have become *alêtai* [wanderers] and beggars, uncertain where to turn and miserable no matter where we happen to live" (14.46). The Assembly must have been used to hearing similar appeals whenever foreigners petitioned for refuge in Athens. Much must have depended on whether they could gain the support of powerful individuals.

If, however, suppliants were likely to expose their hosts to risk at the hands of a third party, particularly a foreign power, their chances of receiving asylum would have been negligible. When the Epidamnians beseeched the Corcyraeans "not to allow them to perish but to arrange peace between them and the exiles, and to bring about an end to the war with the barbarians . . . while seated as suppliants in the sanctuary of Hera," the Corcyraeans rejected their appeal for fear of antagonizing the Corinthians (Thuc. 1.24.5–7; see earlier, chapter 5).

Asylum-seekers might resort to intimidation to get their way. In the 420s about 400 Corcyrean oligarchs, suspecting that they would be massacred by the democratic faction, took refuge in the sanctuary of Hera—probably the same Heraeum referred to a moment ago. The democrats, fearing that the asylum-seekers were sufficient in number to instigate an insurrection, persuaded them to retire to an offshore island and agreed to supply them with provisions (Thuc. 3.75.5).

Granting Asylum within a Sanctuary

Although Zeus was the general overseer of asylum, every Greek sanctuary, regardless of which deity it belonged to, could provide refuge to those in need. It was considered an act of sacrilege to remove a suppliant from a sanctuary by force, since to do so was tantamount to stealing divine property—the verb *sulan* (to steal) that gives us the word *asulia*. Well-frequented sanctuaries offered the best prospects for refugees, as it was all too easy to drive them away from a sanctuary that was rarely frequented. There was, however, a structural flaw in the system. Once a suppliant had gained access to a sanctuary, he or she could use the threat of starvation to blackmail the temple authorities. For if a death occurred within the sanctuary precincts, this caused pollution, which would be certain to arouse divine anger. The temple authorities would therefore have to weigh their options carefully, taking into account the religious consequences of their decision. In practice, however, they probably allowed those with political authority to decide.

Some sanctuaries, like that at Taenarum in the Peloponnese, provided rudimentary accommodation for asylum-seekers (Thuc. 1.133). Long-term residency, however, other than in the case of those who were seeking a cure for a chronic illness or those who, like Ion, were brought up as temple servants, was highly exceptional. Even so, we cannot rule out the possibility that a handful of individuals remained at a sanctuary for an extended period of time, surviving on charitable donations from visitors. There is, however, little evidence to indicate that those who ran the sanctuary were under any obligation, sacred or otherwise, to provide sustenance to those whom they admitted into their precincts, though they may well have provided them with scraps of food in return for work. For the most part suppliants were probably expected to shift for themselves.

Some of the most popular sanctuaries for asylum-seekers were situated either on the coast or on an offshore island, no doubt because many of them arrived by boat, while others, using it as a way station, sought to escape by sea. They include the sanctuary of Artemis at Ephesus, the sanctuary of Hera at Perachora, and the sanctuaries of Poseidon at Geraestus (southernmost Euboea), Calauria (an island off the coast at Troezen), Sunium (on the south coast of Attica), and Taenarum (at the tip of the Mani peninsula).

Settling Asylum-Seekers Long-Term

Once asylum-seekers had successfully petitioned to become long-term residents within the state, what became of them? The only detailed discussion of this question occurs in Aeschylus's *Suppliants*. Following the passing of the decree permitting him and his daughters to reside permanently in the land, Danaüs makes the following announcement (ll. 609–14):

> We are to reside freely as permanent immigrants in the land. We cannot be seized as surety [?] and we are to enjoy *asulia* from all men. No resident or alien has the right to carry us off as slaves. If anyone uses force against us, any *gamoros* [landowner] who fails to render us assistance will be *atimos* [deprived of civic rights] and driven into exile by public decree.

Danaüs's words are obviously intended to reproduce the phrasing of the decree. Indeed they may well be a paraphrase of an actual decree granting immigrant status to asylum-seekers. Later in the play the Argive king Pelasgus deals with the practical question of how to accommodate the new residents in his community. He suggests that they should take up residence in what he calls *dômatia dêmia* (public dwellings). This presumably means either public hostels or, more plausibly, privately owned houses belonging to wealthy individuals that are capable of accommodating a large number of guests for an extended period. The Danaids, it seems, will be allowed to either cohabit as a group or live in separate houses. Pelasgus does not indicate whether the separate houses would constitute a ghetto of sorts or be scattered throughout the city. He makes much of these seemingly trivial details, which are repeated about a hundred lines later in the play, where he states that the Danaids will not be charged rent (ll. 1009–1011). He ends by announcing that he and the citizen body will act as their official *prostatês* (legal representative), the title, incidentally, of an Athenian who represented the interests of a metic (see later, chapter 9).

Mistreating Asylum-Seekers

Despite the belief that the gods punished those who violated *asulia* with extreme severity, the plight of suppliants was uncertain at best. Trickery, deception, and other forms of entrapment were used to entice them away from their place of refuge. In fact the earliest instance of asylum-seeking in the historical record also happens to be the earliest instance when asylum was violated. In ca. 632 an Athenian named Cylon made an abortive attempt to establish a tyranny. When it failed, he and his supporters took refuge at an altar on the Acropolis. Just when they were on the point of starving to death, the suppliants were encouraged to leave the sanctuary under promise of safe conduct. But instead they were slaughtered. The instigator of these killings was Megacles, a member of the highly prestigious Athenian *genos* (noble kin group) known as the Alcmaeonids. As punishment for this sacrilege, the Athenians pronounced a curse on the *genos* and its descendants in perpetuity. In consequence, all its living members were driven into exile and the bones of their dead were disinterred and cast out of Attica, though the curse was later rescinded (Hdt. 5.71; Thuc. 1.126.3–12).

A similar instance occurred in Sparta in ca. 471 when the regent Pausanias took refuge in the sanctuary of Athena on the Spartan Acropolis to escape arrest by the ephors, who had charged him with offering citizenship to helot rebels. The ephors barricaded him inside the temple and when Pausanias was on the point of starvation they dragged him outside so that his corpse should not pollute the sanctuary (Thuc. 1.134). What made their action especially offensive was the fact that they had previously tricked him into making a confession by having a former servant of his pose as a suppliant. Again, when an unnamed Aeginetan, along with 700 others, was being led to his execution by the ruling oligarchical faction on Aegina, he managed to break his shackles and escape to the sanctuary of Demeter Thesmophorus. The Aeginetan grasped the door handles so tightly that his would-be captors resorted to the desperate remedy of "chopping off his hands and leading him in that manner, with his hands still attached to the door handles" (Hdt. 6.91.2).

The weakness of the institution of *asulia* is further illustrated by examples of suppliants who narrowly escaped massacre. In 427 the oligarchic party in Corcyra, fearing that the democrats were going to draft them as rowers in the fleet and ship them off to Athens, sought asylum in the sanctuary of the Dioscuri. The democrats were barely restrained by the Athenians from using violence against "any whom they encountered" (Thuc. 3.75.2–4). Left to their own devices, they would evidently have put their enemies to the sword, including those inside the sanctuary itself. Especially horrendous is what happened shortly afterward. Members of the oligarchic faction who had fled to the sanctuary of Hera, now realizing that they would be massacred by the democrats, "proceeded to slay one another within the sanctuary, while some hanged themselves on the trees and others took their own lives as best they were able" (3.81.3).

Whenever a city was taken by siege, it was common practice for noncombatants to seek refuge on sacred property in the hope that their lives would be spared. Rarely, however, do we hear of compassion being extended to them. On the contrary, both in literature and in vase paintings, it is the mistreatment of those seeking refuge at altars and other holy places that is insisted upon repeatedly. When, for instance, Alexander the Great took Thebes in 335, we are told that "women, children, and the elderly who had fled to the shrines were dragged off and subjected to the utmost outrage" (D.S. 17.13.6; cf. Arr. *Anab.* 1.8.8). Alexander's treatment of Thebes was perhaps exceptional only in the sheer number of suppliants who were treated in this way.

To conclude, it seems doubtful whether *asulia* and the attendant and related institution of *hikesia* served the interests of migrants and refugees to any appreciable degree. It has been suggested that by the end of the fifth century "supplication ... was becoming increasingly a ritual whose binding force was weakening in face of the counter-strain of political realities" (Gould 1973, 101). Overall the evidence tends to indicate that this was true.* Then as now, those whose request for sanctuary had failed were either deported or simply disappeared into an underground world, subject to various forms of exploitation.

Athens's Exceptionalism

When the Attic dramatists reshaped traditional Greek myths to foreground Athenian preoccupations and concerns, they created an idealized

---

* Chaniotis (1996, 83) offers a slightly more nuanced assessment: "At the latest from the early fifth century *asulia* and supplication were increasingly becoming claims which ought not to be respected automatically, but only after a close examination of each individual case."

image of their city that embodied the civic virtues that their country-men professed to espouse. It was Athens, their plays proclaimed, that practices justice, opposes tyranny, demonstrates compassion for the weak, and provides sanctuary for the oppressed, not least by offering asylum in courageous defiance of threats from those communities from which the suppliants have fled. Aeschylus's *Eumenides*, Sophocles' *Oedipus at Colonus*, and Euripides' *Madness of Heracles*, *Descendants of Heracles*, *Suppliants*, and *Medea* all demonstrate (in varying nuanced ways) Athens standing up for the weak and oppressed.

The heated exchange between Demophon, king of Athens, and Copreus, herald of Eurystheus, king of Argos, in Euripides' *Descendants of Heracles* (possibly dated 430) reveals the pride that the Athenians took in their reputation for resisting attempts by foreigners to secure the handover of asylum-seekers. The dialogue takes place inside the sanctuary of Zeus at Marathon, where the refugees are currently sheltering (ll. 252–66):

DEMOPHON: You will never take these men away with you.

HERALD: What if my cause is just and my argument prevails?

DEMOPHON: How can it be just to drag away a suppliant by force?

HERALD: What if it brought no shame to me and no harm to you?

DEMOPHON: But it would indeed harm me, if I let you drag them off.

HERALD: Just leave them outside your borders. We'll handle them from that point.

DEMOPHON: You're stupid if you think you can hoodwink the god.

HERALD: This is obviously the place where outlaws find refuge.

DEMOPHON: This holy spot affords protection to all . . .

HERALD: I wouldn't like to see you having us as your enemy.

DEMOPHON: Nor would I. But I'm not going to hand these men over.

Brave words indeed, though we should note that Euripides never presents things in black and white terms. Eurystheus, the villain of the piece, when caught, admits that he has mistreated the refugees, but Alcmene, Heracles' mother, is objectionable in the way that she bays for his blood. Demophon is not entirely principled either. He makes it clear that his primary motive for providing asylum is concern for his honor, "which I chiefly have to think about" (l. 242). He later tells the Chorus: "Some say that it is right to help strangers, others claim that I am acting like a fool" (ll. 416–18). Public opinion, in other words, is very much to the fore in his calculation.

When the blind and elderly Oedipus in Sophocles' *Oedipus at Colonus* appeals to the chorus to be allowed to reside within their territory, he commends Athens for being "the city that has more power than any other to give me, the wronged stranger, refuge, and more power than any other to come to my rescue" (ll. 261–62).

The literary topos of Athens offering a secure haven for the oppressed also occurs in oratory, as in the appeal by a Plataean representative discussed earlier (Isoc. 14.1):

> Since we Plataeans are aware, Athenians, that you are accustomed eagerly to come to the help of those who have been wronged and since we know too that you most generously reward your benefactors, we come as *hiketeusontes* [suppliants] in the hope that you will not overlook the fact that we have been uprooted from our land in peacetime by the Thebans. And since many people have fled to you and have received all they required, we think that it is especially proper that you show consideration for our city.

Elsewhere Isocrates describes Athens as offering "the securest *kataphugê* [refuge]" to those who are oppressed, conclusive proof being that the city provided succor for the descendants of Heracles when they were returning to the Peloponnese after many generations (4.41, 54–56). It is perhaps telling that no more recent example of any note came to his mind.

The Athenians were clearly susceptible to the image of themselves as a humane society that was uniquely protective of the oppressed. No doubt it filled them with a sense of gratification and pride. We know, too, that they successfully promulgated it outside their borders and that it endured over time. Plutarch, writing in the late first century CE, states that Athens had already secured its reputation for hospitality to asylum-seekers by the time of Solon (that is, early sixth century BCE), when "the city was teeming with people constantly flooding into Attica from all over the Mediterranean seeking refuge" (*Sol.* 22.1).

Did the Athenian *dêmos* live up to this vision in reality? I strongly suspect that, like every other community, it was receptive to refugees only when it suited its purpose to be so and that there was no more compassion in the breast of an average Athenian than there was in that of any other ancient Greek. The sobering fact remains, moreover, that there are virtually no historical instances of foreign asylum-seekers being granted residency in Athens. The 212 pro-Athenian Plataeans who escaped from their besieged city and were permitted to settle in Athens in 428/7 were accorded this right because their city was a valued ally (Thuc. 3.20.2). And when in 421 the Athenians resettled these same refugees in Scione on the western headland of Chalcidice, hundreds of miles from their homeland, they did so only after they had slaughtered all the men and enslaved the women and children who were living there (5.32.1). Other instances of Athenian "exceptionalism" were strictly *quid pro quo*. The Samians were offered Athenian citizenship in 405 because Samos had served as Athens's main naval base in the Aegean during the Peloponnesian War and had remained a loyal ally even after the crushing defeat at Aegospotami (*ML* 94.12–15 = Fornara 166). Similarly the exiled Acarnanians were permitted to reside indefinitely in Athens because they had fought alongside the Athenians against Philip II of Macedon at the Battle of Chaeronea in 338 (*IG* II² 237 = *SIG*³ 259 = Rhodes and Osborne 77). In sum, what chiefly differentiated Athens from other *poleis* was not its treatment of refugees and asylum-seekers per se, but the fact that it was bound by a more complicated set of alliances than any other city-state.

Xenia and Proxenia

"Stranger, it is not right that I should disrespect a stranger, not even one who comes here who is more wretched than you," declares the swine-herd Eumaeus to Odysseus, when the latter returns to Ithaca in disguise. He then adds, "All strangers and beggars are under the protection of

Zeus" (Hom. *Od.* 14.56–58). Eumaeus is alluding to the religiously sanctioned institution known as *xenia*, a term loosely translated as "guest-friendship," which placed both guest and host under the protection of Zeus Xenios, as well as under a reciprocal obligation to treat each other respectfully. I justify its inclusion in this chapter on the grounds that *xenia* is a species of asylum that may well have developed out of the same impulse to provide protection for those who were unprotected as that which promoted *asulia*.

Xenia bound aristocrats and their direct descendants together in perpetuity. Just before the Greek Diomedes and the Trojan Glaucus are about to engage in single combat, they realize that their grandfathers were linked by *xenia*. "For this reason I am your *xeinos philos* [friend and host] in the heart of Argos, and you are mine in Lycia, when I come to your land," says Diomedes. They then exchange armor "so that others may know that we are guests and friends from the time of our fathers." Glaucus, it turns out, comes off by far the worse, handing over his gold armor and receiving bronze in return (*Il.* 6.224–31).

But though *xenia* primarily served the needs of mobile aristocrats, Eumaeus's suggestion that it was occasionally practiced by persons of no social distinction, though idealistic, may not be wholly fantastical. After all, any Greek who was on the road would have had to throw himself at times on the mercy of strangers. There were few if any wayside inns, and sleeping under the stars would have been extremely dangerous. In fact it is highly likely that *xenia* came into being as a response to widespread mobility. And as we have seen already, it bound together Greeks and non-Greeks, particularly at the high end of the social scale. Herodotus informs us that when Croesus, king of Lydia, sent a messenger with gifts and requested an alliance with the Spartans, the latter "rejoiced in the arrival of the Lydians and swore oaths regarding both guest-friendship and an alliance" (1.69.1–3).

By the first half of the fifth century many states, including Athens, had placed the care of their members when traveling abroad in the hands of local citizens known as *proxenoi* (literally "those who represent *xenoi*"). *Proxenoi* were expected to provide those whose state they represented with hospitality and other services, particularly if they were visiting dignitaries. They also represented them in court, when they fell foul of the law. For obvious reasons the ideal candidates for the position were wealthy aristocrats who had extensive connections abroad and were themselves well-traveled. A number of *proxenoi* were honored by the city they represented, at times by the grant of citizenship.

It is generally believed that *proxenia* had its origins in guest friendship, the plausible theory being that private ties of hospitality gradually evolved into public ones (Walbank 1978, 2–3). Like *xenia, proxenia* testifies to the prevalence of travel in the ancient world. From the archaic period onward there was an increasing flow of travelers moving throughout the Greek world, some to cities that were centers of trading activity, others to those that sponsored athletic games, and still others to cities that possessed a sanctuary of international repute. *Proxenia* offered those travelers who resided temporarily abroad some measure of protection and support.

8

THE FUGITIVE

Fugitives in Archaic Literature

Murderers and homicides, condemned to live either on the margins of society or completely outside it, are prevalent in Greek literature. We already encounter them in Homer, often in hauntingly abbreviated passages that leave us uncertain as to what has brought these individuals to such a pass. All that we know about Bellerophon, for instance, is that Proteus of Argos drove him into exile "because he was far stronger" (*Il.* 6.157–59), although a later version states that he was falsely accused of attempting to seduce Proteus's wife. Having incurred the hatred of the gods, Bellerophon wandered along the Aleian or Wandering Plain, "eating his heart out, avoiding the path of men" (*Il.* 6.200–202). It sounds like a fate worse than death—solitary confinement in a boundless space where he and others of his kind traipse back and forth endlessly to no purpose and with no outcome. Was Bellerophon condemned to search out this path or did society's rejection force it upon him? Elsewhere we learn that he is a homicide, but the details are not spelled out.

Bellerophon was, to his cost, a loner, but Tlepolemus, the son of Heracles, enjoyed divine support, and that made all the difference to a man on the run. Having murdered his father's elderly uncle Licymnius, he assembled a small fleet, gathered a sizable company, and fled from his brothers and nephews. Eventually he arrived at Rhodes, "an *alômenos* [wanderer] and a man of sorrow," where his luck changed dramatically. He was able to establish a settlement on the island with three tribal groupings. It clearly helped that he was "beloved of Zeus," especially since Zeus turned a blind eye to his crime. In fact Tlepolemus prospered so

FIGURE 12 Silver *drachma* from Rhodes, ca. 205–190. The obverse depicts the sun god Helios, to
whom the island was sacred. (The Colossus of Rhodes, built in 282, was a statue of Helios.) The
reverse depicts a rose, for which the island is named. A budding sprig is visible to the right. A
bow case lies to the left. The letters R–O flank the stem of the rose. Rhodes originally consisted
of three independent cities, Lindus, Ialysus, and Camirus. All were allied to Athens in the fifth
century. In 408 they underwent what Strabo (*Geog.* 14.2.10) called a synoecism and a new city
called Rhodes was founded at the northern tip of the island.

much that he was able to contribute nine ships to the expedition to
Troy, which indicates that he had managed to turn his life around (*Il.*
2.653–70).

Tlepolemus is not the only fugitive who manages to turn his life
around in the *Iliad*. Another is Phoenix, who was cursed with infertil-
ity by his father after the latter discovers that he has slept with his slave
mistress, which he did at the bidding of his jealous mother. Though
his relatives tried to prevent him from fleeing, Phoenix managed to
evade detection one night and "fled far away through Greece of the
broad choruses" (9.478). He eventually arrived in Phthia, where Achilles' father Peleus granted him shelter. Peleus, we are told, "loved him as
a father loves his only son, an only son who is brought up among many
possessions"—an extraordinarily warm endorsement of his affection
for the fugitive (9.481–82). He even gave him a small kingdom to lord
over. In return, Phoenix acted *in loco parentis* to Achilles, who became
devoted and regarded him as his mentor. Being incapable of procreat-
ing, Phoenix doted upon Achilles as if he were his own child, evidently
in the forlorn hope that Achilles would look after him in old age.

Peleus, it seems, had a reputation for befriending fugitives. He took in Epeigeus, a Myrmidon who had unintentionally killed his own cousin. Epeigeus accompanied Achilles to Troy, though they do not seem to have been close friends (16.569–76). The infant Patroclus also found a warm reception under Peleus's roof when he was brought there by his father. He had killed one of his playmates, "not intentionally but in a rage when playing knucklebones," as his ghost reminds Achilles when it is requesting that their ashes be interred in the same cinerary urn. Far from exhibiting any distrust toward Patroclus on account of his violent temper, Peleus nurtured the child and allowed him to be his son's playmate (23.83–92). Though Peleus may have been unusual in his readiness to take in fugitives, we should not discount the possibility that there were other aristocratic households willing to do the same if the fugitive in question could be put to use.

In the world of the Homeric poems, and no doubt in archaic Greece in general, encounters with a fugitive must have been relatively commonplace. When Telemachus is about to sail back home to Ithaca after seeking news of his father in Sparta, he encounters the seer Theoclymenus, who informs him that it is his fate "to wander among men to avoid being killed on account of having slain a fellow-tribesman." "Take me on board," he pleads, "since I supplicate you as a fugitive. Don't let them kill me—I know they're after me." Telemachus agrees, saying, "I won't drive you from my ship. Come with me. You'll be looked after when I get home, with all I have" (*Od.* 15.271–82). What is striking is that Telemachus offers Theoclymenus more than he is asking for—temporary, if not permanent refuge under his roof. It is tempting to suppose that Telemachus's generosity would have been endorsed by the poet. Homer's point seems to be that fugitives may still have a useful function to fulfill, whether as the founder of a new settlement, as childminder, as seer, or merely as manual worker.

The fact remains that a fugitive could hardly predict what kind of reception he would receive when he knocked on the door of a great house. When Priam unexpectedly enters the tent of Achilles and supplicates him for the return of his son's body, it was "as when oppressive *atê* [destructiveness] has taken hold of a man who has committed murder in his native land and who has arrived in a foreign country at the house of a wealthy man" (*Il.* 24.480–82). The type of person who is called to the audience's mind has suffered intensely from social rejection and the point of the simile is that scarcely any condition was more wretched than that of a murderer on the run. The simile also exemplifies the unpredictability of a fugitive's lot. Priam put his life at risk when he entered Achilles' tent, just as many fugitives did when they ventured to knock on a stranger's door.

Fugitives, for obvious reasons, were hardly to be trusted. Often they sought to ingratiate themselves by purporting to offer a commodity that was in short supply in virtually every Greek household—namely, news. The swineherd Eumaeus observes to the beggarly Odysseus that he has long since ceased to trust anyone who prophesies his master's return "from the time when an Aetolian deceived me with his story, a murderer who came to my house after wandering far and wide over the earth, to whom I gave a kindly welcome" (*Od.* 14.379–81). His experience would no doubt have been all too familiar to Homer's audience, many of whom are likely to have been deceived by a vagrant spinning a plausible tale to earn a bed for the night. It is a mark of Eumaeus's uncompromising humanity that he is still prepared to offer hospitality to a stranger, one, incidentally, who is in the very act of deceiving him by assuming a false identity, even though he has already been badly burned in the past. He does so because he fears Zeus Xenios and pities his guest more than he resents being deceived by him. The only reason why princess Nausicaä is not suspicious of Odysseus when he supplicates her on the seashore is, as she tells him, because Scheria is too remote to be attacked by enemies (Hom. *Od.* 6.204–5). The stranger cannot therefore have any ulterior motive. Otherwise it is highly unlikely that she would have trusted him.

Homer's attitude toward fugitives is mainly positive. Herodotus by contrast uses the example of a fugitive to demonstrate the principle that some individuals, despite their best efforts, personify bad luck. He conveys this depressing moral in an anecdote about a Phrygian called Adrestus, who was exiled by his father for accidentally killing his brother (1.35–45). In the course of his wanderings Adrestus arrives at the court of the Lydian king Croesus, where he requests ritual purification for his crime. Croesus, being a man of principle, duly obliges and, having discovered that Adrestus's family and his are bound by ties of *xenia*, offers him refuge in his palace. Later, being plagued by a dream that prophesies his son's death, the king requests that Adrestus take care of his son while he is out hunting boar. Inadvertently Adrestus kills the son when taking aim at the boar. The story is perhaps expressive of the latent fear that many Greeks would have experienced at the thought of accommodating a killer under their roof, even one who was guilty of involuntary manslaughter. What makes it all the more tragic is that Adrestus warned Croesus of the bad luck that attended him. Croesus was just too decent to take his warning seriously. Not for nothing the name Adrestus is cognate with *adrasteia* (necessity, inevitability). Overcome with guilt at having committed involuntary manslaughter a second time, Adrestus took his own life.

Exile as Punishment for Crime

In Athenian law, and in the laws of other city-states, exile was used to punish those guilty of voluntary and involuntary homicide, politicians who had committed treason, and generals who had suffered a military defeat (see appendix D). Depending on the circumstances of the crime, it might be imposed either for life or for a fixed term of years. It frequently involved loss of civic rights and/or confiscation of property. However, when we read the word *phugê* in a literary text or inscription it is often unclear whether it signifies a sentence that has been passed in a court of law, or the voluntary flight of an accused individual engendered by fear of prosecution or violence at the hands of the murder victim's enraged countrymen. A case in point is the *phugê* of the historian Thucydides, who may either have been exiled or have fled in advance of prosecution (5.26.5).

The Athenian lawcode ascribed to Dracon (ca. 621/620) contains several provisions relating to exile. It recommended that exile should be the punishment for both voluntary and involuntary homicide (*IG* I³

104 = *IG* I² 115 = *ML* 86 = Fornara 15), though a republication of this lawcode in 409/8 seems to have potentially ameliorated the situation for a person guilty of involuntary homicide by decreeing that he could be pardoned if the victim's immediate relatives unanimously voted in his favor (ll. 11–16). If a person found guilty of homicide returned illegally, he could be killed with impunity. If he was accused of another crime while living abroad, he had to make his defense in a boat moored off shore at the court known as "in Phreatto" near the Piraeus (Dem. 23.77–78; [Arist.] *Ath. Pol.* 57.3–4). On his return to Attica the exile was required to make a sacrifice and purify himself before being readmitted into the community (Dem. 23.72).

After the first speeches had been delivered and before judgment had been pronounced, Athenian law permitted those who had been charged with homicide to go into voluntary exile. Only in egregious cases would a posse be dispatched to hunt a convicted fugitive down. While this might seem a humane alternative to capital punishment, in practice it must have been an excruciatingly hard decision to make, since it involved second-guessing the jury (MacDowell 1963, 115). In addition, the plaintiff might propose exile as an alternative to the death penalty after a guilty verdict had been delivered—an option Socrates rejected on the grounds that he would be as unpopular abroad as he had been in Athens and so "constantly exchanging one city for another" (Pl. *Ap.* 37d).

Plato in the *Laws* recommended exile as a punishment for those guilty of homicide, but with a view to rehabilitating the criminal. He proposed two years for a man convicted of involuntary homicide in order that he should "learn to control his temper," whereas if his crime had been intentional his period of exile should last three years (9.867c–e). In the interim a group of twelve men were to be appointed to review his case, and when his term of banishment had expired they were to assemble on the borders of the land and inform him whether he was deemed fit to return. We may wonder whether Plato expected him to be subjected to a test, too. If the convicted man committed a similar crime in the future, he was to be banished in perpetuity. Plato also recommended banishment lasting three years for a husband or wife who kills his or her partner, a father or mother who kills a son or daughter, or a sibling who kills another sibling (9.868c–e). Anyone who struck his father or his mother was to be banished from the city and exiled to the countryside, with the further restriction that he should not be permitted to enter any sanctuary (9.881b–d).

Once the decree of banishment had come into effect, it was illegal for anyone to befriend or give hospitality to an exile. The exile became in effect a nonperson, a condition graphically described by Orestes in Aeschylus's *Libation Bearers* (ll. 290–95):

> His back is scarred by a bronze whip; for such people there is neither a share in the mixing-bowl nor in libations poured in love. . . . There is no hospitality for him, but despised by all and friendless he eventually dies.

Plato paints an equally dark picture in the *Laws* (9.881de):

> If any free person eat, drink, or have any dealings whatsoever with a criminal [that is, sentenced to exile], or even so much as take his hand in knowledge of who he is, he shall not be permitted to enter any sanctuary or any agora or any part of the city whatsoever, without first purifying himself, as he is one who has been infected by contact with an accursed horror.

Exile was the punishment for serious crimes in cities other than Athens. A fragmentary decree from Miletus dated between 470 and 440 preserves the names of three men (more names were inscribed, but they have perished), who, along with their descendants, were exiled in perpetuity perhaps for attempting to establish a tyranny (*ML* 43 = Fornara 66). Bounty amounting to 100 *statêres*, extracted from their confiscated property, is to be paid out to "whoever kills any of them" (l. 3). If, on the other hand, they fall into the hands of the city-state—presumably by returning illicitly—they are to be put to death (ll. 7–9).

Few human conditions would have been worse than lifelong exile, for which there is hardly any modern equivalent. Following the murder of his wife and children in Euripides' *Madness of Heracles*, Heracles contemplates the anguish of such an existence (ll. 1281–98):

> It would be an offense against religion to remain with those I love in Thebes. What shrine could I visit, what religious festival could I participate in? The deadly curse that I am afflicted with means that no one can come near me. Shall I make my way to Argos? How can I, since I am an exile? Should I head toward some other city? If I did, I'd be spotted and looked at suspiciously, kept in check by bitter gibes, like, "Isn't that the son of Zeus who murdered his wife and children? Let him die elsewhere...." I have reached such depths of misfortune that even the earth will groan if I walk upon it, and rivers and seas if I see to cross them. My fate is like that of Ixion, bound perpetually to a wheel.

Ostracism

The importance that the Athenians attached to exile as a safety valve in a political crisis is indicated by the fact that the oath that was taken by jurors serving in the *hêliaia* (lawcourt) contained the following words (Dem. 24.149):

> I will cast my vote in accordance with the laws and decrees of the Athenian people. I will not cast my vote for tyranny or oligarchy.... I will not restore *pheugontes* [exiles or fugitives] or persons condemned to death. I will not drive into exile nor allow anyone else to drive into exile *menontes* [presumably "metics"] in contravention of the established laws and decrees of the Athenian people.

In a class of his own was the politician who was sent into exile for a period of ten years, though he had not been accused of committing any crime. The procedure, known as *ostrakismos*, is thought to have been introduced into Athens in ca. 508 at the prompting of Cleisthenes, though the first known victim of ostracism was Hipparchus in 487.

Once a year the *dêmos* was formally asked if it wished to invoke the process. If it answered in the affirmative, two months later a kind of negative election took place between any number of candidates. If a minimum of 6,000 votes were cast in total—the alternative possibility of 6,000 votes for (or more strictly against) one of the candidates is less likely—the candidate who received the highest number of votes was required to leave Attica within ten days and take up residence beyond the promontory of Geraestus on the island of Euboea. The votes in the election were inscribed on potsherds known as *ostraka*, from which the name *ostrakismos* derived.

Ostracism may be viewed in part as an alternative to mass exile and was probably used at times to preempt *stasis* or civil war. Diodorus Siculus (11.55.3) states, "The Athenians introduced ostracism . . . in order to reduce by means of exile the arrogance of those who had risen too high." Indeed it has been argued that ostracism performed an important symbolic function "[by] reminding élites annually of the potential of non-élites to intervene decisively in violent intra-élite conflict" (Forsdyke 2005, 151)—conflicts that would have traditionally resulted in mass expulsions by one body of supporters or another, such as we examined in chapter 5. Certainly what we know about the circumstances that led to the ostracism of Aristides, Cimon, and Thucydides, son of Melesias, suggests that a major motive underlying the removal of all three was to defuse political conflict.

But though the desire to eliminate rivalry between two élite politicians was one objective, the institution did not exclusively serve a political agenda—or at least it was not treated solely as a political safeguard by the *dêmos*. Graffiti on a few *ostraka* reveal that some voters were guided by religious concerns, as in the case of those indicating that the candidate was either accursed or polluted (Parker 1983, 269–70). Other voters targeted individuals for personal reasons. Callias, son of Cratias, who was probably ostracized in 485, may well have owed his exile in part to the fact that he had adopted easternizing customs (Hall 2009, 616–17). Objectionable sexual practices were also occasionally instanced in graffiti. Thus ostracism, whatever its original intention, became a way of venting popular anger. The classic instance is the story of the illiterate country bumpkin who voted to ostracize the general and politician Aristides simply on the grounds that he was fed up hearing him always referred to as "the Just" (Plu. *Arist.* 7.5–6). It was also used frivolously by some voters. There are some *ostraka*, for instance, that were cast against *Limos* (Hunger). In short there was a wide variety of reasons that might induce an Athenian to want to see the back of a prominent individual, though responsible and informed citizens would probably have concerned themselves chiefly with his polarizing effect upon the decision-making process. The restraint of the *dêmos* in its use of this safeguard is in fact quite remarkable. Only ten Athenians are known for certain to have been ostracized. Five of these were ostracized in the years between 487 and 482, when the city was undergoing intense political upheaval. The last politician to be ostracized was Hyperbolus in ca. 417.

High-Profile Exiles

Narratives of politicians on the run captured the popular imagination. One of the most exciting has to do with Themistocles, architect of the Greek naval victory at Salamis. No doubt the fugitive had recounted it in later years himself, with of course appropriate embellishments (see map 7). Under the pronouncement of ostracism from the Athenian Assembly in ca. 472, Themistocles first settled in Argos, where he had powerful friends. From there he "visited" other places in the Peloponnese. The Spartans, who hated the Argives, found his presence irksome and insulting, and they persuaded the Athenians to condemn him to death on the trumped-up charge of conspiring with the Persians. Accordingly a posse of Athenians teamed up with some Spartans with orders to "seize him wherever they might find him" (Thuc. 1.135.3).

Catching wind of their approach, Themistocles fled to Corcyra, where he expected to receive a warm reception, since he had done good service to the islanders in the past. The Corcyreans were fearful of antagonizing both Athens and Sparta, however, so they immediately sent him back to the mainland. He sought refuge with Admetus, king of the Molossians, despite the fact that the two of them had not previously

FIGURE 13 Silver *triôbolon* (coin worth three obols) from Argos, ca. 490–70. The obverse depicts the forepart of a wolf, the symbol of Apollo Lykeios, who was worshipped in Argos. On the reverse is the letter "A" with two incuse (that is, recessed) squares containing pyramidal sections. Argos's king Pheidon, who reigned some time between the eighth to sixth centuries, was credited, improbably, with being the first to strike coins in Greece. The *polis* claimed to be "the longest continuous occupation of any place in Greece" (Cartledge 2009, 38). It was a stable democracy throughout the classical period, apart from two brief periods when the oligarchs seized control.

been on good terms. When his pursuers turned up at Admetus's palace soon afterward, the king ordered them to leave (see chapter 7).

Themistocles then journeyed to Pydna, a coastal town in Macedonia, where he was hospitably received by its king, Alexander. Without revealing his identity he later boarded a merchant vessel bound for the coast of western Asia Minor. As luck would have it, however, the boat ran into a storm and was diverted to the island of Naxos, which was currently under blockade from the Athenian navy. Themistocles proved to be as quick-witted as ever. He immediately revealed his identity to the captain of the vessel, warning him that, if he handed him over to the Athenians, he would claim that the captain had accepted a bribe to take him on board. Themistocles also promised to reward him if he succeeded in making his escape. The latter agreed and a day or so later the boat set sail for Ephesus.

After disembarking, Themistocles journeyed inland toward Persia. By now he had been on the run for about three years. En route he wrote a letter to Artaxerxes I, the Persian king, claiming that he had become a

MAP 7 Themistocles' flight to Persia.

fugitive because of his friendship for Persia and requesting permission to reside within its borders for the space of a year. The king agreed. However, before presenting himself at court, Themistocles took the sensible precaution of familiarizing himself with the Persian language and customs so as to make the best possible impression on his host. The strategy worked to perfection, and Themistocles came in time to be held "in higher honor than any Greek before or since" (Thuc. 1.138.2). The king appointed him governor of Magnesia, where he resided until his death. He remained at heart an Athenian, however. When he died, his friends, in accordance with his wishes, succeeded in smuggling his bones back to Attica, where they buried them secretly, since it was forbidden to bury in Attic soil an outlaw who had been condemned for treason.

The narrative of Alcibiades' flight is equally thrilling and contains even more twists and turns. In 415, shortly before the departure of the Sicilian Expedition to which he had been appointed as one of its three generals, he was accused of being implicated in the mutilation of the herms —stone pillars of Hermes with carved heads and erect penises that stood at street corners—and of profaning the Eleusinian Mysteries. His request to be put on trial before he sailed was denied and he was ordered to proceed forthwith to Sicily, together with his colleagues, Nicias and Lamachus. Soon after his arrival in Sicily, however, he was recalled to Athens at the insistence of his accusers. Alcibiades was taken on board ship but succeeded in escaping from his warders when they docked at Thurii. Very likely some of the ship's crew were sympathetic to his cause or alternatively were under the spell of his magnetic personality. He then fled via Elis to Sparta, where he proceeded to ingratiate himself with his hosts. The Athenians condemned him and his associates to death *in absentia*, whereupon he memorably remarked, "I'll show them that I'm still alive" (Plu. *Alc*. 22.2). They also confiscated his property and placed him under a curse (Thuc. 6.61.4–7; Isoc. 16.9).

Alcibiades now proceeded to give military advice to the enemy that was highly damaging to Athens. In fact his defection to the Spartans is merely the most spectacular example of what was a very common practice among political exiles—the exaction of revenge on one's native land for being declared a traitor. He urged his hosts to fortify Decelea in the north of Attica, which now became a haven for runaway slaves a mere 13 miles from Athens. "This above all brought about the ruin and destruction of his city," Plutarch (*Alc*. 23.2) caustically observed. But though Alcibiades won the goodwill of the Spartans in the short term by adapting to their austere way of life, they eventually began to suspect his loyalty and he was compelled to flee again, this time to Ionia. It certainly did not help his relationship with them that he was accused of having seduced Timaea, the wife of King Agis, when the latter was stationed at Decelea.

He now began to intrigue with the Persians. In 412/11 he managed to secure a position as advisor at the court of the satrap Tissaphernes in Sardis, where, in an attempt to bring about his recall, he tried to secure the support of Persia on Athens's behalf. Tissaphernes fell under the spell of Alcibiades' personality, but in the end the hope of acquiring aid came to nothing (Thuc. 8.52; Plu. *Alc.* 24.3–25.2). Shortly afterward, Alcibiades, along with a number of other exiles, was recalled by the Five Thousand, Athens's government at the time (Thuc. 8.97.3). He decided not to accept their offer, however, fearing that if he did, he would again have to face criminal charges. Instead he was appointed general of the Athenian fleet at Samos. It was in this capacity that he now won a significant naval victory at Cyzicus in 410. Finally convinced that he had nothing further to fear from his fellow-citizens, Alcibiades returned to Athens in 407. His most memorable accomplishment was the restoration of the procession to Eleusis that took place on the final day of the major annual celebration of the Eleusinian Mysteries. Ironically, it was the Spartan occupation of Decelea that had made the overland journey extremely dangerous for initiates, and so the Athenians had temporarily suspended the procession and replaced it with a voyage along the coast.

Alcibiades was now formally cleared of the charges that had been lodged against him eight years previously (Xen. *Hell.* 1.4.12). Even so, he remained a highly controversial figure. His enemies continued to scheme against him and eventually succeeded in depriving him of his generalship. So in 406 he threw in the towel and withdrew to the Thracian Chersonese. The following year he made an appearance at the Athenian encampment in the Hellespont to inform the generals that he was on good terms with the Thracians and could secure their services on Athens's behalf. They rebuffed his offer and the Athenian fleet was heavily defeated at Aegospotami soon afterward (Xen. *Hell.* 2.1.25–6; D.S. 13.105.3–4). Alcibiades fled yet again, this time to the court of the Persian satrap Pharnabazus in Hellespontine Phrygia. Acting on the advice of the Thirty Tyrants and of the Spartans, Pharnabazus had him assassinated in 404/3.

Both narratives are extraordinarily rich in detail. They not only indicate a deep fascination with high-profile fugitives but also testify to the existence of a world of possibilities for enterprising individuals on the run that extended beyond the confines of the Greek-speaking world. As the double-dealing of Alcibiades indicates, moreover, exile could have profound, even catastrophic consequences for the exile's city-state, if the exile placed his expertise at the service of the enemy. But whereas high-profile political fugitives might have found a warm welcome abroad, nonpolitical exiles of no social rank were exposed to dangers and threats wherever they went. Those most at risk were the ones who were guilty of the most notorious crimes. One such was a Phocian called Phalaecus, who had pillaged the sanctuary at Delphi and who in Diodorus's words "passed his long life wandering about in considerable fear and danger . . . and became famous because of his misfortune" (16.61.3).

Runaway Slaves

We have no means of knowing what percentage of the servile population chose flight with all its attendant dangers in preference to slavery. Though the Athenians occasionally employed *drapetagôgoi* (runaway-catchers), it is likely that they hired them on a strictly temporary basis (Ath. *Deipn.* 4.161d). Sometimes, too, the slave-owner would set off in hot pursuit of his own *drapetês* (runaway) (Dem. 53.6).

Papyri from Ptolemaic Egypt indicate that in the hellenistic period and no doubt earlier the risk of a slave taking flight was sufficiently common for vendors to make it their practice to stipulate on a bill of sale that the merchandise they were selling "was neither a wanderer nor liable to flee nor susceptible to epilepsy" (*PTurner* 22, dated 142 BCE). Other papyri of similar date announce rewards for their capture. One of these runaways was a Syrian called Hermon, who is described in great detail as follows:

> About 18 years old, of medium stature, beardless, with good legs, a dimple on the chin, a mole by the left side of the nose, a scar above the left corner of the mouth, tattooed on the right wrist with two barbarian letters. He has taken with him three *octadrachmae* of coined gold, ten pearls, an iron ring on which an oil flask and strigils are represented, and is wearing a cloak and a loincloth. Whoever brings back this slave shall receive 3 talents of copper. If he points him out in a shrine [where he is presumably seeking asylum], 2 talents. If he points him out in the household of a substantial and actionable

man [who has presumably taken him in as a slave], 5 talents (*PPar*. 10 dated 156 BCE, adapted from the translation of Hunt and Edgar [1963, no. 234]).

I sincerely hope Hermon evaded his captors.

Since we have no testimonia from runaways themselves, we can only speculate as to what compulsion would have driven them to abscond. Other than in time of war, they seem for the most part to have fled singly, the overwhelming majority of them no doubt being males. If they were caught, it is possible that they were branded like livestock, either on the forehead or on the shoulder, to indicate that they were a flight risk. Though escape from a harsh master or mistress would seem to be the primary motivation for absconding, it may be that the indignity of the institution was insufferable to some. We know nothing about how a runaway might have identified potential harborers or how he selected a final destination. We never hear of the equivalent of an underground railway. The obvious recourse would have been to merge into the background and pretend to be free (Lys. 23.7). Even if a slave escaped abroad, however, it would have been difficult for him to remain at liberty, since foreigners were an inevitable source of curiosity, even in an accommodating *polis* like Athens. Some, therefore, as intimated by the papyrus just quoted, probably threw themselves on the mercy of another slave-owner in the hope that they would receive better treatment. Others might have committed serious crimes while on the run, simply in order to stay alive. The one advantage that slaves in the Greek world had over African-American slaves in the antebellum South was that they did not conform to a single racial group and therefore could not be automatically identified. In fact [Xenophon], aka the Old Oligarch, goes further and claims that the clothing and general appearance of slaves made it impossible to distinguish them from free on the streets of Athens (*Ath. Pol.* 1.10).

At least from the classical period onward an Athenian slave who was harshly treated could take refuge in the Theseum, or sanctuary of Theseus, which was situated close to the heart of the city. The runaway could then request to be sold to another master. In other words, she or he did not seek refuge in the hope of gaining freedom but of acquiring a more humane owner. The choice of the Theseum derived from the fact that the legendary founder of Athens was deemed sympathetic toward exiles and fugitives. This at least was the view of Plutarch (*Thes.* 36.2), who states, "[Theseus's tomb] is a *phuximon* [place of refuge] for slaves and all those wretches who fear people who are stronger, since Theseus himself was both their champion and supporter and responded in kindly fashion to the needs of the downtrodden." The decision to establish a slave refuge in Athens, whenever it was taken, is likely to have been a response to an essentially economic problem. It was probably intended to encourage disgruntled slaves to seek redress by a change of ownership—a clearly preferable option from the state's point of view to that of their deserting Athens altogether.

Similar sanctuaries for runaway slaves existed elsewhere in the Greek world and may have been more common than the few references in our sources suggest (Plu. *Mor.* 166e). An inscription dated ca. 92 BCE, which describes cult regulations relating to the Andanian Mysteries of Messene, includes the following provision for the welfare of runaways (*IG* V.1 1390.80–84; Meyer 1987, 51–59):

> There is to be a *phugimon* [place of refuge] for slaves. Let the sacred area be the refuge, according to wherever the priests designate it. Let no one harbor *drapetai* [runaways] or give them food or provide them with goods.... The priest shall sit in judgment over cases involving runaway slaves, specifically those who sit there from our city-state. If he does not hand one over, the runaway is to be permitted to leave the master who is in charge of him.

It is revealing that the decree forbade providing runaways slaves with nourishment, evidently to prevent them from becoming long-term residents. It also excluded runaway slaves from elsewhere being granted *asulia*. Other popular refuges were the sanctuary of Zeus on Mount Ithome and that of Poseidon at Taenarum, though it may be that only the latter was an acknowledged place of asylum (Thuc. 1.128.1 and 133; Schumacher 1993, 72).

For the most part a *phugimon* or *phuximon* can only have been a temporary solution, though occasionally we hear of runaways being granted permanent refuge inside a sanctuary. Those who were granted this privilege inside the Egyptian sanctuary of Heracles at Canopus were branded with *hiera stigmata* (sacred markings) to signify that they were under the god's protection (Hdt. 2.113.2). Perhaps in Athens, too, slaves who had been granted asylum in the Theseum and not been sold were permitted to reside there indefinitely. We never hear of any equivalent to the maroon societies in the Caribbean, Latin America, and the United States, viz autonomous and self-sufficient communities that comprised runaway slaves. The nearest equivalent is Naupactus, in which the Messenian helots settled after ca. 460, but since it had a mixed population of free and former slaves it is hardly a particularly apt parallel (Cartledge 1985, 46).

The disorder of wartime presented the most favorable conditions for flight, not least because slaves formerly belonging to the enemy now became a valuable asset. Sometime before the outbreak of the Peloponnesian War the Athenians established a watch post consisting of three archers at the entrance to the Acropolis to prevent *drapetai* and other undesirables from gaining access to the sanctuaries within (*IG* I^3 45; Wernicke 1891, 51–57). The fate of those who did manage to enter the sanctuaries is not known. Around the same time the Athenians accused the Megarians of harboring runaway slaves (Thuc. 1.139.2). When civil war broke out on Corcyra in 427, both the democrats and the oligarchs scoured the countryside for slaves, promising freedom to those who joined their ranks (3.73). The majority of their recruits would have been runaways. With the resumption of hostilities in 413 more than 20,000 Athenian slaves deserted to Decelea, which the Spartans occupied as a forward base inside Attica (7.27.5; cf. 6.91.6). This figure may represent as much as one-fifth of the entire slave population. A year or so later some Chian slaves fled to Athens, when the Athenians began besieging their island (Thuc. 8.40.2). Slaves who accompanied their masters on campaign were also likely to desert, particularly if they suspected that they were facing defeat (7.13.2 and 75.5).

Occasionally prisoners of war managed to escape as a group. Many of the Athenians who were taken prisoner in 413 after the failure of the Sicilian Expedition gained their freedom by fleeing from Syracuse to Catania, approximately 100 miles to the north (Thuc. 7.85.4). Being a powerful body, they no doubt terrorized the locals along the way. They presumably managed to board ships, which took them back to Athens. Likewise Syracusan prisoners working in the stone quarries in the Piraeus managed to escape to Decelea and Megara in 409 (Xen. *Hell.* 1.2.14).

9

THE ECONOMIC MIGRANT

Reasons for Becoming an Economic Migrant

In the modern world economic migrants tend to be both entrepreneurial and dynamic, having demonstrated their willingness to take risks and leave their homes in order to create opportunities for themselves and their families. They tend to plan their departure well in advance and are likely to have a well-established network in their new place of residence, whereas other migrants are forced to leave their homes suddenly and without any advance planning. There is every reason to suppose that economic migrants in the ancient world would have been equally entrepreneurial and dynamic. The first economic migrant in the western canon is the patriarch Abraham, the archetypal upwardly mobile wanderer. Abraham left his homeland in order to achieve a higher standard of living, even though the very considerable fortune that he acquired en route after departing from Ur of the Chaldees in southern Mesopotamia was incidental to the purpose of his journey, which was to demonstrate evidence of the Lord's favor.

A primary motivation for the movement of people in the modern world, too, is the desire to escape financial destitution and starvation, though distress caused by political upheavals runs a close second. In a world like ours, where cheap labor is at a premium, economic migrants at the bottom of the ladder can easily be lured abroad by the promise of prosperity. In the ancient world by contrast, where servile labor was readily available, merchants and craftsmen were the ones most likely to better their economic circumstances by migration.

Economic survival often depends on a willingness to migrate. It was no doubt under duress that Hesiod's father abandoned his unprofitable life as a trader in Cyme, a town on the Anatolian coast south of Lesbos, and moved to the remote inland village of Ascra in Boeotia, "fleeing evil poverty, which Zeus gives to men" (*Op.* 638). Why he chose Ascra, which he describes as "a miserable village," is anyone's guess. Perhaps he had heard that land was easy to come by. He then turned his hand to farming, though with what success is unknown. Hesiod unflatteringly describes the region as "bad in winter, stifling in summer, and unpleasant at all times" (*Op.* 640). He reminds us that the decision to better oneself economically often comes at a high price, not least for the offspring, and perhaps, too, for the spouse, of immigrants. I can't help wondering how Hesiod's mother dealt with the change in their circumstances, assuming she was alive when they migrated. Did she, like her son, perpetually complain about the weather?

Of the tens of thousands of economic migrants who populated the Greek landscape hardly any have left us any indication as to why they chose to settle abroad. Even the most basic question—did they leave home out of necessity or in order to seek new opportunities?—cannot be addressed. Nor do we know what percentage of economic migrants settled abroad with their families. Did some of them occasionally find ways to send remittances back home, as is frequently the case today? Did others arrive singly and then summon their families to join them? We are equally poorly informed about the social networks that must have facilitated and encouraged migration in ancient Greece, as they do in the modern world, providing migrants with a temporary place to stay and assisting them while they struggle to get on their feet. We do not know how many migrants remained abroad and how many returned to their place of birth at the end of their working lives. Did Hesiod make it back to Cyme in later life? Did he actually want to? Or did he eventually adjust to the dreadful weather?

In the ancient world as in the modern, economic migration had benefits for both parties. Indeed the migration of artisans and professionals from one *polis* to another was an essential factor in Greece's cultural, economic, and political development. As Aristotle observed, "It is necessarily the case that city-states contain a large number of slaves, metics, and foreigners" (*Pol.* 7.1326a 18–20). This state of affairs is likely to have been true of "even the smallest, most isolated, most 'backward,' most agriculturally-oriented *polis*," as Whitehead (1984, 50) notes. Certainly the quality of life in Athens, as well as its culture, depended to a large degree on a continual influx of migrants. The citizen body understood this, for it certainly would not have permitted this influx unless it judged it to be in its best interests, even though it is unlikely to have understood the relationship between migration and economic growth. And although Athens is a special case, it was by no means unique.

The size of the immigrant population obviously varied from one city-state to another. Some *poleis* were highly restrictive, others less so. At the high end of the scale was Athens; at the low end, Sparta. Herodotus claims that until his day only two foreigners had been awarded Spartan citizenship, and this was because one of them was a highly valued seer (9.35.1). (The other was his brother.) Likewise the Megarians proudly maintained that they had granted citizenship only to two non-Megarians (Plu. *Mor.* 826c). Sparta had a reputation for being extremely xenophobic, a circumstance that drew disparaging comments from other Greeks, the Athenians especially (Thuc. 1.144.2; 2.39.1; Plu. *Mor.* 238e). No doubt foreigners stuck out like a sore thumb in a Spartan street. Another *polis* that exhibited xenophobic tendencies "in accordance with Spartan law" was Apollonia in northwest Greece, and there may well have been others (Ael. *VH* 13.16). Xenophobia, after all, operates along a sliding scale.

It goes without saying that no Greek state had anything resembling an "official" immigration policy or imposed a quota, and the extent to which it accommodated permanent settlers from abroad has to be understood in terms of its relationship with Greeks of different ethnicity in general. The fact that Athens was more receptive to foreigners than any other state was due largely to its imperial role in both the fifth and fourth centuries. In the modern world societies that absorb migrants successfully become more dynamic, even though the frequent consequence of that dynamism is social inequality and deep cultural divides (Scheffer 2011, 319). We are in no position to judge whether this was the case, too, in Athens, and in fact we can hardly begin to estimate the contribution that metics made to its culture and economy, other than to acknowledge the self-evident fact that foreigners would have been evident in all aspects of Athenian society (Cohen 2000, 18). Part of Athens's appeal for foreigners lay in the fact that it would have scored higher than any other *polis* on the Human Development Index, which ranks countries according to the criteria of income, health, and education. Athens, in other words, was the prototype of the modern cosmopolitan urban center like London, New York, and Hong Kong, whose vitality and dynamism depend largely on their sizable immigrant population.

A state's outlook toward the foreigners living in its midst is hardly likely to have been constant and unchanging. In wartime latent tensions and hostilities between citizens and foreigners are likely to have resulted in persecution, as happened in Syracuse when its ruler Dionysius I declared war against Carthage in 396. The Sicilian Greeks responded by persecuting many wealthy Carthaginians who dwelt among them, "not only by plundering their property but also by seizing them and subjecting their bodies to all manner of torture and insult" (D.S. 14.46.3). Though we hear of such occurrences only rarely, there may well have been many such instances that have gone unrecorded.

Immigration scholars identify two related phenomena as the catalyst for migration: a "push" from the country of origin due to its unfavorable internal conditions and how those conditions impact upon specific individuals and groups; and a "pull" to another country or region that holds out the expectation, promise, or hope of a better existence. As noted already, the evidence rarely permits us to determine what drove tens of thousands of Greeks to exchange one city-state for another. In fact it is often impossible to differentiate economic migrants from refugees. We have no means of knowing what percentage of Athens's metic population was motivated to leave its place of origin because of economic considerations and what percentage left, whether voluntarily or under compulsion, because of political discontent or persecution. Scholars tend (tacitly for the most part) to assume that economic improvement was the primary incentive and that most economic migrants were free to return at will. However, this hardly permits us to conclude that a "push" from one's place of origin played no part at all in the decision to emigrate.

The Origins of Economic Migration

We have evidence that city-states were permitting economic migrants to settle permanently within their borders from the sixth century onward, though the legal status of these migrants in the archaic period is obscure. While some of the professional *dêmiourgoi* (literally "those who work for the people") whom Homer identified as itinerants probably became permanent settlers abroad (see chapter 10), we do not know in what way that might have affected their legal status in their country of adoption—assuming they were accorded any status whatsoever. Most itinerants are likely to have settled abroad on a purely informal basis, perhaps at the invitation of an appreciative employer.

The first economic migrants of whom we have note are the aristocrats who left their homes to marry into wealthy foreign families of similar status. Dynastic marriage is already a feature of life in the *Odyssey*, as we see from the fact that the Phaeacian king Alcinoüs is eager for the stranger Odysseus to become his son-in-law (7.311–15). Whether dynastic marriage was as central to alliance-building in archaic Greece as it has been at other periods of history, is, however, impossible to determine. When suitors travel vast distances to compete for the hand of the daughter of Cleisthenes, tyrant of Sicyon, the latter goes out of his way to thank them "for their willingness to marry into my family and leave behind their own homes" (Hdt. 6.126.2–130). His complimentary remark seems to suggest that a willingness to relocate was the exception rather than the rule among the élite.

Plutarch reports that it was Solon who first permitted skilled workers to settle in Attica and that he did so on condition that they brought their families with them (*Sol.* 24.2). Though he denies that Solon's motivation was to drive undesirable foreigners away, he claims that he

took note of the fact that Athens was "filled with people who were constantly flooding into Attica from elsewhere in order to find security"
(22.1). In other words, it is unclear whether the lawgiver intended to
implement a pro- or an anti-immigration policy (Whitehead 1977, 141–
42). Plutarch, moreover, is writing hundreds of years after the event,
and it would be naïve to assume that he had any insight as to what had
prompted Solon's legislation.

Though many scholars believe that it was the reforms of Cleisthenes
that first granted official recognition to Athens's immigrant population, the word *metoikos*, which most frequently describes an economic
migrant to Athens, does not occur in a literary context until 472 (Aes.
Pers. 319). Other data suggest that the *terminus ante quem* for the introduction of metic status was ca. 460.

The Legal Status of the Athenian Metic

Metoikos means literally either "a person who has changed his *oikos*"
or "a person who lives with others of the same standing." Aristotle defined metics as "citizens only in the sense in which children who are too
young to be inscribed in the list and old men who have been removed
from the list can be called citizens" (*Pol.* 3.1275a 14–16). They would
no doubt have been subject to controls and restrictions of the kind
Aristotle has in mind in every community, but it is Athens alone that
has provided us with a relatively full account of what these controls and
restrictions actually amounted to. We learn, for instance, that foreigners seeking permanent immigrant status in Athens were required to
record the fact that they were residing in Attica after a statutory period
of time. Their chances of escaping detection in a close-knit and self-
policed society like Athens were obviously slim. We do not know the
length of the statutory period, but it was probably a month at most.
Registration meant enlisting in one of Attica's 140-odd demes. Failure
to do so meant either immediate expulsion (Lys. 23.2) or enslavement
(Sud. *s.v. pôlêtês*). There is no evidence that an immigrant was required
to undergo any form of scrutiny to determine his or her worthiness

to reside long-term in Athens. Plato recommended that "any foreigner who pleased" should be permitted to take up residence in his ideal polity, so long as he or she practiced a craft (*Laws* 8.850ab).

Metics were required to secure the goodwill of an Athenian citizen, who would act as their *prostatês* (patron, guardian). The role of the *prostatês* is only vaguely understood, but the person so charged probably acted both as their legal representative and as their supervisor. This simple and rather informal arrangement would have guaranteed that most metics were law-abiding, since the reputation of their sponsors would have been seriously compromised otherwise. There is no indication as to whether there was any limit to the number of metics whom a single *prostatês* could sponsor. It is not inconceivable that some had very large numbers under their charge. The close relationship between metic and *prostatês* seems to have remained in effect until around the middle of the fourth century, when much of the power invested in the *prostatês* was transferred to the courts (Gauthier 1972, 133–35; Demetriou 2012, 200–201).

Metics had to pay a regular, presumably monthly, poll tax, known as the *metoikion*. This amounted to one *drachma* for an adult male and half a *drachma* for an adult female living on her own. Though this was a relatively modest fee, it may have been sufficient to induce a substantial proportion of metics to return to their homelands once their working lives were over. Metics also had to pay a market-tax known as *xenika telê* (foreigners' tax) for permission to trade in the agora (Dem. 57.34). Those who performed some special service for the state might be granted *isoteleia*, which meant that they had the right to pay the same taxes as an Athenian citizen. Those who were in the equivalent of the super-tax bracket were required to subsidize important and costly public programs called liturgies, just as wealthy citizens had to do. These programs included the financing of dramatic choruses, triremes, and gymnasia. Like citizens in the same wealth bracket, in times of war and other emergencies they had to pay a property tax known as the *eisphora* (Lys. 12.20). Overall, the financial burden borne by metics would have greatly enriched the state, as Xenophon fully appreciated (*Vect.* 2.1), quite aside from the benefits accruing from their skills and their entrepreneurship.

Metics were also required to perform military service, either as hoplites or as rowers. It seems they were not permitted to serve in the cavalry (*Vect.* 2.5). Metic hoplites may have numbered as many as 13,000. So far as we know, they did not receive any military training, so their service may have been minimal. They seem to have played little part in the Peloponnesian War. In fact the only occasion that we hear of them serving in the ranks is at the Battle of Delium in 424. Perhaps they mainly functioned as the Greek equivalent of the British Home Guard in World War II. As such, they would have been called upon to defend the city only as a last resort (Duncan-Jones 1980, 103–5). Given the fact that most metics were artisans and small traders, however, most of them probably served as rowers in the fleet, for which they would have received pay. Indeed they may have constituted a very sizable proportion of Athens's rowers, particularly if we take seriously an observation by [Xenophon], the author who goes under the modern name of the Old Oligarch, that Athens needed metics in order to man its fleet (*Ath. Pol.* 1.12).

Until the 350s metics were not permitted to own land or property in Attica. From this date onward, however, they occasionally received *gês enktêsis* ("the right of land tenure in a country or district by a person not belonging to it" [*LSJ⁹*]). One important consequence of this was that metics were now permitted to establish permanent sanctuaries in honor of their gods in Attica. An inscription dated 333/2 granted permission to merchants from Citium, a Phoenician town in Cyprus, to buy land on which to build a sanctuary of Aphrodite (Tod 189 = Harding 111 = Rhodes and Osborne 91). The importance of this measure can hardly be exaggerated. The freedom to worship one's own gods in a permanent sanctuary specifically designated for that purpose would have accorded both migrants and immigrants a wholly new sense of belonging, even though the main motive on the part of the Athenians may well have been economic self-interest. We should note, moreover, that this was a reward for good behavior, if not good service, and not an entitlement. Sanctuaries provided the ideal setting for social and organizational networks. Such networks not only enabled metics to mix freely with others of the same ethnicity, but also to plan joint business ventures.

The inscription relating to the merchants from Citium cites as a precedent a previous grant of *gês enktêsis*, which Egyptians had received to establish a sanctuary in honor of their goddess Isis. The only other metic community known to have been accorded such a right is that of the Thracians—in their case, in honor of the goddess Bendis. However, the fact that none of the many cults that made their entry into Athens from 350 onward alludes to this privilege may simply be due to the fact that within a short space of time *gês enktêsis* was no longer seen as a privilege to be remarked upon. That said, several sanctuaries that served the interests of the metic community were established on land that was leased out by the Athenian state in this same period. It is also striking that a number of inscriptions relating to foreign religious associations were discovered on the outskirts of the residential area, an indication perhaps of their somewhat marginalized status.

Marriage between metics and Athenians seems to have been officially discouraged. A law ascribed to Pericles (dated 451/450) decreed that "a man could not have a share of the *polis* unless he was born from two *astoi*" ([Arist.] *Ath. Pol.* 26.4), which meant that if a metic married an *astos*, their offspring was not eligible for citizenship.* Though this law was rescinded during the Peloponnesian War when Athens faced a manpower crisis due in large part to the plague, it was renewed immediately afterward ([Arist.] *Ath. Pol.* 26.3; Plu. *Per.* 37.3–4). If a metic was killed, the crime would be treated as the equivalent of an unintentional homicide, irrespective of the circumstances (Lape 2010, 48–49). Though this denied metics the full protection of the law, since the maximum penalty for unintentional homicide was exile rather than execution, it may at the time of its passage have signaled an improvement in their legal status, viz from no legal protection at all to at least partial protection. Metics were also incorporated into the religious life of the community, notably by being required to participate in the Panathenaic festival held in honor of Athena. Very likely this was seen as a duty rather than a privilege, intended to remind the metic population

---

* For discussion of the terms *astos* and *politês*, both commonly translated "citizen," see Cohen (2000, 62–63 with n. 84).

that they were invested in the welfare of the state. They also played a significant role in the affairs of the demes to which they belonged (Cohen 2000, 74).

Once a foreigner had been identified as a metic, he or she was free to reside in Athens indefinitely—much to the displeasure of Plato, who recommended in his imaginary lawcode that the entitlement be limited to twenty years (*Laws* 8.850b). It would tell us a great deal about the level of comfort and acceptance enjoyed by metics if we knew what percentage of them remained in Attica till their death. Like productive and hard-working immigrants in general, some at least would have achieved considerable social standing. It is hardly fortuitous that Plato chose the house of the elderly and wealthy metic Cephalus as the setting for the *Republic*. Cephalus had evidently chosen to end his days abroad, like many long-term immigrants.

Incidentally, the Piraeus, which is where Cephalus lives, was particularly popular as a residential center for metics, accounting for about 20 percent of their total number. Fourth-century sepulchral inscriptions that have come to light there testify to the presence of immigrants from at least 60 different *poleis* (Garland 2001, table 1, p. 64; *IG* II² 7882–10530). The popularity of the Piraeus derived from the fact that it was both a port city and a manufacturing center. We should note, however, that metics settled throughout Attica, many of them in rural areas, and few demes had no metic residents at all (Cohen 2000, 122–23). A substantial number of Athenian citizens internally migrated to the Piraeus as well, attracted by its economic opportunities. The scale of this movement is indicated by the fact that out of 240 funerary inscriptions commemorating Athenian citizens discovered in the region only 8 belong to demesmen of the Piraeus (Garland 2001, 60).

The Composition and Size of Athens's Metic Population

In the contemporary world "migrants are not only employed in jobs that nationals are reluctant to do, but are also engaged in high-value activities that local people lack the skills to do" (Koser 2007, 10). The

FIGURE 14 Silver *statêr* from Istros, ca. 430–350. Istros, a *polis* on the western shore of the Black Sea, takes its name from Ister, a word of Thracian origin, which the Greeks gave to the Lower Danube River. It was founded by settlers from Miletus in 657. The obverse depicts two young heads, *tête-bêche* (that is, with heads reversed). It has been variously suggested that these represent the two branches of the Danube, the rising and setting sun, or the Dioscuri. The reverse, which bears the legend *ISTRIÊ(NÔN)*, depicts an eagle clasping a dolphin in its talons. Originally an oligarchy, Istros became a democracy in the second half of the fifth century as the result of *stasis*.

same is likely to have been true of Athens's metic population, with the proviso that many of those engaged in high-value activities would have been short-term residents. Certainly some of those who resided in the Piraeus were high-earners, like Lysias and Polemarchus, the sons of Cephalus, who owned a shield factory, three houses, and 120 slaves (Lys. 12.18–19), or Cephisodorus, implicated in the mutilation of the herms, who owned at least 16 slaves (*IG* I³ 421.33–49 = *ML* 79A = Fornara 147). Further evidence of the wealth that was in the hands of metics is provided by a sumptuous grave monument, dated ca. 330, that was found at Kallithea and erected in commemoration of Niceratus and his son Polyxenus, metics from Istros.

Undoubtedly the majority of metics, however, were considerably less wealthy. In contemporary western society immigrant workers undertake low-paid jobs. Many, too, are in semiskilled or skilled employment. Very likely that was true of Athens as well. The decree dated ca. 401/400, which granted citizen rights to metics who had helped liberate Athens from the rule of the Thirty, lists farmers, a cook, a muleteer, a carpenter, a sculptor, a builder, and a laborer among their ranks (*IG* II² 10 = Harding 3). Women, too, immigrated to Athens, many of them no doubt as the helpless victims of sex trafficking.

Greeks from the eastern Mediterranean migrated to Athens in larger numbers than those from the western Mediterranean, probably because the Piraeus was better situated for trading with the East than with the West. Attic gravestones honoring metics dating mostly to the fourth century indicate that they came chiefly from the Black Sea coast, the Hellespont, the Propontis, Thrace, Thessaly, central Greece, and the Peloponnese (*IG* II² 7882–10530; Garland 2001, 64–65). But though the overwhelming majority of metics were Greek, many non-Greeks also migrated to Athens. Xenophon claimed that in the first half of the fourth century "Lydians, Phrygians, Syrians, and other barbarians" settled in large numbers (*Vect.* 2.3). Judging from the variety of foreign gods who were worshipped in the Piraeus, many Carians, Egyptians, Phoenicians, and Thracians also resided there.

The size of Athens's metic population doubtless fluctuated in line with the city's changing political and economic fortunes, though we should bear in mind that it would not have been easy in any circumstances to relocate at short notice. When the city was at the height of its power in the years leading up to the outbreak of the Peloponnesian War, there might have been as many metics as citizens (Duncan-Jones 1980, 102). It is likely that there was a reduction in numbers just before hostilities began, particularly if Thucydides is right in claiming that the Greek world expected that Athens would be brought to its knees within three years (7.28.3). This decline in numbers would have accelerated once the evacuation of the Attic countryside got under way and again when conditions in the city deteriorated in consequence of the plague. As metics were not yet permitted to own property, those who were resident in Athens presumably had to vacate their rented homes to make way for citizens. These evacuees, as we might call them, would in consequence have been competing with the rural population for temporary accommodation on previously unoccupied land.

There was probably an influx of foreigners when peace was declared in 421. However, a sizable number of metics left Athens following the disaster in Sicily and others about a decade later in response to the xenophobic policies of the Thirty Tyrants (see later). When the Macedonians installed a garrison in the Piraeus in 322, following the eclipse of Athenian naval power at the end of the Lamian War, the number of metics again began to decline. Even so, a census conducted by Demetrius of Phaleron probably in 317 BCE revealed that there were almost half as many metics as citizens residing in Attica even at this time, viz 10,000 as compared with 21,000 citizens (Ath. *Deipn.* 6.272c).

Prejudice against Immigrants

It is perhaps inevitable that metics would have had to face prejudice at times, like immigrants the world over, though the degree and extent of prejudice would have depended upon their individual status and identity. Polls conduced in Britain between 1998 and 2002 discovered that "respondents are significantly more likely to be hostile to migrants and minorities if they are older, poorer, and less well educated, and live in northern England" (Saggar 2003, 185). Comparable inequities probably existed in Athens and elsewhere, particularly for those who were either at the lower end of the economic scale or non-Greek.

Though supportive of metics in general, Xenophon was uncomfortable with the large number of non-Greeks who were claiming metic status. He thought it highly inappropriate that citizens were required to serve in the army alongside "all sorts of barbarians" (*Vect.* 2.3). His purpose in recommending that "approved" metics be permitted to own freeholds in Attica was to attract "a larger and better class of persons desirous of living in Athens" (2.6). Metics, in other words, were expected to uphold the law and conform to the social norms. No doubt Xenophon was typical of many of his class. It is highly improbable, however, that there was anything equivalent to the fear which the famous "Polish plumber," a symbol of cheap labor, struck into the French workforce in 2006, when it was suspected that he and his like would put hardworking native plumbers out of work. That is because metics would rarely have been in competition with Athenians for jobs, though as merchants and manufacturers they might well have been in competition for profits.

Some Athenians, perhaps even the majority, held highly ambivalent views of metics. [Xenophon] objected, on the one hand, to the fact that they, like slaves, were undisciplined and could not be distinguished in appearance from slaves or commoners. On the other hand, he acknowledged their vital contribution to the fleet and thought it appropriate that they should be permitted freedom of speech (*Ath. Pol.* 1.10 and 12). By contrast Dicaeopolis in Aristophanes' *Acharnians* (l. 508) called metics "the useless part of the *astoi* [local population]."

Which takes me to the next point. It is probably safe to say that metics were accepted so long as they kept a low profile and demonstrated loyalty toward their adoptive country. The ideal type is exemplified by Parthenopaeus, originally a native of Arcadia, who, following his death in battle, received this glowing eulogy from the Argive king Adrastus, in whose country he had resided (Eur. *Supp.* 891–900):

> Being born and bred in Arcadia, he behaved as resident foreigners should behave. He did not make himself objectionable or troublesome to the city —characteristics that would have rendered him loathsome whether as a citizen or as a foreigner. He stood in the ranks of battle like a native-born Argive and defended his country. He rejoiced when Argos prospered and grieved when misfortune overcame it.

In the following passage the orator Lysias fleshes out the definition of what constitutes model metic behavior, and in so doing reveals much about the constraints that metics were placed under (12.4):

> Neither my father nor my brothers nor myself ever appeared as prosecutors or defendants in any lawsuit. On the contrary, we conducted ourselves under the democracy in such a way as neither to cause nor to receive offence.

The loyalty of metics was suspected in wartime, seemingly irrespective of ethnicity. When Nicias sent a report to the *dêmos* instancing reasons for the decline in the strength of his fleet in Sicily, he mentioned that the *xenoi*—presumably a reference to metics—"were at the first opportunity deserting to their respective cities" (Thuc. 7.13.2; cf. 7.63.3). Though this may have been an extreme case—the Sicilian Expedition was a doomed venture by the time Nicias dispatched his letter to Athens—it is unlikely to be without parallel. In a speech dated 330–24 the orator Hyperides refers to an Athenian law of uncertain date which "forbids metics from emigrating [*exoi(kein)*] from Athens in wartime" and warns that any metic who does so will be denounced and arrested if he returns later (*Ath.* 29, 33). Aeneas Tacticus indicates that it was common practice in wartime to limit the freedom of movement of both citizens and foreigners (10.8).

The remaining evidence for hostility toward metics is rather inconclusive. Though personal animosity between citizens and metics surely existed, and though some metics must have been subjected at times to abuse if only for their accent, our sources are virtually silent on this point. So far as we know Aristotle, who was Athens's most celebrated metic, did not experience prejudice in the years preceding Athens's defeat at the Battle of Chaeronea in 338, even though his close connections with the Macedonian court made him an obvious target of anti-Macedonian sentiment (Whitehead 1975, 97f.). After the death of Alexander the Great in 323, however, and in the wake of overt demonstrations of hostility toward Macedon, he thought it prudent to go into voluntary exile. Foreign deities were often the butt of humor, but it would be tendentious to translate this into hostility toward metics.

When the Thirty Tyrants came to power in 404 they arrested ten metics and appropriated their property (Lys. 12.5–7; cf. Xen. *Hell.* 2.3.21 and 40). Two of the ten were the orator Lysias, who managed to escape, and his brother Polemarchus, who was executed. What makes the action of the Thirty all the more egregious is the fact that Lysias's father, Cephalus, who had originally migrated from Syracuse at the invitation of Pericles, had been a law-abiding metic for thirty years (Lys. 12.4). The Thirty probably took this action not because they were hostile to the metic population as such, but because they were seeking to remodel Athens along xenophobic Spartan lines (Krentz 1982, 66–68). In other words, confiscating their property was a way of signaling the direction they would be taking the state. Incidentally, though many metics probably took to their heels when the Thirty came to power, the community did not abandon Athens en masse. On the contrary metics fought valiantly against the Thirty for the restoration of the democracy—proof indeed that they identified closely with the fortunes of the *dêmos*. Without their contribution in fact Thrasybulus might not have succeeded in overthrowing the Thirty. Such was the esteem in which these foreign freedom fighters were held that in ca. 401/400 a decree was passed granting both them and their descendants citizen rights. In consequence, citizen rights (not quite the same thing as citizenship) were granted to perhaps as many as 1,200 metics.

Emigrant Workers

The reverse phenomenon of Athenians emigrating from Athens for economic reasons is also recorded. Those whom we can track most easily are the potters and painters. The earliest evidence dates to ca. 440, when émigrés established a potters' workshop in Lucania in southern Italy, around the time of the foundation of the Athenian colony at Thurii. A decade or so later an important workshop was established in

FIGURE 15 Silver *nomos* (coin equivalent to a *statêr*) from Thurii in Lucania, fourth century. The obverse depicts the head of Athena wearing a helmet with the monster Scylla pointing on top. The reverse depicts a bull butting. The inscription reads *THOURIÔN*. Thurii was established perhaps principally under the leadership of Athens in 444 as a panhellenic settlement on the site of a previous Greek foundation called Sybaris. It seems likely that this was in response to an appeal from Sybarite refugees. Founded initially as a democracy, Thurii experienced three instances of *stasis* in the Peloponnesian War period and possibly two more in the fourth century.

Apulia, which almost certainly included Attic-trained craftsmen in its ranks. Other sites where Attic-trained potters and painters are believed to have settled include Olympia, Taras, Corinth, Falerii in Etruria, and Syracuse (MacDonald 1981, 159–68).

It is important to note, however, that we do not know what proportion of these émigrés were citizen craftsmen, what proportion had formerly been Athenian metics who now decided that there were richer pickings to be had elsewhere, and what proportion were slaves. In fact it is entirely conceivable that the majority were slaves. Thucydides reports that the largest number of the slaves who escaped to Decelea following the Spartan occupation of the fort in 413 were *cheirotechnai* (skilled craftsmen), and that designation may well have included potters and painters (7.27.5).

The migration of potters and painters from Athens continued after Athens's defeat in 404, in line with the state's changing political and economic fortunes. Though the numbers involved were small—a few hundred in total over a period of half a century—they are likely to have been representative of a much more general trend involving perhaps thousands of émigrés. It is also probable that a large number of other skilled workers, including the sculptors, masons, and painters who had been working on the Acropolis, emigrated at this time too, since the state could no longer afford to finance large-scale building projects.

10

THE ITINERANT

Itinerants in Archaic Greece

Outside the confines of the city walls a very different life existed, one beset by all manner of danger, yet one too that held out the tantalizing possibility of reward. Odysseus, though eager to return home, tells the Phaeacians, "If you were to suggest that I remain here for a year—on condition that you provide me with an escort home and furnish me with splendid gifts—I should be willing to do that, since it would be much better for me to return home with my hands amply filled" (*Od.* 11.356–59). Returning home with one's hands "amply filled" was the reason, too, to become an itinerant. It was a lifestyle to which many different entrepreneurial individuals were committed—peddlers, trinket vendors, seers, bards, physicians, merchants, entertainers, prostitutes, and others whose skills or commodities were in high demand, not to mention brigands, footpads, pirates, and the like. Markets, fairs, and festivals would have provided the ideal venue for the sale of their wares or the hire of their talents. In later times intellectuals became itinerants. Journeymen, too, filled their ranks, as did transhumance pastoralists. By far the largest group, however, were the mercenaries.

Itinerants are differentiated from the economic migrants whom we investigated in the previous chapter by virtue of the fact that they regularly moved from one place to another, some making only a brief stop, others staying a month or more. Some might have a home to which they periodically returned, others presumably did not. Even so, their lifestyle had points in common with that of the migrant, which is why it deserves inclusion in this study. The ubiquity of itinerants in the

Greek world, as Purcell (1990, 44) has noted, is a reflection of the relative scarcity of the human resource in the Mediterranean world.

The earliest evidence occurs in the *Odyssey*, where we learn of a group of highly valued itinerants whose reputations were such that they are "invited from the ends of the earth"—a turn of phrase that already in Homer's day meant from south Italy and Sicily to Asia Minor. They include "seers, healers of ills, builders in wood, and bards," among whom we should of course number Homer himself (17.382–86). The noun that Homer uses to describe this specialized group is *dêmiourgos*, which literally means "one who works for the community or the *dêmos.*"

This brief mention of *dêmiourgoi* leaves many questions unanswered. How and by whom were they remunerated? Did they receive a fixed income? Were they available for hire by each family in the community or were they "invited" (and reimbursed) at the bidding of the entire community? Did they move from place to place according to a fixed annual schedule or did they come and go either as they pleased or as the "invitation" went out? Who made up the majority of their clients? If they were employed by the *dêmos*, as their name suggests, what was their relationship with the aristocracy?

As long-distance travel became more common, the reputations of a few highly gifted individuals became widespread, as Herodotus makes clear. A few examples will serve. Arion of Lesbos was credited with transforming the dithyramb, a song in honor of the god Dionysus, into a vehicle for avant-garde musical showmanship. Having performed at the court of Periander tyrant of Corinth, Arion visited Italy and Sicily, where he earned a considerable fortune before returning to Corinth—famously on the back of a musically inclined dolphin after he dove into the Aegean to escape pirates (1.24.1). The physician Democedes of Croton, who acquired expertise in treating injured athletes, was wooed successively by Aegina, Athens, and Samos, his salary increasing each time he moved, before he was captured and pressed into service by the Persian king Darius I (3.131). Several other renowned Greek physicians practiced medicine at the Persian court, including Apollonides of Cos, Ctesias of Cnidus, and Polycritus of Mende. Though Democedes and Apollonides both owed their appointment to the fact that they were taken prisoner, their reputations, like those of Ctesias and Polycritus, no doubt preceded them. Underlying many such stories (Arion's included) is the dangers that beset itinerancy.

In wartime all Greek travelers, itinerants included, would have been at grave risk. When at the outset of the Peloponnesian War some Peloponnesian ambassadors were passing through Thrace on their way to solicit help from the Persians, the Thracian king handed them over to some Athenians who happened to be at his court. The latter escorted them to Athens, where upon arrival they were summarily executed and their bodies cast into a pit (Thuc. 2.6).

Itinerants in Classical Greece

Dêmiourgoi remained a feature of the classical landscape. Given the increase in population from the archaic period, they would have become much more numerous. They are also the first celebrities whose reputations owed nothing to either birth or privilege.

Homer's classification of itinerants begins with *manteis* (seers) or charismatic religious specialists, as we might call them. *Manteis* comprised both women and men, traveled extensively, and sometimes received high honors. Teisamenus of Elis, for instance, was granted Spartan citizenship for his services as a military seer—virtually a unique privilege in that closed society (Hdt. 9.35.1). Though it no doubt helped to be able to trace one's lineage back several generations to a legendary diviner, all one actually needed to set oneself up in business was a collection of prophecies. It is hardly surprising, therefore, that some *manteis* abused their position of trust. One such was Thrasyllus of Siphnos, who, after being bequeathed a set of scrolls by a childless seer called Polemaenetus, "became an itinerant, passed his time in many cities, and had intimate relations with several women, some of whom gave birth to children he never recognized as legitimate." Having acquired a fortune abroad, he returned home to Siphnos, where he became its wealthiest citizen (Isoc. 19.5–9). In the absence of what we would call today "quality control," fraudulence must have been rife within the profession. Oedipus's taunting of the blind seer Teiresias for having "eyes only for profit" no doubt drew appreciative nods from some members of Sophocles' audience (*OT* 380–89; cf. *Ant.* 1033–47). Plato, too, was scathing toward the profession, castigating "*agurtai* [begging priests] and *manteis* who go to the houses of rich men and persuade them that they hold power from the gods by virtue of their sacrifices and spells" (*Rep.* 2.364b).

Rhapsodes or song-stitchers, probably so-named because they provided extempore performances, were also perpetually on the move, competing for prizes at public festivals. Plato's *Ion* is named for a famous rhapsode from Ephesus who tells Socrates at the beginning of the dialogue that he has just arrived in Athens from Epidaurus. Ion has won first prize in the quadrennial games held in honor of the healing god Asclepius and is confident that he will be equally successful in the forthcoming Panathenaic Games. The ubiquity of rhapsodes throughout the Greek world is indicated by the claim of one aficionado that he listened to their recitations "almost every day" (Xen. *Symp.* 3.6). From the fourth century onward, actors also traveled widely, often specializing in set-piece renditions, such as Timotheus of Zacynthus, who became famed for his memorable rendition of Ajax's suicide (Sch. *ad* Soph. *Ajax* 864).

A number of big-name sophists were itinerants, delivering public lectures and offering formal instruction to students, for which they were handsomely rewarded. They include Protagoras of Abdera, Gorgias of Leontini, Hippias of Elis, and Thrasymachus of Chalcedon. Though Athens was their primary venue, it was by no means their only destination. Hippias of Elis, for instance, claimed to have earned twenty *minae*—a very considerable sum of money—by lecturing to the inhabitants of a small Sicilian village (Pl. *Hp. Ma.* 282e). Sophists made appearances at the Panhellenic games, and it may well be that something akin to the modern lecture circuit was established by the middle of the fifth century. Though the length of their sojourn in any one place varied, it is likely that those at the top of their profession were constantly on the move. Philosophers were also in high demand. Diogenes the

Cynic is known to have visited Megara, Myndus, Samothrace, Olympia, Sparta, Delphi, as well as Athens (D.L. 6.41, 57, 59–60). They were often accompanied by an admiring group of pupils, as we know from the fact that Aeneas Tacticus recommended keeping a register of foreigners who were resident "for education or any other purpose" (10.10).

Celebrity dramatists became the equivalent of present-day artists-in-residence at prestigious universities. Aeschylus accepted an invitation from the tyrant Hieron I of Syracuse in ca. 476 to visit his court and write a play in celebration of the foundation of Aetna (see earlier, chapter 5; *Vit. Aes.* 8–11). Euripides' *Andromache* (dated 425) received its first performance abroad, no doubt with the poet in attendance (Sch. *ad* l. 445). Later Euripides visited Magnesia in Thessaly, where he was treated as an honored guest. Toward the end of his life he accepted an invitation to reside at the court of Archelaus, king of Macedon, where he wrote a lost play called *Archelaus*, which sought to justify the king's shaky dynastic claim to the throne. He remained in Macedon until his death two or three years later (*Vit. Eur.* 21–25).

Last, sculptors and other kinds of artists were itinerants. The Athenian Phidias, who was the most celebrated sculptor of his generation, undertook important commissions both at Delphi and Olympia. And when a famous sculptor like Lysippus of Sicyon undertook one of his many commissions abroad it is natural to suppose that he was accompanied by a small army of apprentices. Noteworthy, too, is the ethnic diversity of the craftsmen who worked on the temple of Asclepius at Epidaurus in the 370s. The chryselephantine statue was the product of ivory workers from Aegina, Ephesus, and Sicyon; of stonemasons from Athens and Corinth; of joiners from Corinth; and of a painter from Corinth. The workforce that constructed the temple consisted of Argives, Athenians, and Corinthians (Burford 1969, 199). And when the city of Thebes was rebuilt in 316 following its destruction by Alexander the Great some twenty years earlier, it was masons from Athens who constructed "the greater portion of its walls," and Greeks from cities in Sicily and Italy who erected buildings "to the extent of their ability" (D.S. 19.54.2).

Long-Distance Traders

From the twelfth to the eighth centuries, trade in the Greek world had contracted sharply, almost to the point of extinction. It revived in the eighth century, as we learn both from Homer and archaeology. At the beginning of the *Odyssey* we encounter Mentes, the lord of the Taphians—actually the goddess Athena in disguise—who has disembarked on Ithaca in search of bronze while en route for Temese with a cargo of iron ingots (1.184). Neither Taphus nor Temese is mentioned elsewhere in Greek literature, so we do not know how far Mentes sailed with his cargo before landing on Ithaca nor how far away is his destination, but perhaps that is Homer's point—these were places off the map.

The Homeric poems lead us to suppose that most long-distance traders were Phoenicians. As Finley (2002, 67) noted, there is no word for "trader" in Homeric Greek. To be a Phoenician meant in effect being either a trader or a pirate. When Nestor greets Telemachus at Pylos, he says, "Strangers, who are you? Where do you come from along the sea lanes? Are you traveling for trade? Or are you roaming like pirates?" (*Od.* 3.71–74; cf. 9.252–55). It is, however, tendentious, to see these two "vocations," as we might call them, as mutually exclusive. On the contrary, many traders would have engaged in piracy when the opportunity offered itself. As scholars have regularly noted, both trading and piracy are forms of redistribution. Given their close association with piracy, it is hardly surprising that the Phoenicians constituted a byword for greed (*Od.* 14.288–89; 15.415–16). The prejudice they experienced subsequently extended to merchants in general and to Greek merchants in particular. It was partly for this reason that wealth accruing from land ownership was judged superior to wealth that had been acquired from (dubious) commercial undertakings.

The contribution that mercantile itinerants made to Greek civilization can hardly be overestimated, however. It was largely due to them that the overseas settlement movement was so successful, that the Greeks became literate, and that their culture became informed and enriched by other cultures. And if for no other reason merchants were to be admired for their enterprise. Herodotus clearly admired Sostratus of

Aegina (ca. 600), whom he describes as the wealthiest trader of his day (4.152.3). Sostratus's trading activities took him from the Aegean Sea to Etruria. His voyage may have been facilitated by the *diolkos* (stone slipway) that was used for dragging ships across the Isthmus of Corinth between the Saronic and Corinthian gulfs, though we do not know the exact date of its construction. His name (or that of his namesake) turns up in an inscription dated to the late sixth or early fifth century on a stone anchor that was dedicated to Apollo at Gravisca in Etruria (Demetriou 2012, 64 with fig. 4). Long-distance traders who transported their wares by sea would mostly have confined their activity to the period from late spring to early autumn. Presumably they remained at home in the winter months or in a port that passed for home.

Pirates and Brigands

Pirates and brigands have been described as "a normal manifestation of Mediterranean production and redistribution" and "a systematic epiphenomenon of connectivity, suppressed by powerful states only for brief periods in Mediterranean history" (Horden and Purcell 2000, 387). Known as *leïstai* or *leïsteres*, they are prominent in the Homeric poems. They frequently traveled long distances in search of plunder, not only stealing movable property but also abducting women and children. Eumaeus, Odysseus's faithful swineherd in the *Odyssey*, is himself a victim of human trafficking. Descended from royal stock, he was abducted by Phoenician raiders while still a child (15.403–484). Odysseus's former nurse Eurycleia, who seems to have been of good birth, was presumably trafficked (1.429). So, too, going back one more generation, was Eumaeus's former Sidonian nurse (15.425–29). In "real life" women and children who were trafficked would have been forced to provide sexual services.

The Phoenicians, as we have just seen, had a reputation for raiding, but they certainly did not monopolize the profession. In fact they may well have been unfairly singled out as perpetrators. The "son of Castor," one of the Cretan personae adopted by Odysseus when he returns incognito to Ithaca, boldly asserts that "much wealth came my way" from being a raider. He further states that he "went among the people of Crete as one who was feared and respected," a claim that tells us much about the morally ambivalent value system that prevailed in Homeric Greece (*Od.* 14.234). Brigands and pirates operated more or less at will in the archaic and classical periods. Though pirates were kept in check in the fifth century, when Athenian naval power was at its height, they seem to have been particularly prevalent in the fourth century and proved largely immune to Alexander the Great's efforts to control them (Str. *Geog.* 5.3.5 C232; McKechnie 1989, 122–26).

Much about the lifestyle of such individuals is shrouded in mystery. We do not know what circumstances might have induced a man to choose such a career path. In some cases the career no doubt ran in the family; in others it was the result of exigency. Many able-bodied refugees must have turned their hand to raiding, whether on land or on the high seas. We tend to think of raiders as living wholly outside the law, but what constituted legality was not the same in antiquity as it is today. We should not rule out the possibility that they were able to retire in comfort and style, as "the son of Castor" claims to have done, particularly if they had enriched their local communities. If this is the case, they must have retained ties with their homeland. Indeed some at least may have led lives of partial domesticity.

Mercenaries

Mercenaries, known variously as *misthophoroi* (pay-earners), *xenoi* (foreigners), or *stratiôtai* (soldiers), comprised by far the largest number of itinerants. They are attested from the second half of the seventh century onward, though they almost certainly existed earlier. One such is Antimenidas, the brother of the lyric poet Alcaeus of Mytilene, who fought in the Babylonian army, possibly under Nebuchadnezzar when he campaigned in modern-day Israel and destroyed Ascalon in 604 (fr. 350 Campbell). From the seventh to the fifth centuries, however, the demand for mercenaries in the Greek world declined and was largely confined to tyrants such as Pisistratus of Athens, whose authority depended on private armies. However, those who practiced a specialized discipline, notably Cretan archers and Rhodian slingers, continued to be in demand. We also know that the Athenians employed mercenary rowers in their fleet, both in the fifth and fourth centuries (Thuc. 1.121.3; Dem. 50.14–18).

Mercenaries, as we have seen, were numerous in Sicily, partly because the *poleis* did not have sufficient manpower to perform all their military duties, largely because of the threat from the Carthaginians from the beginning of the fifth century onward. It was the worsening economic conditions at the end of the Peloponnesian War and, later, in the fourth century that generated the rise of mercenaries on an unprecedented scale. This was aggravated by the frequency of *stasis* consequent upon the unstable conditions that resulted from the weakened condition of Athens and Sparta, since this drove large numbers of able-bodied men into exile. Yet another reason for the rise of mercenaries was the increased dependency upon light-armed troops known as "peltasts." (Their name derived from the *pelta*, a crescent-shaped shield made of wicker.) Unlike the hoplite, whose equipment represented a substantial financial investment, a peltast could be armed with little financial outlay.

Though the extent to which individual city-states used mercenaries varied considerably, only the most backward and isolated parts of the Greek world were spared what many commentators, Isocrates most vociferously, saw as a menace to civilized society. From his privileged perspective and that of others like him, mercenaries were the dregs of society and they deserved nothing but contempt. In his *Address to Philip* (dated 346) he wrote (5.120–21):

If we do not put a stop to those who wander about without the means to support themselves and who assault all those whom they encounter by providing them with an adequate livelihood, they are in danger of becoming so numerous without our realizing it that they will become as formidable as the barbarians.

Although Isocrates was no doubt exaggerating, he obviously expected his scaremongering to work, which indicates that there was a genuine alarm at the prospect of a breakdown in the political and social order provoked by vagrants armed to the teeth and capable—in the hysterical hype of Athens's equivalent of a tabloid journalist—of dealing the deathblow to civilization. There is, of course, at least a kernel of truth to what he says in that unemployed mercenaries—an unidentifiable percentage of their total—would have had little option but to turn their hands to extortion and intimidation. Mercenaries also contributed to political instability, notably in Syracuse, where 20 out of 27 outbreaks of *stasis* saw their involvement (Berger 1992, 90).

It has been estimated that between 399 and 375 BCE, "there were never fewer than 25,000 mercenaries in service, and often more" (Davies 1993, 199). Faced with a severe demographic shortfall, even Sparta with its proud tradition of militarism came to rely on their services (Xen. *Hell.* 4.4.14). Aeneas Tacticus, who was writing in the middle of the fourth century, assumed that mercenaries would be in the employ of every Greek state (10.7, 12.2–5). His recommendation that they should never be more numerous than those who serve in the citizen militia is a clear indication of how much their services were in demand.

Greek mercenaries served abroad as well as in their homeland, and it was in fact the hiring of the Ten Thousand—or to be more precise, the hiring of 10,400 hoplites and 2,500 peltasts—by the Persian prince Cyrus the Younger in 401 that thrust them into the limelight and demonstrated their unrivaled excellence as fighters. The band did not come exclusively from the most underdeveloped and impoverished parts of the Greek world, as had generally been the case up to now. This may have been in part due to the Peloponnesian War, which had thrown many parts of Greece into economic turmoil. Indeed many of those who signed up for service under Cyrus had probably fought in that war. Owing to its duration, they might in some cases have been ill-suited to any other career. They included Athenians, Boeotians, and Spartans, as well as Achaeans, Arcadians, and Thessalians. The peltasts comprised Cretan archers and Rhodian slingers. Few of the Ten Thousand came from East Greece. Their leadership was primarily in the hands of Athenians and Spartans.

Cyrus's objective was to seize the throne from his brother King Artaxerxes II, though he seems to have kept that fact secret as long as he could, so as not to discourage recruits from enlisting (Marinovic 1988, 27). His bid failed due to his death in battle, but this in no way tarnished the image of the Greek mercenary. Quite the contrary in fact, since the Ten Thousand—or more accurately about half that number—succeeded, despite hunger, exhaustion, and frostbite, in making their way through hostile territory to the port city of Trapezus on the shores of the Black Sea, while being buffeted by the snows of central Anatolia—a journey of some 1,900 miles—in effect "a *polis* on the move," as they have been aptly described (Austin and Vidal-Naquet 1977, 380).

This event, which was immortalized in Xenophon's *Anabasis* or *March Up-Country*, marks the beginning of an era in which the mercenary became central not only to Greek warfare but also to the political and social life of the city-state. Henceforth a floating population numbering in the tens of thousands was perpetually available for hire. Consequently, there were probably more Greeks in the fourth century on the move looking for employment, or, failing that, scouring the landscape for the means of survival, than there had been at any time previously.

Some seventy years after Cyrus's campaign, Greek mercenaries served in the army of Darius III, when he was defending his empire against Alexander the Great. Though Alexander vilified them as traitors, they saw themselves as patriots defending Greek freedom against Macedonian oppression. They had a point. When Darius was defeated, some of them were conveyed to the equivalent of labor camps in Macedon, others fled, and a number of them fought to the last. Still others switched their allegiance and enlisted in Alexander's army.

Though primarily attracted by the prospect of adventure and plunder, mercenaries sought to acquire some degree of social respectability as soldiers of fortune. After all, even a man of means could take pride in the fact that he had served with a distinguished mercenary general. The defendant in a speech by the Athenian metic Isaeus (2.6), who fought in Thrace under Iphicrates, saw fit to boast of this fact before an Athenian jury. Likewise Lycomedes of Mantinea took pride in the fact that no mercenaries were more sought after than the Arcadians, amongst whom he himself numbered (Xen. *Hell*. 7.1.23).

Though mercenary generals amassed fortunes, this was hardly true of those who served in the ranks. Most signed up because they could not find better employment. Cyrus was unusual in having a reputation for being generous. The truth is that much about a mercenary's job was lousy. The pay was often irregular, the conditions of service harsh in the extreme, and one's paymaster a law unto himself. We know nothing about the fate of career mercenaries who sustained a serious, perhaps crippling injury. Was any provision made for them? Aeneas Tacticus, who was probably an Arcadian, recommended that before a campaign got under way the terms of their contract should be proclaimed, and if any mercenary found them unacceptable, he should be free to withdraw, whereas if he attempted to do so afterward he should be sold into slavery (10.18–19). We do not know whether this practice was ever adopted, though some basic contractual agreement advertising the rate of pay and outlining the campaign's objective would surely have been essential.

Some mercenaries, like modern professionals, had families awaiting them back home. This included many of the Ten Thousand, who, as Xenophon informs us, "longed to return safely to Greece" (*Anab*. 6.4.8), rather than establish a settlement on the southern shore of the Black Sea, as he had hoped. We can only speculate as to what might have been the domestic circumstances of those who chose not to return to Greece. Marriage to a local woman was obviously the best option, but we have no way of knowing how long a career mercenary might have remained in one place. It is a fair assumption that many of them would have served for a strictly limited period of time before being hired by a different employer and dispatched to another region—a situation hardly conducive to domesticity.

Mercenary settlements were sometimes established in foreign territory, either to provide a base for support, to serve as a garrison, or to reward mercenaries who had reached the end of their careers. The first two factors were certainly to the fore when Dionysius I of Syracuse established his mercenary settlements at the beginning of the fourth century (see earlier, chapter 4). Alexander the Great, too, had similar objectives when he settled his mercenaries in the East. When a rumor broke out that he had died, 3,000 of them abandoned settlements in Bactria and Sogdiana and headed back to Greece, whether to be massacred by the Macedonians (D.S. 17.99.6) or to make good their escape (Curtius 9.7.11). Sometimes, however, mercenaries chose to settle abroad, like those of the Ten Thousand who were eager to establish a foundation at Calpe Harbor, midway between Heraclea Pontica and Byzantium (Xen. *Anab.* 6.4.1–7).

Being temperamentally unfit for civic responsibility and inclined by training to impose their will by force, mercenaries posed a serious threat to settled urban life. Diodorus Siculus reports a particularly egregious example of bad behavior on the part of Dionysius I's Campanian mercenaries that occurred at the end of his war against Carthage in 404. The mercenaries in question journeyed to Entella, where they "induced" the citizen body ("bullied" might be a better word) to admit them as *sunoikoi* (fellow citizens). Once inside, they "fell upon all the men of military age by night, married"—presumably by raping—"the wives of the men with whom they had broken faith, and took possession of the city" (14.9.8–9). This, however, is an extreme case, and though it remains questionable how effectively settlements occupied by mercenaries functioned overall, the desire for land and citizenship at the end of one's working life was logical and understandable. Since, moreover, many thousands of them were non-Greek, their incorporation in the life of the *polis* contributed significantly to the hellenization of Sicily (Berger 1992, 91–92).

Persons of No Fixed Abode

Itinerants include those whose livelihood depends on begging and casual employment. Since, moreover, borders were highly porous, there must have been a large number of people who were in effect stateless.

Both Hesiod (*Op.* 299–302, 395–400, 498–99) and Tyrtaeus (10 *IEG*) suggest that the prospect of becoming homeless in the archaic world was an ever-present reality, though what percentage of the population sunk to this level is impossible to determine. It is not improbable that the number increased dramatically in the fourth century, as a result of the political upheavals and economic problems that we discussed a moment ago. Vagrants not only faced hardship but also opprobrium. Plato, like many educated and wealthy Greeks, believed that beggary was the consequence of idleness, and he refused to admit such people into his ideal state on the grounds that "they make their livelihood by endless entreaties" (Pl. *Rep.* 552a–e). Significantly, *ptôchos* (beggar), derives from *ptôssô* (shrink from, skulk, cringe). In other words, the very attitude and appearance of the beggar, quite apart from his or her circumstances, aroused both loathing and fear.

Though a few persons of no fixed abode may have been able to attach themselves to a noble household, such as Irus, who has a regular position as beggar-in-residence in Odysseus's palace, the majority would have been vagrants in the literal sense of the word. There is, of course, no knowing how many Greeks slept rough, but the number may well have been considerable. Though many who were infirm and elderly had no option but to eke out a slender living by begging on street corners, the able-bodied probably sought employment as casual laborers. As such, however, they would have been highly vulnerable to exploitation. The god Poseidon worked for a year under Laomedon, king of Troy, only to be sent packing without recompense when his period of service had come to an end (Hom. *Il.* 21.441–52). The suitor Eurymachus pretends to offer Odysseus employment as a casual laborer, building walls and planting trees in exchange for grain, clothes, and shoes, but he does so only to mock him (Hom. *Od.* 18.356–61). Both in wartime and in time of famine vagrants would have been particularly at risk, since they were perceived as a drain on the state's (and family's) limited food supply. For this reason Aeneas Tacticus recommended that such people, whom he typified as *talapeirioi* (the much-suffering), should be periodically "banished by proclamation" (10.10).

11

REPATRIATION

L'Esprit de Retour

L'esprit de retour consumes even those who have lived most of their lives abroad. Many people envisage returning to the place of their birth long before it is a distinct possibility. *L'esprit de retour* certainly consumed the Greeks, as numerous passages in their literature indicate, even though relatively few migrants would have returned to their place of birth, compared with the large number who return eventually today. It is hardly surprising that Alexander's attempt to establish mercenary settlements in the East ran into such difficulties and that many of his veterans ultimately began the long trek home. There is hardly a more poignant picture than the one that Homer invokes in the first scene of the *Odyssey*, where Odysseus, detained on the island of Ogygia by the nymph Calypso, is described as "longing for his home and his wife" (1.13) and "yearning to see the smoke rising from his own land" (1.57–59). When we meet him later, still a prisoner of Calypso's desire, we are told that he

> never stopped weeping so that his sweet life was draining from him, as he mourned for his return home. . . . Every day he sat on the rocks beside the sea, his heart bursting with tears and grief and sadness, as he looked over the barren deep, weeping (5.151–58).

It is no consolation to him that he sleeps each night in the arms of a "queenly nymph who is bright among the goddesses" (1.14). Odysseus's state of mind is one of nostalgia, a pathological sickness for one's homeland, a word that is derived from but does not exist in ancient Greek (*nostos* = homecoming, *algia* = sickness). It is safe to assume that his yearning would hardly have been less intense if he happened to be an overseas settler sitting in a cave on some unfamiliar island or promontory, pining for his family. Homer's image is, in other words, grounded in the experience of contemporary Greeks, for whom the feeling of acute loss was mediated neither by distance nor by time. *L'esprit de retour* also haunts Achilles when he recalls his father back in Phthia, whom he will never set eyes on again (*Il.* 24.507–11).

A similarly moving image of homesickness is evoked by Herodotus's story of the Paionians, a Thracian people who were deported from their homeland to Phrygia in 511 by Darius I, allegedly because the Persian king was so impressed by the industriousness of their women (5.12–15). Some twelve years later, Aristagoras, deputy tyrant of Miletus, offered to help repatriate them if they could make their way independently to the coast. Despite being pursued by the Persian cavalry, their courage and determination were such that they made it to the coast, whereupon the Chians graciously ferried them to Lesbos. The Lesbians in turn conveyed them by boat to Doriscus, from which they returned on foot to Paionia (5.98). Seemingly they were not subjected to abuse.

In many cases, however, a returnee represented a serious threat to his or her city-state, since it was likely that his return would reignite the *stasis* that had initially provoked his expulsion. This in effect is the situation that prevails on Ithaca when Odysseus returns home after an absence of twenty years. Not for nothing the oath that each Athenian juror had to swear included the following statement: "I will not bring back either exiles or those under sentence of death" (Dem. 24.149). It was obviously intended to head off the political instability that would ensue in the event of an exile exacerbating the kind of factional squabbling that had led to his banishment in the first place.

No less problematically, the return of exiles also created legal battles, notably when their property had been acquired by new owners—the situation that Odysseus manages to head off just in time. Not for nothing the amnesty between the opponents and former supporters of the Thirty Tyrants made in 403 specifically prohibited the remembering of past grievances, described in Greek by the verb *mnêsikakein* ([Arist.] *Ath. Pol.* 39). Though the circumstances under which exiles returned to their former *polis* are rarely recounted, the state probably authorized a general distribution of all the land that was vacant (Lonis 1991, 103). It can hardly have been the case that all returnees were able to repossess their original homes, especially when large numbers of them returned. Whatever procedure was adopted, however, we may suspect that recriminations would have been commonplace, if not the norm.

None of this diminishes the intensity of the homecoming itself. One of the most thrilling events in Athens's history was the return of the exiles following the overthrow of the Thirty. The democrats staged a triumphal entry into Athens under arms that culminated in a sacrifice to Athena performed on the Acropolis. It was a highly charged and deeply moving spectacle that not only symbolized the restoration of unity throughout Attica but also acknowledged the contribution of "the men of the Piraeus" to the restoration of democracy.

The Mentality of the *Émigré*

To understand the mentality of someone yearning passionately to return home we can do no better than consult the late-fifth-century Athenian orator Andocides. Andocides was implicated in the mutilation of the herms on the eve of the departure of the expedition to Sicily and he turned informer to avoid execution. He was subsequently deprived of civic rights and barred from entry to Athens's sanctuaries. Though he was not formally banished, he felt obliged to go into voluntary exile in order to improve his finances, hoping that he would eventually be invited to return as the city's benefactor. The speech titled "On His Return," which he delivered to the Assembly in ca. 409 when he was petitioning to recover his civic rights, encapsulates with disarming frankness the mindset of someone who spends years waiting to return home:

> I realized it would be for the best if I lived in a place where I should be least noticed by you. In time, however, as was only natural, I was seized by a desire

for my old way of life as an Athenian citizen—so much so that I thought
that the best course of action was either to die or to perform such beneficial
service to Athens that my rights as a citizen would be restored to me (2.10).

Andocides could hardly express his yearning to return home more convincingly, and though hyperbole is the stuff of forensic oratory there is
little reason to doubt his sincerity. He had previously attempted to gain
the good graces of his fellow-citizens in 411 by providing the Athenian
fleet at Samos with essential supplies, which he sold at cost price. An oligarchic coup occurred, however, and he narrowly escaped death by taking refuge at an altar. "On His Return" was his first formal request for
the restoration of his civic rights. It failed.

Andocides eventually returned to Athens at the end of the Peloponnesian War, when the *dêmos* passed a decree granting amnesty to political exiles. Then in 400 or 399 he successfully defended himself against
an attempt to debar him from entering either a sanctuary or the Agora.
A decade later in 392/1 he was again exiled, this time for being a member of a delegation to Sparta that had negotiated peace terms that were
considered excessively favorable to the enemy. We do not know whether
he went into exile alone or with his family. Nor do we know how closely
he kept in contact with his compatriots while abroad, though he may
well have ended his life embittered toward Athens.

The fact that so many groups of refugees returned to their place of
origin is testimony to the strength of the bonds that united them. These
bonds were fostered in part by preserving the worship of the ancestral gods and retaining the sense of a religious community. Perhaps,
too, there were traditions that kept communal bonds alive. There were
other, more informal ways of preserving the sense of ethnic identity,
as the speech that Lysias wrote for a litigant titled "Against Pancleon,"
delivered shortly before 387, indicates. The plaintiff reveals that on the
last day of each month all the Plataeans living in Athens gathered together in the Agora at the place where cheese was sold (23.6–7). It was
here that they gossiped, exchanged news about events back home, did
business deals, and generally hung out together. Doubtless every ethnic
group living abroad collected regularly at a designated meeting place.

The "Return" of the Messenians

No people proved more resilient in exile or more determined to retain their ethnicity than the Messenians, for whom, at the instigation of the Theban commander Epaminondas, a *polis* was founded on the western slope of Mount Ithome in 369—no fewer than 287 years after their ancestors had first been driven from their homeland according to Pausanias's calculation (4.27.9). They had been wanderers from their homeland far longer than any other Greek people. Their nearest rivals were the Plataeans, whose exile had lasted a mere two generations. Pausanias goes on to tell us that the Messenians "did not abandon the customs they brought from their homes in any way and did not lose their Doric accent" and that "even to this day [ca. CE 150] have kept the purest strain of Doric among the Peloponnesians" (4.27.11).

Or so the legend went. But what truth is there in it? It has recently been characterized as "an impressive reshaping of the past if there ever was one" (Luraghi 2008, 3). Even Pausanias, who was clearly an ardent admirer of the Messenians' tenacity, expressed doubts about the reliability of the stories they told about their past, as this passage indicates:

> The disasters which they suffered and the length of their exile have obliterated many of the events of their past even after their return, and since they are ignorant it is possible for anyone who wishes to dispute the facts with them (3.13.2).

Evidently there were others besides Pausanias who were skeptical of Messenia's claims. And what exactly were the "customs" that they supposedly preserved? We know of none of them. The only religious cult that we know was specific to the Messenians is the Andanian Mysteries. Thucydides, moreover, writing over half a millennium before Pausanias, tells us that the Messenians and Spartans were *homophônoi* (sharing the same dialect) (4.41.2). We will never learn to what extent the Messenians managed to preserve an accurate historical memory of their ancestors prior to the Spartan conquest of their land in the eighth to seventh centuries BCE and to what extent they dreamed it all up. There is, however, no evidence that the people had ever constituted themselves into a *polis* prior to 369, which was the year when the Theban general Epaminondas settled them.

There is a strong likelihood that the helots, who comprised the greatest number of the exiles, created an imaginary Messenia only in ca. 464, when they revolted from their Spartan masters and took refuge on Mount Ithome, following an earthquake that had rocked Sparta, literally and metaphorically, to its foundations (Thuc. 1.101.2; D.S. 11.63.1–4, 65.4). The death toll was said to be 20,000. After a protracted siege, the helots finally surrendered on condition that they "be permitted to depart from the Peloponnese under a truce and never set foot in it again." They also agreed that "if any of them was caught, he would become the slave of his captor." The duration of the revolt, reputedly as long as ten years, may have enabled the establishment of "semi-permanent communal institutions" on Mount Ithome (Cartledge 1985, 46). Spending long nights huddled over their campfires would have provided the rebels with the ideal context for creating and strengthening Messenian ethnicity.

Accompanied presumably by their families, the helots, after their surrender, trekked north to Athens. It must have been an extremely arduous and hazardous journey, like all such journeys undertaken by refugees. They were on the road for many days, as Athens is 150 miles from Mount Ithome. The Athenians agreed to receive the refugees because they were now on hostile terms with the Spartans, since the latter had refused their offer for help in suppressing the revolt. We may wonder how the Athenians accommodated the refugees, since they must have numbered in the hundreds, if not the thousands.

Later, in ca. 457–56, the Athenians transported them to Naupactus, a port at the entrance to the Corinthian Gulf which they had recently seized from the Ozolian (or Western) Locrians (Thuc. 1.103.1–3; cf. D.S. 11.84.7–8; Paus. 4.24.7). Naupactus thus became a kind of colony of runaway slaves, though the analogy is not entirely apt. An unpublished inscription suggests that the exiles coexisted peacefully with the indigenous population, both groups placing themselves under the protection of Athena Polias (Lewis 1992, 118).

The descendants of the refugees fought alongside the Athenians both against the Spartans at Pylos in 425 and against the Syracusans in Sicily in 413 (Thuc. 4.9.1; 7.57.8). Following Athens's defeat at the Battle of Aegospotami in 405, however, the Messenians, as they continued to call themselves, were expelled from Naupactus by the Peloponnesians. Pausanias (4.26.2) claims that some of them went to live with their relatives in Sicily and Rhegium, but that the majority departed for Libya, where they gave military assistance to the inhabitants of Euesperides (modern-day Benghazi). And there they remained for at least a generation.

After the defeat of the Spartans at the Battle of Leuctra in 371 Epaminondas advocated that a *polis* should be established for the Messenians in the foothills of Mount Ithome. He evidently chose this site both because it was the strongest natural fortress in the region and because it was a site of great patriotic significance. He was hardly motivated by humanitarian concerns for a dispossessed people, any more than the Athenians had been in the 460s when they settled the Messenians at Naupactus. On the contrary he envisaged Messene, allied to Megalopolis, as a way of containing the Spartans in the southeast Peloponnese (see earlier, chapter 4). His plan succeeded brilliantly, and the Spartans were reduced to a power of minor military significance.

What percentage of those who settled in Messene claimed descent from those who had been exiled in 464 is unknown. Pausanias reports the tradition that when summoned back to their homeland the Messenians "collected together more quickly than anyone might have expected, due both to their longing for their homeland and to their hatred for the Spartans" (4.26.5). This seems highly dubious, to put it mildly. Recalling a people who had been dispersed over a wide geographical area would have been an arduous and time-consuming task. Nor is it by any means obvious that repatriation would have seemed a particularly attractive proposition, involving as it did living in close proximity to the hated Spartans. Many who lived abroad may well have been content to recount tales of Messenian prehistory and stay rootedly put. After all, very few—if any—had ever set foot in Messenia, and they can hardly have felt much attachment to its soil.

Most of the settlers probably came from the ranks of those who were already living in Laconia and Messenia, and from soldiers who were serving in Epaminondas's army. We know that some of those who took up the offer were of proven non-Messenian ethnicity because Diodorus Siculus, following the contemporary historian Ephorus, explicitly states that Epaminondas did not restrict citizenship to those claiming to be of Messenian stock but registered "all those who wished"—a further indication that the offer of resettlement may have had only limited appeal (15.66.1).

As ever in this study, many questions remain unanswered. How long did it take to build the wall and the houses, and to provide the new city with a proper water supply and other essential facilities? Who footed the bill? (Probably Epaminondas did, on behalf of the Boeotian Confederacy, but we do not know this for certain.) Assuming that the city was still being completed when the first settlers began to arrive, how were they domiciled? Was any upper limit put on the number that was permitted to relocate? How were they distributed inside the *polis*? Were social and/or ethnic distinctions observed in the allocation of allotments? (Presumably those claiming descent from the original exiles had first choice, though again we do not know this for certain.)

Mass Enforced Repatriation

The enforced repatriation of large groups of people was sometimes used by a besieging army as a weapon of war, in part because the swelling of the citizen body increases the number of mouths that need to be fed, thereby fomenting unrest, if not a complete breakdown of the social and political order. Xenophon, for instance, tells us that toward the end of the Peloponnesian War, the Spartan admiral Lysander, following his naval victory at Aegospotami in 405:

> sent the Athenian garrisons [that is, the cleruchs] and every other Athenian whom he saw anywhere back to Athens, granting them safe conduct on condition that they sailed to that destination alone but not if they sailed anywhere else, in the conviction that the more people who gathered in the Piraeus and Athens, the sooner there would be a scarcity of food (*Hell.* 2.2.2).

The tactic was successful, and a few months later Athens was forced to surrender. Likewise, after the Thirty Tyrants had established their rule, the Spartans decreed that "Athenian exiles should be returned from everywhere and that those who prevented their return should be deemed enemies of Sparta" (Plu. *Lys.* 27.2). In this case enforced repatriation was intended to keep the city weak and divided by increasing the number of Spartan sympathizers.

Enforced repatriation inevitably causes massive legal and logistical problems. A case in point involves the repatriation of the oligarchs of Phlius, a town in the northwest Argolid, who had been driven out by their democratic opponents in 382. Eventually the democrats voted to reinstall the exiles because they feared that the Spartans, who sympathized with the oligarchs, would exact reprisals. So they agreed to restore their property and compensate those who had acquired it in the interim at public expense. Disputes between the current owners and the returning exiles were to be settled in a court of law (Xen. *Hell.* 5.2.10).

Once their fear of Spartan military intervention had receded, however, the democrats reneged on the deal (5.3.10). They refused to hear any complaints in an impartial court (viz one made up equally of democrats and oligarchs) as they had originally promised. Instead they made the exiles plead before a popular court. Since this was composed of the same people who had previously refused to hand over the confiscated property, it was unlikely to deliver a fair verdict. "What kind of justice is this," the oligarchs indignantly demanded, "where the guilty are also the judges?" So saying, they went into exile a second time, this time voluntarily, accompanied by others who were sympathetic to their cause.

The oligarchs presented their case to the Spartans, who agreed to come to their rescue. When Phlius fell in 379 after an eighteen months' siege, the Spartan king Agesilaus proposed peace on the following terms (5.3.25):

> Fifty men from the restored exiles and fifty men from those at home [that is, the democrats] should first determine who should be left alive and who should be condemned in accordance with due process, and secondly establish a constitution under which to run the state.

The episode starkly reveals the problems that returning exiles sometimes caused, particularly when they were able to seek support from an
outside power. Even without that complication, however, their attempt
to repossess their property would have put enormous strains on the
social fabric of the *polis*, as it does at the end of the *Odyssey* when Odysseus seeks to repossess his home.

The Exiles' Decree of Alexander the Great

The most comprehensive instance of mass enforced repatriation was
that undertaken by Alexander the Great. At the beginning of his reign
Alexander had taken steps not to aggravate the refugee crisis that he had
inherited as the leader of the Greek world. So in 335 he summoned a
convention at the Isthmus of Corinth and declared that there should
be "no executions or *phugai* [banishments] contrary to the laws of the
city-states, no seizing of property, no parceling out of land, no cancella-
tion of debts, and no freeing of slaves for the purpose of bringing about
a revolution" ([Dem.] 17.15). In the spring of 324, however, facing the
threat of insurrection, he announced to his army at Opis in Mesopotamia that all his generals and satraps were to disband their mercenary
armies. The consequences of this action were dire. The release of mercenaries always presented a threat, but Alexander's disbandment was
on an unprecedented scale. As a result, as Diodorus Siculus reports,
"mercenaries released from service were running wild throughout the
whole of Asia, supporting themselves by plunder." Many of them gathered at Taenarum, a major center for mercenary recruitment, where
they placed themselves under the command of the Athenian general
Leosthenes, Alexander's sworn enemy (17.111.1–4).

Had Alexander not foreseen the implications of his decision? Perhaps he determined that there was no alternative. At any rate he sought
a public venue to make his ruling binding on all those Greek cities—
how many we do not know—that now would have to deal with the
consequences of exiles returning en masse. Accordingly at the com-
mencement of the Olympic Games in late July 324 he promulgated

FIGURE 16 Silver *tetradrachma* struck in the name of Alexander the Great, 325–23, though as Price (1991, vol. 1, 88) notes, "the attributions of lifetime issues are purely tentative." The obverse depicts the head of either Heracles or the deified Alexander in the guise of Heracles, wearing the skin of the Nemean lion, which the hero had slain. The reverse depicts Zeus, Heracles' father and Alexander's ancestor, seated on a throne holding a staff in his left hand with an eagle perched on his extended right hand. A wreath is to the left. Alexander coins were minted principally to pay soldiers.

what is known as the Exiles' Decree. The decree established a panhellenic amnesty for all refugees by requiring them to return to their native cities and regain possession of their property. It took the form of an open letter that Nicanor of Stagira, Aristotle's adopted son and future son-in-law, handed to the winner of the heralds' competition to read to the assembled audience. Diodorus, who quotes a contemporary historian called Hieronymus of Cardia, has preserved the text of the letter, which was concise to the point of terseness (18.8.4):

> Alexander the king to refugees from the Greek cities. We were not responsible for your exile but we shall be responsible for your return to your own homelands, with the exception of those who are under a curse. We have written to Antipater [Alexander's viceroy in Europe] about these matters so that if any of the cities are unwilling to receive you back he will compel them to do so.

"Those who are under a curse" included an unknown number of felons and other criminals, as well as others whom Alexander himself had

driven into exile. Of these the largest group comprised the Theban deportees whom he condemned to a life of wandering when he laid waste
their city the previous year. Many of them had probably fought against
Alexander as mercenaries in the Persian army.

The reaction of the crowd is said to have been ecstatic. Diodorus
alleges that all the exiles had assembled in Olympia and that they numbered more than 20,000. But he can be thinking only of those who were
within easy reach of Olympia (Badian 1971, 28). The total number is
likely to have been considerably larger, especially if we include women
and children, because only men were permitted to attend athletic con-
tests. Alexander also took the opportunity to pension off 10,000 veterans who were serving in his army (D.S. 17.109.1–2).

The contents of the letter had no doubt been leaked well in advance
to give time for a large and appreciative crowd to assemble. Alexander was nothing if not a consummate self-publicizer. In fact Diodorus
claims that his purpose was "to enhance his fame and to win the support of many people through favors in the event of revolution and rebellion among the Greeks." We should therefore perhaps see the Exiles'
Decree as intended to win him partisan support throughout Greece.
He had previously been solicited by exiles from Heraclea Pontica and
Samos for permission to return to their homeland, so he would have
been fully aware of the potential benefits of gratifying the returnees. He
may even have hoped that their assimilation would prove a distraction.

Implementing the terms of the Exiles' Decree must have been a bu-
reaucratic nightmare, however, involving as it did the return of landed
property that had been appropriated by those who were politically at
odds with the returnees. It has been suggested that the procedures governing the reinstatement of the exiles were set forth in a more extensive
document than the proclamation itself (Poddighe 2011, 118). Even if
this were the case, however, each city-state would have been left to its
own devices to work out the messy details.

To comprehend the legal complications, let us turn to a decree that
relates to the repatriation of exiles to Tegea in Arcadia. "The returning
exiles are to be furnished with the paternal property away from which
they went into exile, and women are to be furnished with their mater-

nal property in the case of unmarried women who owned property and did not have brothers," it declares (ll. 4–7, Heisserer 1980, 205–18 = *SIG³* 306 = Harding 122 = Rhodes and Osborne 101). It then goes on to state that each returning exile is to receive a house. If the house has no garden, the returnee is to be assigned one that is nearby. If there is no adjoining garden, she or he is to receive half a garden. The current resident, viz the person who had acquired ownership of the house, is to be paid two *minae* in compensation (ll. 10–21).

The Tegean decree made a distinction between (1) daughters and widows who had gone into exile with their fathers and husbands but who had returned after their fathers and husbands had died, and (2) daughters and widows who had remained in exile after the latter's death and were only now returning. The former group, having already had their marriages annulled, were to be treated preferentially, and had already, it seems, been permitted to inherit their former husbands' property; the latter group, however, were to be subject to investigation regarding their entitlement to inherit (ll. 49–56).

Given the limited nature of written records, many disputes must have come down to verbal claims about ownership. The lawyers, or rather the speechwriters, must have had a field day trying to settle all the claims. Violence no doubt occurred when the previous owner was forced to evict the family that had taken possession of his property. Many of those who were evicted may even have found themselves homeless—hardly a recipe for amicable relations.

For the sixty days following the promulgation of this decree, a "court composed of foreigners" in nearby Mantinea was to adjudicate the settlement of disputes (ll. 24–36), evidently because it was thought more likely to exercise impartiality than a court composed of Tegean citizens. To alleviate tensions, the decree ends with an oath taken in the name of Zeus, Athena, Apollo, and Poseidon, in which the citizenry promises "to be well disposed toward the returning exiles . . . and not to bear a grudge against any of them" (ll. 58–60)—a pious hope if ever there was one and one that reminds us that when returnees reconnect with their former friends, communities, and ancestors, much pain and anger will come to the fore, since "there is no such thing as a genuine, uncomplicated return to one's home" (Edward Said, quoted in Long and Oxfeld 2004, 15).

The Exiles' Decree represented a flagrant violation of the cherished autonomy of the Greek city-states. That autonomy had been enshrined in the charter of the League of Corinth, established by Philip II after the Battle of Chaeronea, which Alexander had pledged to honor. He had certainly interfered in the inner workings of individual cities on previous occasions, but this was on an unprecedented scale. Evidently he no longer cared to mask his contempt for public sentiment. To make matters worse it was around this time that he either requested or demanded that the Greeks recognize him as a god. Hardly surprisingly, some six months later a number of cities sent ambassadors to his court to present arguments against the return of exiles. Diodorus tells us that Alexander "did his best to send all of them away satisfied" (17.113.4). What exactly this amounted to is anyone's guess. We do know, however, that some states were successful in petitioning to introduce changes in line with their individual circumstances. The decree from Tegea, for instance, states explicitly in the introduction that it was promulgated "in accordance with corrections that were made by the city-state regarding issues in the *diagramma* (regulation) to which objection had been made" (ll. 2–4).

In conclusion, though the Exiles' Decree addressed a very great social evil, it would be naïve to assume that a humane concern for the welfare of his subjects featured remotely in Alexander's thoughts, as some modern commentators have suggested. It is equally clear, too, that Alexander never thought through the devastating practical consequences of this measure for the recipients of the exiles—or that if he did, decided he had little choice but to propose their return.

The Return of the Samians

We may well wonder how many exiles returned to their homes as a result of Alexander's decree. Diodorus's claim that "most Greeks welcomed the exiles" seems highly improbable. Clearly many Greeks would have deeply resented the turmoil that their return occasioned, particularly those who had to relinquish their residences. The most vigorous protest came from the Athenians, who were required to give up an important overseas possession (18.8.6).

In 365 the Athenians had conquered Samos and expelled its population. Four years later they established a cleruchy on the island, composed exclusively of Athenian citizens. Then in 324, acting on the advice of one of his generals, Gorgus of Iasus, Alexander announced to his army that he was "giving Samos back to the Samians." It was an evocative turn of phrase and one calculated to earn the goodwill of exiles everywhere, especially those who were serving in his army. Gorgus's goodwill toward the Samians went further. He took it upon himself, presumably with the agreement of his *polis*, to proclaim that Iasus would cover the travel expenses of the returning exiles. We learn this from an inscription passed by the Samian *dêmos* some time between 334 and 321, honoring him and his brother Minnion for the services they had rendered to the exiles (*SIG³* 312.20–23, rev. Heisserer [1980, 184–86] = Rhodes and Osborne 70).

The Athenians had probably heard of Alexander's promise to the Samians shortly before the promulgation of the Exiles' Decree. Being "in no way willing to give Samos up," they promptly sent a delegation to Alexander, hoping to make him change his mind. The Samians meanwhile had taken Alexander at his word, and a number of them now crossed from the mainland, where they had been living, to Samos. Learning this, the Athenian *dêmos* ordered the general in charge of the island to round them all up and send them back to Athens to stand trial. On their arrival, they were imprisoned and sentenced to death. We learn of these events from a decree honoring a certain Antileon of Chalcis for his support in securing their release (Habicht 1957, no. 1).

When Alexander died in 323, the Athenians promptly revolted from Macedonian rule. They did so largely because of their resentment at his interference in their internal affairs. Though the origins of the so-called Lamian War that gives its name to the revolt can be traced back to Alexander's execution of his court historian Callisthenes of Olynthus in 327, it is fair to state that hostility toward the Exiles' Decree played a major part. The Roman historian Curtius (first or second century CE) tells us that the Athenians claimed that Alexander's objective had been to repatriate "a cesspool of social orders and people" and that they "preferred to tolerate anything rather than receive back what was once the filth of their own city, and was now the filth of their place of exile" (10.2.6).

Perdiccas, who succeeded to the throne on Alexander's death, upheld the ruling in favor of the Samians. Athens was eventually defeated and the Samians returned home in 322/1, "after an exile that had lasted 43 years" (D.S. 18.18.9). It must have been a profoundly emotional occasion, especially if there was a handful of elderly survivors among the returnees. Given the lapse of time, however, most of those who repossessed the island would have been the sons, if not the grandsons, of the original exiles.*

Very likely the Athenian cleruchs living on Samos fought tooth and nail for what they, too, saw as their homeland (Shipley 1987, 168). After all, most of them had lived their entire lives on the island. We do not know what reception they received when they returned "home." Habicht (1966, 401) estimated that the number of cleruchs who were displaced was equivalent to "almost a third of all adult male citizens of Athens." For them, too, it was a humanitarian crisis—and for us one more whose details elude us.

---

* One of the refugees was the philosopher Epicurus, who eventually founded the philosophical school known as "the Garden," where he and his followers lived in seclusion. As Paul Cartledge has suggested to me, his desire for seclusion may have been a response to the violence that his parents had experienced as refugees.

CONCLUSIONS

Targeted by Death Squads, Raped by Soldiers, Tortured by the State; More Than 40 Million People around the World Have Been Forced out of Their Homes and into Exile.

—*GUARDIAN WEEKLY* (JANUARY 11, 2013)

Horrific events, comparable to the preceding, occurred repeatedly in the Greek world. Yet terrible though the sufferings of the Greeks were, the thesis of this investigation has been that migration, displacement, and relocation, both forced and voluntary, were central to the survival, viability, and (it necessarily follows) phenomenal success of Greek societies. Though population movements in antiquity were for the most part modest by modern standards, many were large in proportion to the total population. In fact they were a persistent feature of daily life, often with devastating consequences for those who were dislocated.

A major problem throughout this survey has been the imprecision of the Greek language, which in important ways fails to distinguish between different types of migrants. The wanderer was none the less central and integral to hellenic identity, witness Homer's *Odyssey* and Xenophon's *Anabasis*. For a variety of reasons, still keenly debated, from the second half of the eighth century to the end of the sixth the *polis* exported a sizable proportion of its population. The desire to extend the frontiers of trade, obtain resources or land, escape famine or destitution, or simply fulfill one's human potential, were among the leading factors. When compelled to do so, moreover, the Greeks were fully capable of putting their roofs on their backs and moving an entire population elsewhere. Flexibility was a necessary part of the Greek, or rather Mediterranean, *mentalité*, though the Greeks were among the leaders in mobility. Both to head off civil strife and to safeguard their interests, political factions and tyrants regularly deported their opponents.

Of the many thousands who became homeless in the Greek world, a few could seek shelter, either temporarily or permanently, through *asulia* and *xenia*, though to what extent either institution did much to alleviate the hardship of the average refugee or migrant is questionable. In wartime those living in unprotected areas sought shelter inside a walled city, thereby engendering disease and fomenting social and political unrest. A number of individuals either went into enforced exile or took to their heels to escape vengeance-seekers or the law. Excepting those with powerful connections abroad, theirs was a daily battle for survival. Slaves, too, occasionally found freedom in flight, though with what frequency or success is impossible to determine. Itinerants and economic migrants were a prominent feature of the Greek landscape from the archaic period onward. They took to the footpaths (there were scarcely any roads to speak of) or to the high seas, motivated primarily by ambition or a taste for adventure. No itinerant was more ubiquitous than the mercenary, whose numbers proliferated in the fourth century.

If anything, the situation may well have deteriorated in the period covered by this survey, with an increasing number of vagrants and out-of-work mercenaries threatening to destabilize the Greek world. To what extent Alexander the Great, who certainly added to the problem, was able to arrest it, is impossible to determine. Finally, as is true of émigrés in all periods of history, the yearning to return to one's homeland remained a vivid and haunting dream. When realized, however, it would often produce serious tensions within the community that sometimes resulted in civil discord.

Unsurprisingly Athens presents a case study that is often exceptional and sometimes unique. The *polis* sent out few overseas settlements until it acquired its empire in the fifth century, when it employed cleruchies and the like partly as a way of exercising control over regions that were critical to its security. Athens also relocated its population from the countryside to the city during both the Persian and the Peloponnesian wars. The state accommodated a far larger population of immigrants than any other *polis*. It employed ostracism seemingly as a way to defuse *stasis* and thereby to eliminate the need for mass deportation. The amnesty that initiated the return of its exiles in 401/400, following the civil war that had seen the overthrow of the Thirty, was exemplary.

In conclusion, it is hardly any exaggeration to state that the brilliance of Greek civilization was predicated in part upon the shiftlessness of its population. Being Greek meant facing the prospect of being displaced at some point in one's life without any certainty of return. Praxithea's comment in Euripides' lost play *Erechtheus* that the populations of all Greeks cities (with the exception of Athens) were "distributed in the same way as by the throw of the dice" is *au point* (50.7–10 Austin). It was also the case that the mobility of the Greeks, and the spirit of adaptability that this bred inside them, encouraged the construction of panhellenic institutions and fostered cultural homogeneity. Greece in sum was a civilization of displaced persons.*

---

* All this said, we should not overlook the fact that the Greeks were merely "one of many actors playing a role within an extensive network of communications spanning the Mediterranean" (Hall 2002, 92). This is the underlying premise to Horden and Purcell's *The Corrupting Sea: A Study of Mediterranean History* (2000). It is also the case that the inbred nature of the *polis* hampered the Greeks from capitalizing on the full potential of their diaspora. As Purcell (1990, 58) eloquently puts it, "The success that came with the currents of Mediterranean mobility was reserved for the people whose first community of shepherds grew by the addition of vagabonds and runaways, which preyed on more stable and involuted neighbours for the procreative resource, and whose first leaders were reared on the milk of the roving wolf."

—καὶ μακρὸς Ὄλυμπος.
—and lofty Olympus.

—HOM. *IL.* 15.193

He rests. He has travelled.

—JAMES JOYCE, *ULYSSES*

ENVOI

This investigation has raised numerous questions that I have been unable to answer adequately, owing to lack of evidence.* The following are some of the most compelling.

1. How large an area would settlers take over when initially settling in a new land?
2. What percentage of overseas settlements ended in failure and with almost total loss of life?
3. What percentage of the wives of first-generation settlers was non-Greek?
4. What percentage of second-generation settlers was bilingual?
5. When a political faction expelled its opponents, what percentage of that faction was typically expelled? Was it merely the most prominent representatives who were driven out, or was a majority of those who were known to be opposed to the interests of the winning faction expelled?
6. What strategies did a portable *polis* adopt to maintain its cultural identity abroad?
7. What was the fate of the relatives of exiles and fugitives who were not themselves expelled? Did they, for instance, face eviction?
8. Would a large group of refugees seek to maintain cohesion, or would it typically be forced to divide into small groups?
9. Given the fact that political exiles were not permitted to take weapons with them, what were their chances of survival once they had been deported?
10. Would sanctuaries sometimes be taken over by desperate refugees?

---

* These questions were provoked by colleagues and friends who attended a talk I gave at the University of Texas at Austin in October 2012. I am most grateful to my host, Lesley Dean-Jones, and to James Dee in particular.

11. To what extent did the sanction of religion provide some protection for refugees?

12. What percentage of economic migrants left their homes to improve the quality of their lives and what percentage left as a result of extreme impoverishment?

13. What percentage of economic migrants settled abroad with their families?

14. What percentage of economic migrants returned to their original homeland at the end of their working lives?

15. What percentage of economic migrants in Athens and elsewhere did short-term residents comprise?

16. After a siege had led to the massacre of all the men of military age, what steps might be taken to protect captive women and children?

17. What was the fate of the sick and the elderly after a siege? Were they abandoned or slaughtered?

18. Did refugees occasionally establish camps in the Greek countryside? What were their chances of survival if they did? What percentage died from sickness or starvation?

19. To what extent were runaway slaves a significant concern to a *polis*? What percentage managed to evade capture and live out their lives in freedom?

20. What strategies did fugitives with no hope of finding permanent refuge abroad adopt in order to survive?

21. What percentage of the Greek population faced displacement as the result of political exile, war, famine, and other catastrophes at some point in their lives?

22. What percentage of the Greek population did persons of no fixed abode constitute?

23. How did the plight of the refugee change over time?

24. Did the size of the refugee population increase over time?

FURTHER READING

Chapter 1. Prolegomena

Ancient and Modern Responses to Migration. See Dummett (2001, Ch. 1) for many of the issues discussed here. For Queen Elizabeth I's views on immigration, see Bartels (2006, 305–22). For a brief history of American naturalization law, see López (2006, 30–34). For a summary of post–World War II migrations, see Goldin et al. (2011, 85–93). For the effects of 9/11 on refugee protection, see Newman (2003, 9–11). It is a truism that strong anti-immigration sentiment persists in most major developed countries today. The year 2012, the centenary of Enoch Powell's birth, saw some attempt to rehabilitate his memory. On Margaret Thatcher's appetite for the word "swamped," see Dummett (2001, 14–17).

The Silence of the Sources. For acknowledgment of the scale of migration in antiquity, see D.S. 12.8.9, who states that in earlier times Sybaris had been so generous with grants of citizenship to foreigners that its population had swelled to 300,000. Its citizenry was able to implement this policy due to the fertility of its land. The commonly voiced claim today that the scale of the current refugee crisis "has never been witnessed before in history," though true in terms of absolute numbers, is not necessarily true in terms of the proportion of settled to unsettled. Plu. *Mor.* 605c, citing several men of letters who wrote in exile, states: "The muses, it seems, co-opted exile as their fellow-worker in perfecting for the ancients the fairest and most esteemed of their accomplishments." Syme (1962, 40), himself an immigrant to the UK from New Zealand, commented: "Exile may be the making of an historian." The proposition is examined by Dillery (2007, 51–70).

Causes of Population Displacement. For a useful summary of the causes of relocation from the geometric to the classical period, see Demand (1990, 165–76).

The Carians are said to have abandoned the island of Syme in the Dodecanese after the Trojan War because of a drought (D.S. 5.53.2). It was drought, too, followed by famine, that allegedly induced the Therans to colonize Cyrene (see later, chapter 3). The Chalcidians are said to have abandoned Pithecusae, partly as a result of "earthquakes, eruptions of fire and sea, and hot water" (Str. *Geog.* 5.4.9 C248). In the hellenistic period the silting up of rivers caused the populations of Atarneus, Myous, and Priene to relocate, but there is no evidence for silting as a cause of displacement prior to this era.

Chapter 2. The Wanderer

The Centrality of Wandering to the Experience of Being Greek. A wandering existence would have been particularly terrifying for a single or divorced woman such as the non-Greek princess Medea, who, on learning that her husband has rejected her, must contemplate what life will be like, "exiled, tossed out of the land, bereft of my friends, with only my children, I and they alone" (Eur. *Med.* 513).

Lyric and Elegiac Poetry. See Bowie (2007, 28–49). The relative paucity of references to exile in sympotic poetry may, as Bowie (p. 21) suggests, be due to the fact that "pursuing the topic at length could well impair a singer's status as a welcome symposiast."

Tragedy. For the intimate association between wandering and wretchedness in Greek tragedy, see Montiglio (2005, 26–30).

Philosophy. For Diogenes the Cynic on the theme of homelessness, see Branham (2007, 71–86). For Teles and Plutarch, see Nesselrath (2007, 88–99).

Myth and Legend. See Hall (2002, 9–19) for a vigorous defense of the importance of what he labels "fictive kinship" as a condition for forging a sense of ethnicity. There may well be some substance to the claim of a Dorian invasion, though the search for material evidence to back it up has so far proved inconclusive. In the nineteenth century archaeologists believed that the Dorian invasion caused the destruction of the Mycenaean palaces. They detected evidence for this in the introduction of iron working, the evolution of the protogeometric style of pottery, the change from cremation to inhumation, and the appearance of new types of weapons and jewelry, all of which they attributed to the arrival of a culturally and ethnically distinct group around the eleventh century. Refinement in dating techniques has, however, conclusively demonstrated that each of these innovations either predated the destruction of the Mycenaean palaces or made its first appearance only in regions that claimed to be of non-Dorian ancestry, notably Athens and Euboea. See Snodgrass (2000, 360–73) for the archaeological evidence relating to the twelfth to tenth centuries. Linguistic evidence pointing to a proto-Doric idiom that was spoken in central and northern Greece is also inconclusive. Even so, some scholars continue to put faith in the legend, on the grounds that it is supported by data principally of a ceramic nature, which point to the arrival of newcomers to Laconia some time around 950. The size of the migratory movement (assuming it occurred) cannot be estimated—Isocrates (*Panathenaicus* 255) claimed that 2,000 Dorians founded Sparta—but we should hardly be thinking in terms of "a single, massive influx" (Hall 1997, 184). For a succinct account of the modern debate, see Asheri (in Asheri et al. 2007, 116–17) and Hall (2007, 43–51). For the Romans as an upstart people, see Livy (1.8.6, 2.45.4, and so on).

Loraux (1986, 148–50) describes the myth of Athenian autochthony as "the Athenian myth par excellence." For the perceived benefits of autochthony in Athenian discourse, see Loraux (2000, 13–27). Montiglio (2005, 13) claims that the idea was based on the notion that migration is a sign either of weakness or of aggression. It was Rosivach (1987, 294–306) who first drew attention to the fact that it is largely a fifth-century invention. For the important part belief in autochthony played in the construction of Athenian ethnicity, see Cohen (2000, 79–103); Isaac (2004, 114–24); and Lape (2010, 17–19 and 99–101). Pl. *Crit.* 112c, speaking of the Athens of his imagination 9,000 years previously, adds an interesting "architectural" element to the myth of Athenian autochthony: "They constructed buildings in which they and the descendants of their descendants grew old and they handed them down unaltered to others like themselves."

Chapter 3. The Settler

Why the Greeks Settled Abroad. For the Ionian migration, see Snodgrass (2000, 373–78), who aptly characterizes it as "a remarkable testimony to the vitality of the Greek communities in the eleventh century" (p. 373). As Lomas (2000, 171) writes of Italy, "The vast range of myths and historical traditions about founders and the processes of settlement and foundation is indicative of the similarly vast range of possible motivations for Greek migration and settlement." See, too, the mix of motives discussed by Hall (2007, 114–17). Though Camp (1979, 397–411) suggested that drought was a major cause of the eighth-century migratory movement, the evidence is inconclusive (Jameson 1983, 14 n. 4). A major problem in our understanding of the archaic movement is that almost all our sources date to the classical period. See, however, Malkin (2009, 374–75), who argues for the reliability of many of the preserved details of these sources. There is further discussion in Hall (2007, 100–106). Murray (1993, 102–23) provides an excellent account of the major themes relating to settlement abroad. For what they are worth, we have a literary foundation date for 73 settlements (Graham 1982a, 160–62). Al-Mina at the mouth of the River Orontes on the Turkish/Syrian border, once thought to be an earlier foundation than Pithecusae, is now known to have been contemporary, though there is some doubt as to whether this was a Greek, as opposed to a mixed settlement (Hall 2007, 97). The Greeks were also visiting nearby Ras-el Basit and Tell Sukas by the second half of the eighth century. See Boardman (1999, 38–

54). For the causes of settlement in the eighth century, see Tsetskhladze (2006, xxviii–xxx). An interesting variant is the foundation of Tarentum by a group of Laconians known as the Partheniae, who had allegedly been deprived of their civic rights because they had been born when their fathers were away fighting the Messenians (Str. *Geog.* 6.3.2 C278 = Antiochus of Syracuse, *FGrH* 555 F 13). For a detailed discussion of the meaning of the word *emporion*, together with a list of all the communities that are classified as *emporia*, see Hansen (2006, 6–39). Naucratis in the Nile Delta, described by Herodotus (2.178–79) as both a *polis* and as an *emporion*, was a special case. See Bowden (1996, 28–31) and Demetriou (2012, 105–52). Murray (1993, 111) interestingly suggests that settlement abroad might actually have indirectly led to an increase in population in the mother-city, as attested by the fact that a number of them sent out several expeditions within the space of a single generation. With reference to Greek settlements in the west, Osborne (1998, 268) argues that private enterprise "should be envisaged as responsible . . . for the vast majority of eighth- and seventh-century settlements."

The Role of Apollo. For a skeptical view of Delphi's centrality, see Londy (1990, 122), who points out that "of colonies founded between 750 BCE and 500 BCE, scarcely one in ten can boast a Delphic response." See further his table I (p. 119) for a list of the fifteen Delphic "colonization responses" dated ca. 750–500. As Malkin (1987, 17) notes, "not one foundation oracle with any claim to authenticity has come down to us from any other oracle." Dougherty (1993, 178–98) suggests that Apollo's importance is due partly to his role as purifier, viz of the violence perpetrated by Greeks against the local population. She writes (p. 180), "The Greeks use Apollo and the purification process that murder demands as a conceptual analogy, a metaphor, to describe colonization." For an interesting parallel in the Hebrew Bible, see the question that is put to a local priest by representatives of the Danites when they are seeking a land to inhabit, "Inquire of God that we may know whether our undertaking will succeed," which receives the instant reply, "Go in peace. The mission you are on is under the eye of the Lord" (Judges 18.5–6).

The Size and Composition of a Settlement. On the panhellenic nature of the movement in general, see Malkin (2011, 53–64). The pirates from Cumae who first settled Zancle (later called Messana) on the Strait of Messina were joined by "large numbers from Chalcis and the rest of Euboea" (Thuc. 6.4.5). The very large number of settlements founded by Miletus and Chalcis are difficult to explain unless we assume that the original nucleus of pioneers was supplemented by others from other city-states (Malkin, 2011, 54). An exception to the rule that most foundations comprised pioneers from a single *polis* in the first generation is Naucratis, which was jointly founded by nine cities (Hdt. 2.178).

Designating the Oikist. For the role of the oikist, see Graham (1983, 29–39). For the connection with Delphi and the posthumous cult of the oikist, see Malkin (1987, 17–91, 190–203). It is indicative of the challenges that the oikist often faced that our first encounter with Aeneas shows him to be so dispirited that he wishes he had died fighting at Troy (*Aen.* 1.94–96). This, however, does not prevent him from delivering a rousing pep talk to his fellow-refugees in the midst of his travails, even though he scarcely believes it himself (1.198–209). For heroic honors being granted to the oikist, see Hall (2007, 104–5), who notes that the literary testimony for this practice is late.

Identifying the Site. For Arganthonius's offer to the Phocaeans and the site of Tartessus (Phoenician Tarshish), see Demand (1990, 37); Murray (1993, 109); and Asheri et al. (2007, 184). Regions where presettlement contacts are very likely to have occurred include the delta of the Rhône, southern Italy and Sicily, and the Black Sea coasts (Graham 1990, 45–60).

Choosing the Pioneers. Plato (*Laws* 5.735e–736a) suggests, not improbably, that in some cases those selected were the equivalent of political exiles, deemed to be the most dangerous and anti-social members of society. For priestesses as pioneers, see Graham (1980–81, 302–13).

Departing. On the questionable veracity of Herodotus's account of the foundation of Cyrene and the ways in which foundation stories served later political agendas, see Osborne (1996, 8–15; 1998, 255–56). For the problematic relationship between the Cyrenean inscription and the Herodotean text, see Corcella (Asheri et al. 2007, 680). Other foundation inscriptions include *ML* 13 = Fornara 33 (Locrian decree relating to an unknown settlement, dated 525–500); *ML* 20 = Fornara 47 (decree of East Locrians relating to their settlement at Naupactus in Western Locris, 500–475); *ML* 49 = Fornara 100 (Athenian decree relating to the settlement at Brea, ca. 445 or 426/5). A fate similar to that of the Therans awaited the Eretrians when they tried unsuccessfully to return home after failing to establish a settlement on Corcyra (Plu. *Mor.* 293b).

Laying the Foundations. Dunbabin (1948, 179–83) rejected the view that in southern Italy and Sicily many of the cults and observances adopted by the *apoikia* were taken over from the Sicels and Italians, though he acknowledged that worship was sometimes established on sites previously venerated by indigenous peoples. Malkin (1987, 185) states, "Presence and familiar protection were felt to be all the more necessary in a new and foreign territory," but he does not elaborate on the consequences that inevitably flow from this insight. For the establishment of cults and *nomima*, see Malkin (2009, 382–90). See also Osborne (1996, 232–42) for archaeological evidence of the physical transformation of three Greek settlements—Thasos, Metapontum, and Megara Hyblaea—each from being a "community with a priority on survival into a community with a distinct civic identity willing to invest in communal facilities, to render its civic face visible by monumental constructions" (p. 242).

Relations between Settlers and Indigenous Populations. See Graham (1982a, 155–57); Lomas (2000, 173–85); and Hall (2002, 97–100). Ridgway (1992, 114) writes of Pithecusae that it was "permeated by Levantine contacts and influences." See further Boardman (1999, 165–68). A special case is Naucratis, where the pharaoh Psammetichus I (r.

664–10) licensed the establishment of a colony of Greeks (Bowden 1996, 17–37; Boardman 1999, 117–35). For relations between Greeks, Carthaginians, and Sicels, see Sjöqvist (1973, 49–72). Dunbabin (1948, 43) states: "At least half the Greek colonies [viz in Sicily and southern Italy] were built on sites previously occupied by native towns, and it is likely that most were. In every case of which we hear, the Greeks drove out the Sicels or Italians by force." He further maintains (p. 187) that "life in the [Italian] colonies was completely Greek in its material aspects." Recently, however, scholars have detected the presence of both Greek and indigenous inhabitants in many settlements. Lomas (2000, 173), for instance, writes, "It is highly likely that the population of [settlements in Italy] was originally mixed even in respect of the Greek population, arising from the fact that the foundation of a colony was not necessarily a single decisive act." For Taras and Sybaris, see Osanna (1992, 118–29). For Emporium, see Demetriou (2012, 24–52). For burials at Incoronata and Policoro, see Osborne (1998, 262–63). For the influence of the Greeks on the Gauls at Massalia "where it seemed as if Gaul had moved to Greece, not Greece to Gaul" (Justin 43.3), see Murray (1993, 109). For relations between the Greeks and the Getae in Dobruja Bulgaria, see Coja (1990, 157–68), who concludes: "[They] coexisted peacefully ... each of them ... living within its own social organization" (p. 166). For Greeks and indigenous populations in the Black Sea region, see Tsetskhladze (1998, 44–50), who maintains that "a small part of the local population formed a component in the Ionian Greek cities from the outset." For relations between Greeks and natives in the Iberian peninsula, see Domínguez (2006, 492). For a brief summary of cultural interactions between the Greeks and non-Greeks in western Asia prior to the arrival of Alexander the Great, see Colledge (1987, 134–48). Dougherty (2003, 187) notes that the Athenian general Nicias likened the challenge of conquering Sicily to "establishing a city among hostile foreigners" (Thuc. 6.23.2). For the Mariandynoi and other subjected indigenous peoples, see van Wees (2003, 45–47). This complicated subject is of interest to scholars working in the emerging field of interaction studies, whose focus is inter-regional relations involving power and exchange (Aubet 2013, 41–77).

Women Settlers. See Graham (1980–81, 293–314); Hall (2002, 100–103); and Asheri et al. (2007, 177). For mixed marriages, see Baslez (1984, 69–74). On the basis of their important role in religion, Graham argues, "The great majority of women in Greek colonies must have been from the beginning Greek" (p. 313). This seems to me highly unlikely, not least because a relatively small number of women would have been selected for religious duties. For intermarriage between Euboeans and Italians at Pithecusae, see Coldstream (1994, 53) and Hodos (1999, 61–64). While conceding that *fibulae* (brooches) in Pithecusan graves can be interpreted as evidence of intermarriage, Hodos suggests that in Sicily the presence of such objects is more likely to be evidence of trade. The abduction of the Sabine women during the reign of Romulus is the most famous instance in Roman history. Livy (1.9) narrates the episode in such a way as to suggest that domestic harmony ultimately prevailed between the women and their abductors. By the Augustan era the story had evidently become something of an embarrassment, though it could not be excised from the record.

Setbacks, Failures, and Eventual Successes. A classic instance of the perils of nostalgia is recorded in the case of the Phocaeans, half of whom gave up the attempt to settle elsewhere and returned to their abandoned city (see chapter 4). For internal strife among settlers, see Verg. *Aen.* 5.636–40, where the goddess Iris takes the form of an elderly woman called Beroë and claims to have had a dream in which Cassandra told her that the Trojans should settle at Drepanum rather than continue on their voyage to Hesperia, thereby stimulating the women to set fire to the ships.

The Athenian Postscriptum. Fifth-century settlements founded by states other than Athens include Siris (Policoro), Heraclea Trachinia, Heraclea Pontica, and Chersonesus. For the difference between early migration and Athens's settlements, see Brunt (1966) and Cawkwell (1992). For her cleruchies and settlements, see Graham (1983, 166–210), Salomon (1997), and Moreno (2009). As Malkin (2009, 376) points out, Athens was internally settled during the eighth and seventh centuries by the "filling" of Attica. Figueira (1991, 171) notes that some *apoikiai* had as many as 5,100–6,100 colonists. By the fourth century no distinction between the terms *apoikia* and "cleruchy" was being observed. For discussion of the socioeconomic class of the populations of Athens's cleruchies and settlements, see Figueira (1991, 60 and 201) and Mattingly (1996, 137 n. 83).

The Alexandrian Post-Postscriptum. See Walbank (1993, 43–45) and Cartledge (2004, 204–6). An example of a foundation that served as a garrison is Alexandria in Caucaso (central Hindu Kush), which Alexander populated with 3,000 Macedonians and Greek mercenaries. For a list of the sources, see Heckel and Yardley (2004, 303–10), who note their inadequacy in helping us to determine the exact nature of each settlement, viz whether it was a *polis*, a military settlement, and so on. Fraser (1996) proposes that the number of *poleis* should be reduced to about six "of whose historical existence . . . there can be no serious doubt" (p. 170). Given their geographical locations, however, even these six meant that Greek culture now spread to parts of the world that were previously entirely ignorant of it, including modern-day Baluchistan, Pakistan, Tajikistan, and Afghanistan. Fraser (p. 185) interestingly suggests that Alexander was partly motivated to establish foundations by the importance he attached to "reducing the damage done to agriculture and livestock by nomadic movements across fertile arable land."

Chapter 4. The Portable *Polis*

Uprooting the City. See Demand (1988, 416–23; 1990); Raaflaub (1991, 565–88); Horden and Purcell (2000, 383–91); and Purcell (2005, 253–59). The other relocations cited earlier are discussed in detail in this chapter. For a taxonomy of synoecism (viz partial, full, and so on), see Hansen and Nielsen (2004, 115–19 with index 21 [pp. 1365–66]). As Demand (1990, 8) notes, even when an entire city was uprooted it may well have been the case that a handful of people remained behind, either because they refused to leave or because they were required to continue tending the shrines.

Instances of Relocation in Early Greek History. For the identity of the Cimmerians, see Corcella (Asheri et al. 2007, 580–81). For the relocation of the Colophonians to Siris, see Demand (1990, 31–32) and Boardman (1999, 184). As Demand (1988, 417) points out, *metoikêsis* "played a role in the structure of [Herodotus's] work as a whole," the proposed relocation of the Persians being an example of ring-composition. Another likely instance of *metoikêsis* is Lefkandi on Euboea, which flourished in the Late Helladic IIIC period. The site was abandoned in ca. 700, perhaps as a result of war, and the population may have resettled at nearby Eretria, whose rise coincides with this event.

The Relocation of the Phocaeans. See Demand (1988, 416–18; 1990, 34–39); Morel (2006, 368–70); and Malkin (2012, 174). Herodotus (1.166.1) states that the Phocaeans "were living together with the original settlers" at Alalia. Hansen and Nielsen (2004, 163) interestingly suggest that, while the Phocaeans saw themselves as undertaking a *metoikêsis*, the Alalians may have regarded them as settlers. Domínguez (2006, 476) and other scholars believe that some of the refugees headed to existing Phocaean settlements in the West, including Massalia on the southeast coast of France and Emporion on the northeast coast of Spain. Antiochus of Syracuse (*FGrH* 555 F 8 = Str. *Geog.* 6.1.1 C252) claims that the refugees first tried to settle at Cyrnus and Massalia but were forced away and eventually founded Elea. The circuitous wanderings of the Phocaeans evoke those of Aeneas in *Aeneid* book 3. For the partial relocation of the Teians, see Malkin (1987, 54–56, 131); Demand (1990, 39–42); and Asheri et al. (2007, 189). Though Herodotus states that all the Teians emigrated, he later tells us (6.8) that they contributed seventeen ships to the combined Greek fleet that fought at the Battle of Lade in 494 over half a century later—an indication that theirs was only a partial relocation. We also hear of Teians founding Phanagoria on the Taman peninsula in southern Russia at approximately the same time as their relocation to Abdera (Arr. *Bithynika* fr. 55 Roos and Wirth). A number of prominent intellectuals decided to leave their homes in the face of Persian expansion. A notable example is Pythagoras of Samos, who fled to Croton on the toe of Italy.

Plans to Relocate "All the Ionians" in the West. A more limited attempt to relocate to the west occurred in 497, some two years after the outbreak of the Ionian Revolt, when Aristagoras, the deputy tyrant of Miletus, suggested to his partisans that they should either establish a colony in Sardinia or take refuge in the city of Myrcinus among the Edonians. He eventually chose Myrcinus but was killed while besieging another city (Hdt. 5.124–26; cf. 6.22). As Asheri et al. (2007, 191) note, such projects "involved the mirage of the Island of the Blest"—the favored island in question being either Sardinia or Sicily. For events consequent upon Zancle's offer to the Ionians, see Finley (1979, 49–50).

Themistocles' Threat to Relocate the Athenians. For Siris, allegedly founded by the Trojans, see Str. *Geog.* 6.1.14 C264. Though some scholars continue to believe that the proposal ascribed to Themistocles is a fiction, Dunbabin (1948, 374) long ago advanced arguments in its defense. As Demand (1990, 66f.) has pointed out, the relocation would have constituted a *sunoikismos*. Elsewhere she plausibly suggests that the Athenians' refusal to relocate in advance of the Persian invasion and Themistocles' threat to do so on the eve of the battle are "crucial elements leading up to the turning point of the war" (1988, 422).

The Synoecism of Olynthus. See Larsen (1968, 62–64); Demand (1990, 74–83); and Hornblower (1997, 102f.). Olynthus's population is thought to have eventually grown to about 30,000.

The Athenian Fleet as the *Dêmos* in Exile. See Forsdyke (2005, 189–91).

Dionysius I of Syracuse's Program of Mass Resettlement. See Stroheker (1958); Finley (1968, 74–87); McKechnie (1989, 35–39); Caven (1990, 49, 86–88); and Demand (1990, 98–106). For Leontini, see Berger

(1991, 138–39). For the factors that gave Greek civilization in Sicily a unique stamp and contributed to its instability, see Sjöqvist (1973, 61–62). Many of the names of the settlers at Entella that have been preserved in inscriptions are Oscan, which is what we should expect given the southern Italian ethnicity of the mercenaries, even though they are inscribed in Greek. As Demand notes (1990, 105), 13 of the relocations effected by Dionysius I are attested by Diodorus Siculus and one by the coinage. Verdicts on Dionysius are mixed. Stroheker (pp. 83–84) points out that, despite all his efforts, at the time of his death Carthage still dominated well over half the island. Caven (1990, 131), by contrast, while acknowledging that there was little to choose between enslavement by the Carthaginians and enslavement by Dionysius, claims that when he died hellenism in Sicily was "probably . . . in better shape than it had been for a decade." Another motive behind the desire to found a new settlement on the part of a tyrant was to receive heroic honors after his death (D.S. 11.49.2).

Timoleon's Revival of Syracuse. See Westlake (1952; 1969, 276–312; 1994, 707–22); Finley (1979, 94–101); Talbert (1974, 146–60); and McKechnie (1989, 39–42). The depopulation of Syracuse raises a number of interesting questions, not the least of which is its principal cause—internal strife, foreign war, disease, decline in the birthrate, or population transfer. Citing archaeological data for the revival of Greek Sicily under Timoleon, Talbert (1974, 146) claims that "the ancient authors' generous praise [of Timoleon] is perhaps not sufficiently lavish." As Westlake (1952, 55) insightfully puts it, "he refused to despair of the city-state." Finley's (1979, 101) is a lone, dissenting voice, seeing his contribution as short-lived, on the grounds that "the autonomous, self-governing Greek city was beyond redemption even in old Greece and there was surely no hope for it in Sicily, where it had never grown strong roots."

Mass Resettlement in the Peloponnese. See Demand (1990, 107–19). For Mantinea and Megalopolis, see Nielsen (in Hansen and Nielsen 2004, 517–22), with important discussion in both cases of the scale and nature of the synoecisms.

The Synoecism of Halicarnassus. See Hornblower (1982, 78–105; 1994, 223, 225–26) and Demand (1990, 120–27; 133–50). As Hornblower (1990, 105) notes, we are prevented from understanding the full-scale of Mausolus's accomplishment by the fact that the city was partially destroyed by Alexander the Great, even though Arrian's claim (*Anab*. 1.23.6) that he razed it to the ground is certainly an exaggeration. Demand (1990, 123) states, "The relocation and synoecism were the necessary first steps to the establishment of Caria as a significant player (i.e., naval power) in the Aegean power game." It is possible that Mausolus planned a number of other changes in settlement patterns in Caria, though the evidence remains inconclusive.

Chapter 5. The Deportee

Political *Stasis* as a Cause of Deportation. The literal meaning of *stasis* is "that which stands, a position in relation to something, a state of affairs." Van Effenterre (cited in Loraux 2002, 93, without reference) commented: "To designate 'sedition,' revolution in the city, Greeks use the word *stasis*, which they borrowed from the root most evocative of ideas of firmness, permanence, and stability. As if *stasis* were an institution for them!" In effect it was, and an essential one at that. *Stasis* in the sense "civil strife" already appears in the poems of Solon, Alcaeus, and Theognis, viz ca. 600. Hansen and Nielsen (2004, index 19 [pp. 1361–62]) list 266 certain instances of *stasis* involving some 120 *poleis*, though not all of these resulted in deportation. Their count updates Gehrke's (1985) pioneering work on the subject. Fifty-four *poleis* experienced more than one outbreak of *stasis*. Heading the list is Syracuse, with twenty-seven instances from ca. 650 to 279/69. For the vicissitudes of this city and other *poleis* in Sicily and south Italy (excluded by Gehrke), see Berger (1992, 34–53). For a linguistic analysis of the application of the term *stasis* in political discourse, see Loraux (2002, 104–8). Forsdyke (2005, 15–29) argues that *stasis* was a key factor in the emergence and development of the archaic *polis*. The Peloponnesian War made the situation between opposing factions immeasurably worse. As Hanson (2005, 104) notes, what in other circumstances would have been "heated, but mostly restrained, civil disputes" now turned into "unchecked bloodletting." From 431 to 406 at least fourteen instances of collusion with the enemy and the subsequent betrayal of their city by both sides occurred (Losada 1972, 16–29; Hanson 2005, 103). A modern instance of mass deportation by a foreign power occurred in 1941 when the Japanese deported approximately 100,000 Hong Kongers to work in munitions factories and the like (Bain and Yu in Adler and Gielen 2003, 57).

Surviving as a Deportee. The moment of departure is vividly captured by Livy, who tells us that, when the Romans decided to transfer the population of Alba to Rome, "The hearts of all the people were seized by a doleful silence as they helplessly debated what to take with them and what to leave behind, asking each other's advice, at times standing on their doorsteps, at times wandering through the rooms of their houses which they would never see again" (1.29.3). On the destruction of cities as a literary theme, see Ogilvie (1965, 120–21), who suggests that Livy's description may derive from Ennius, as did Vergil's description of the fall of Troy in *Aeneid* book 2. For evidence that women were deported, see Tod 202.49–56 = Heisserer 1980, 206–8 = Harding 122 = Rhodes and Osborne 101. For decrees passed by the Samian *dêmos* honoring individuals who had assisted deportees during their time of exile, see *SEG* I 350–60, with Heisserer (1980, 187) and Shipley (1987, 162). Presumably the reason why Herodotus is uncritical of the Colophonians is because he greatly admired their shrewdness (Asheri et al. 2007, 179). He tells a similar story of how the Samians acquired Zancle (6.23–24). For Aeneas Tacticus, see Whitehead (1990), who provides a useful commentary on the passage cited. Paranoia about the presence of foreigners in one's country in wartime has its echo in recent history. Following the attack on Pearl Harbor in 1942, President Franklin D. Roosevelt signed into law Executive Order no. 9066, which authorized the internment—in harsh conditions, as it turned out—of Japanese Americans and those of Japanese descent on grounds of "national security."

Deportations by the Sicilian Tyrants Gelon, Hieron, and Theron. See Dunbabin (1948, 415–18); Finley (1979, 51–52); and Demand (1990, 46–50). For brief histories of the Greek cities of Sicily, see Guido (1967).

As Dunbabin notes, it is possible that an inscription found at Olympia refers to the deportees from Megara Hyblaea being received at Selinus. The town of Euboea is not heard of again. For the resettlement of Aetna and Himera, see Asheri (1992, 150–51). The table of population redistribution in Sicily provided by Lomas (2006, 98–99) puts Gelon's initiative in a larger context. The mass resettlement program of the Sicilian tyrants anticipated Julius Caesar's plan to resettle 80,000 Roman poor in *coloniae* throughout the Mediterranean.

Deportations during the Peloponnesian War. For the Athenian settlement on Aegina, see Figueira (1991, 30–39). Thucydides does not specifically mention the political affiliation of the Megarian deportees but they were almost certainly oligarchs in light of the fact that they enjoyed the support of Sparta (Legon 1981, 236). The 110 women who remained in Plataea after all other noncombatants had been evacuated may well have been slaves already, since their purpose was to make bread (Thuc. 2.78.3). Nearly a decade after settling in Athens, those Megarians who were still of military age fought alongside the Athenians in the Sicilian Expedition. As Thucydides notes, there was an odd irony in the fact that Syracuse, which the Athenians were seeking to destroy, was allied to Selinus—a city that had been founded in part by settlers from Megara (7.57.8). For the date of the treaty between Athens and Leontini, see Berger (1991, 135–36).

Deportation by the Thirty Tyrants. Krentz (1982, 69) provides a list of all the testimonia relating to the flight of deportees from Athens under the Thirty Tyrants. For the presence of deportees in the Piraeus, see Garland (2001, 32–37). Whitehead (1982–83) equates the Thirty's action with Sparta's policy of *xenêlasiai*, being intended "to purge Attike of its dangerously cosmopolitan immigrant population." For the conflicting testimonies in our sources, see Wolpert (2002, 15–28). For the *dioikismos* of Athens and Eleusis, see Rhodes (1993, 462–72) and Wolpert (2002, 30–32).

Laws Ordering the Expulsion of Foreigners. The Megarian exclusion decree was prompted by a dispute both about sacred property near

Eleusis, on the borders between Attica and Megara, and about the harboring of runaway slaves (Thuc. 1.139.2). The first known instance of *xenêlasiai* was the expulsion of Maeandrius of Samos from Sparta (Hdt. 3.148). However, this was not a general prohibition but an action that targeted a specific individual. See Forsdyke (2005, 297–98) for discussion of the reliability of the tradition of Spartan *xenêlasiai*. A rare Athenian case involves Arthmius of Zelea, who was expelled from Athens and all the territory under Athenian control for scheming to make war between Athens and Persia (Aeschin. 3.258; Din. 2.24).

The Massacre and Enslavement of Prisoners of War. See Ducrey (1968, 131–40) and Hanson (2005, 182–84). Hansen and Nielsen (2004, 122 with index 20 [pp. 1363–64]) identify 46 *poleis* that underwent *andrapodismos*, though "only five or perhaps six disappeared for good." In some cases those who had been enslaved later returned to resettle the *polis*. Thucydides' use of the verb *edoulôthê* (was enslaved) to describe the fate of the Naxians after the failure of their revolt in ca. 471 is doubtless metaphorical (cf. Gomme 1945, I, 282). Female prisoners of war feature in Greek tragedy (cf. the choruses in Aes. *Ch.* and Eur. *Phoen.*) and are clearly intended to evoke pity in the audience. Male prisoners of war never appear. References to the outrageous treatment of enslaved women among the orators is self-serving (cf. Dem. 19.196–98, 305–6, 309; Din. 1.24). Panagopoulos (1978, 219) argues that the treatment of prisoners of war by both sides progressively deteriorated during the course of the Peloponnesian War. For Philip II's treatment of prisoners, see Rosivach (1999, 134–36). For hostages, a group incidentally that lacked any legal definition in Greek law, see Amit (1970, 129–47) and Panagopoulos (1978, 187–217).

Chapter 6. The Evacuee

The Evacuation of Attica before the Battle of Salamis. See Strauss (2004, 59–62 and 65–70). For Athens's connection with Troezen, see Barrett (1964, 2–3). The legendary Athenian king Theseus was born in Troezen and was the son of Aethra, daughter of Pittheus, king of

Troezen. On the authenticity of Themistocles' Decree, *ML* (pp. 51–52) writes, "Relatively few of the points of detail which have been raised against the decree have turned out to be decisive." Diodorus Siculus (11.13.4) says only this of the evacuation: "The Athenians, comprehending that every single inhabitant of Athens was now at risk, embarked their wives and children and every useful object they could and conveyed them to Salamis."

The Evacuation of Attica at the Outbreak of the Peloponnesian War. Hansen (2005, 337 n. 36) notes that there are references to the devastation of Attica in a majority of Aristophanes's extant contemporary plays. He estimates (p. 57) that in the decade from 431 to 421 the Peloponnesians remained in Attica only 150 days in total. Even so, I agree with Hornblower's (2011, 190) description of the evacuation as "a change in immemorial living habits" for the inhabitants of rural demes. See also Demand (1990, 95–97). The only other reference to the evacuees occurs in Ar. *Knights* (produced in 424), where the Sausage Seller, with typical comic exaggeration, upbraids Paphlagon (in "real life" the demagogue Cleon) for demonstrating no pity for those who had been living in "barrels, shacks, and garrets for eight years." Instead, Paphlagon continues, "You lock them up and steal their property" (ll. 792–94). This suggests that the evacuees were treated as second-class citizens. For the debate about migration from the Attic countryside to the urban areas in the classical era, see Moore (1975, 238); Whitehead (1986a, 352–57); and Damsgaard-Madsen (1988, 55–68). Irrespective of the scale of internal migration at this time, the evidence does not permit us to conclude that the bulk of it occurred in response to the Peloponnesian War. The Athenians were again forced to evacuate Attica when the Spartans occupied Decelea in 413, though it is doubtful whether this was on such a large scale as the evacuation that took place in 431 and the years immediately following. For "those living within the Long Walls," see the fragment from Eupolis's *Dêmoi* in Page, no. 40, ll. 12–13, where it is suggested that evacuees have more to eat than those who remained in the countryside, which Page takes to refer to the so-called Decelean War. For the evacuation of Boeotia, see Demand

(1990, 83–85). For the formal relationship between Athens and Plataea, see Figueira (1991, 149–54).

Evacuations during the Punic Wars in Sicily. See Caven (1990, 47–49, 72–74). The historical accuracy of Diodorus Siculus is somewhat questionable. It is entirely conceivable that he is describing what he supposes "must have happened" when a city evacuated overnight.

Chapter 7. The Asylum-Seeker

Asylum as a Sacred Obligation. For supplication in the Hebrew Bible, see briefly Naiden (2006, 89). Many of the most important studies of Greek asylum are by Sinn, of which the latest is *ThesCRA* III, pp. 217–32 (pp. 218–19 for bibliography). Ogilvie (1965, 62–63) sees evidence of Greek influence in Livy's claim that a place of asylum existed on the Capitoline Hill in Romulus's day.

Qualifying for Asylum. Chaniotis (1996, 67–69) provides plentiful evidence to indicate that those guilty of lesser crimes could claim *asulia*. For *kakourgoi* (felons), see Phillips (2008, 124–25). Incidentally, in the second play of Aeschylus's trilogy of which *Suppliants* is the first, the Danaids, forced to marry their cousins, commit murder, which raises questions retrospectively about their entitlement to asylum (Dreher 2003, 65–67). Because it did not in principle differentiate between innocent and guilty, *asulia* presented a severe conflict between *themis* (divine law) and *nomos* (secular law).

Supplication. *Hiketês* (suppliant) means literally "one who comes." The noun is cognate with *hêkô*, *hikneomai*. See Gould (1973, 74–103); Pedrick (1982, 125–40); Freyburger (1988, 501–15), and Canciani et al. ("Hikesia" in *ThesCRA* III, pp. 193–216). As to why suppliants grasped the chin, knees, and beard, see Freyburger (1988, 508–10). For *asulia* and *hikesia* in Aes. *Supp.*, see Dreher (2003, 59–84). Five of the 32 surviving Greek tragedies fall into the category of suppliant plays, viz those in which the homeless take refuge in a sanctuary where they make formal application for inclusion within the community. The plays in question are Aes. *Supp.* and *Eum.*; Soph. *OC*; and Eur. *Heracl.* and *Supp.* As Dreher (2003, 61) points out, they take the form of a "triangular relationship model," consisting of suppliants, enemy, and savior. For Admetus's reception of Themistocles and embellishments of the tale in other authors, see Hammond (1967, 492–93). The motif of clutching an infant as a form of extreme supplication also occurred in Euripides's lost tragedy *Telephus* (*ThesCRA* III, p. 197 with no. 29). In Athens it was customary at some meetings of the Assembly for "anyone who wishes" to place a suppliant branch on the altar in order to claim the right to speak on any matter, whether private or public ([Arist.] *Ath. Pol.* 43.6). Supplication could also be made to the Council (Aeschin. 1.104). It seems unlikely, however, that this right would have extended to foreigners.

The Politics of Offering Asylum. For the involvement of the Athenian Assembly in awarding asylum, see Naiden (2006, 173–83). Another interesting instance involves the 500 wealthy exiles from Sybaris who sought refuge in Croton. When the Sybarites responsible for their exile turned up and demanded that the Crotonians hand them over or face war, the latter, though wavering, eventually declined to do so, interestingly on the advice of the philosopher Pythagoras. In the ensuing war they were victorious and went on to destroy Sybaris utterly (D.S. 12.9.2–10.1).

Granting Asylum within a Sanctuary. Excavations conducted in the sanctuary of Hera at Perachora have brought to light cisterns and wells that could accommodate large numbers of people and cattle. For the possibility that a specific area within a sanctuary was designated for the use of asylum-seekers, see Maffi (2003, 15–22). For sanctuaries of Poseidon as places of refuge, see Schumacher (1993, 62–87). For the sanctuary of Poseidon at Calauria, see Sinn (2003, 107–25). For that at Taenarum, see Naiden (2006, 207–10).

Mistreating Asylum-Seekers. For Cylon, see Rhodes (1993, 79–84). Though many scholars are skeptical of the effectiveness of asylum, Sinn

(1993, 93) floats the possibility that "every violation against this indispensable institution was recorded with misgivings and at the same time branded with sharp disapproval, whereas all mention of the cases with positive outcomes were [*sic*] omitted because they were normal." See Naiden (2006, table 3.1 [pp. 163–65]) for instances of rejected supplication in Greek sources.

Athens's Exceptionalism. In four of the five surviving suppliant plays (Aes. *Eum.*; Soph. *OC*; Eur. *Heracl.* and *Supp.*), the suppliants petition for residence in Athens, a further indication of the city's professed compassion for asylum-seekers. Though the plot of Aes. *Supp.* seems *prima facie* to advocate giving refuge to asylum-seekers, the next (missing) play in the trilogy dealt with the outbreak of a war between Argos and Egypt due to Argos's reception of the suppliants. In it Pelasgus was almost certainly killed in battle. What the trilogy may have explored, therefore, were the unforeseen and disastrous consequences of a good faith decision. Rather than advocating kindness to strangers, it might reasonably be interpreted as a warning *against* giving asylum to suppliants, even when their case is justified on humanitarian grounds. For the topos of Athens's hospitality to foreigners, see the bibliography cited in Montiglio (2005, 31 n. 26). Isocrates (12.94) cites Athens's generous treatment of both the Messenians and the Plataeans as examples of her support for those in need.

Xenia and Proxenia. For both *xenia* and *proxenia*, see Herman (1987). For *xenia*-based relationships in the *Odyssey*, see Finley (2002, 100–104). Other examples of *xenia* between a Greek and a non-Greek include Polycrates, tyrant of Samos, and the pharaoh Amasis (Hdt. 3.39–43); and Pharnabazus, the Persian satrap, and Agesilaus, the king of Sparta (Xen. *Hell.* 4.1.34–35). The institution of *xenia* remained in force into the hellenistic period and beyond. For *proxenia*, see Walbank (1978, 1–9); Baslez (1984, 111–25); and Davies (1993, 69–71). As Davies notes, the honors that were paid to *proxenoi* by the state whose citizens they represented indicate they sometimes put their lives at risk, for which reason they were given legal protection (cf. *IG* I³ 19, ca. 450). *Proxenia* is first attested in the late seventh century BCE in a decree of the people of Corcyra (*ML* 4) and continued into the first century CE. In the fifth century it became an instrument of Athenian imperialism that enabled Athens to be kept apprised of seditious activity among her allies (*IG* I³ 18, 19, 27, 28, 91, 92). For its evolution into a communal institution based on the model of *xenia*, see Herman (1987, 132–42).

Chapter 8. The Fugitive

Fugitives in Archaic Literature. Herodotus (6.95) indicates that the Aleian Plain was located in Cilicia. Tlepolemus's division of his men into three tribes is thought to be a reference to the three major city-states that existed on the island in Homer's day—namely, Lindus, Ialysus, and Camirus. Schlunk (1976, 201) sees the murderer who flees from his homeland to escape the exaction of blood vengeance by the relatives of his murdered victim and who is received in a rich man's house as an important "minor motif" in the *Iliad*. Priam's supplication is, moreover, a memorable instance of ring composition. As Schlunk further notes, the poem begins with a suppliant Trojan father appealing on behalf of his daughter to Agamemnon, who rejects his appeal, and ends with a suppliant Trojan father appealing on behalf of his son to Achilles, who answers his entreaty. Fugitives in myth include Alcmaeon, Cadmus, and Orestes. In each case their wandering ends because of intervention from Apollo (Montiglio 2005, 31). The classic instance of upward mobility on the part of a fugitive and his family in early Roman history involves Demaratus of Corinth, who fled to Tarquinii because of political upheavals and whose son Lucumo became the fifth king of Rome (Li. 1.34.2). No less upwardly mobile was Jephthah, who was driven from his father's house by his half-brothers because he was the son of a prostitute, and who later became commander and judge of all Israel (Judges 11–12).

Exile as Punishment for Crime. For Athenian homicide law, see Mac-Dowell (1978, 73–75, 114) and Phillips (2008). For the court in Phreatto, see MacDowell (1963, 82–84). For Socrates, see Forsdyke (2005, 273).

For exile as a punishment imposed on members of the Delian League, see *IG* I³ 14.29–32 = Fornara 71 (Erythrae, mid-460s or late 450s) and *IG* I³ 40.6–7 = Fornara 103 (Chalcis, mid-440s or mid-420s). Pl. *Laws* 9.865de claims that the reason why a homicide is exiled is to avoid giving offense to the dead man "by seeing his killer frequenting the same places he had frequented." In fifth-century Syracuse several sentences of exile were passed by *petalismos* (see later). After Syracuse's defeat at the hands of the Athenians at the Battle of Cyzicus in 411 all the generals were exiled (Xen. *Hell.* 1.1.27). In Greek tragedy voluntary exile is occasionally the preferred fate of those who regard themselves guilty of crimes that put them outside the human fold. Examples are Oedipus, who requests that Creon send him into exile (Soph. *OT* 1381–82, and so on), and Medea, who announces that she will depart from Corinth for Athens and reside with King Aegeus (Eur. *Med.* 1384–85). Exile was imposed on Spartan kings who were found guilty of accepting bribes or performing inadequately on military campaign. See Forsdyke (2005, 295–97). Several Euripidean tragedies end with exile being pronounced upon an offender. Apollo orders Orestes to depart from Argos and go into exile in Parrhasia for one year because he has murdered his mother Clytemnestra (*Or.* 1643–45); the Dioscuri pass a similar sentence upon Orestes (*El.* 1250–51); and Hecuba becomes an enslaved exile (*Tro.* 1271).

Ostracism. *ML* 21 includes a list of 61 candidates, together with the total number of *ostraka* that are assigned to each, up to date of publication. See most recently Brenne (2002, 36–166). The total now stands at over 10,000 *ostraka*. The largest single cache, 191 in all in only fourteen hands, was intended for use against Themistocles. Literary sources include [Arist.] *Ath. Pol.* 22.3–8; D.S. 11.55.2; Plu. *Arist.* 7.4–6; and Poll. 8.20. For discussion, see Rhodes (1993, 267–71) and Forsdyke (2005, 144–204). Forsdyke (p. 283) argues that the annual posing of the question before the Assembly as to whether the *dêmos* wanted to hold an ostracism had the consequence in and of itself of quelling inter-élite conflict. There was a learned debate in antiquity as to whether ostracism was the equivalent to exile. The Scholiast on Aristophanes *Wasps* (l. 947) defined ostracism as the equivalent of a species within the genus exile.

The chief difference between the two, the Scholiast explained, lay in the fact that those who were ostracized kept their property, whereas those who were exiled forfeited theirs. A form of ostracism was practiced in Syracuse, where the process was called *petalismos*, literal meaning "leafing," so called because the names of those to be exiled were inscribed on leaves (D.S. 11.87.1–2). There is also evidence for the practice at Argos, Chersonesus, Cyrene, Miletus, and Megara (Forsdyke 2005, 285–88). For Megara, see also Hansen and Nielsen (2004, 464). It is unclear whether any of these cities was inspired by the Athenian model.

High-Profile Exiles. For other versions of Themistocles' flight and exile, see the sources cited in Frost (1980, 200–218). Diodorus Siculus (11.56–58) is particularly detailed. For a full account of Plutarch's narrative of Alcibiades' exile, see the relevant sections in Verdegem (2010). For Alcibiades as a traitor, see Bottineau (2010, 118–49). A decree that was passed by the *dêmos* of Amphipolis (dated 357/6) exiled in perpetuity, along with their children, two high-profile Amphipolitans who had favored an alliance with Athens in preference to one with Philip II of Macedon, and further declared that if they were apprehended they were to be killed (*SIG³* 194 = Tod 150 = Rhodes and Osborne 49; cf. D.S. 16.8.2).

Runaway Slaves. See Christensen (1984, 23–32); Kudlien (1988, 232–52); Chaniotis (1996, 79–83); Andreau and Descat (2011, 138–41); and McKeown (2011, 155–57). For the protection of the Acropolis against runaway slaves, see Wernicke (1891, 51–57). On the branding of slaves, see Ar. *Babylonians* fr. 88 in *CAF* I, p. 414 and—more dubiously— Eupolis fr. 318 in *CAF* I, p. 342, though neither of these explicitly refers to runaways. It is unclear whether the individual who bore the imprint of a stag was a runaway slave, though such a marking would, of course, have been appropriate and ironic (Lys. 13.19). As McKeown (2011, 160) notes, runaways do not feature in Greek comedy, though some slaves consider the possibility of flight. In addition, there was a comedy by Antiphanes called the *Drapetagôgos* (Ath. *Deipn.* 4.161d). For asylum for slaves, see *ThesCRA* III, 219 with nos. 70–78. Similar regulations to those of Messene are known from Samos and Ephesus (Chaniotis 1996, 80–81). Though it lies outside the time frame of this investigation, the story told by the third-century BCE ethnographer Nymphodorus of Syracuse of a bandit-slave named Drimacus, who led his fellow-runaways "as a king leads his army," terrorized the population of Chios, and exercised awesome power, is highly instructive (*ap*. Ath. *Deipn*. 6. 265d–266e). The slave-owners came to an agreement that Drimacus would receive into his ranks only runaway slaves who had been grossly mistreated and would return all others to their owners. See further Forsdyke (2012, 37–46, 74–85, and so on). For the Hebrew treatment of runaway slaves, see Deuteronomy 23:15–16: "You shall not give up to his master a slave who has escaped from his master to you; he shall dwell with you, in your midst, in the place which he shall choose within one of your towns, where it pleases him best; you shall not oppress him."

Chapter 9. The Economic Migrant

Reasons for Becoming an Economic Migrant. See Dummett (2001, 44f.) for the modern use of the term "economic migrant" as a propaganda device intended to blur the distinction between refugees and immigrants and to suggest that the motives of those claiming asylum are deceptive and trivial. Hornblower (1991, 13f.) believes that Thuc. 1.2.6 indicates an awareness that prehistoric Athens benefited from an influx of foreigners. For Hesiod's father's move to Ascra, see West (1978, 30). Scheffer (2011, 319) rightly states, "The dynamism of [the United States] is closely connected to its ability to integrate people of extremely diverse backgrounds." It would, however, be presumptuous to suppose that the ancient world duplicated the modern in this regard. Overall, we lack the means even to begin to assess the effects of immigration on Athenian culture and can only surmise from a distance, so to speak, its impact on the Athenian economy. For a useful survey, see Cohen (2000, 17–22). De Ste. Croix (1983, 95) assumed a priori that metics were "living by choice in their city of residence." The Spartans were unusual in the fact that they were "not permitted to reside abroad, for fear they would acquire foreign customs and undisciplined lifestyles" (Plu. *Mor.* 238e; cf. Xen. *Lac.* 14.4). For Athenians living as metics in Megara, see Hansen and Nielsen (2004, 464 [entry by Legon]).

The Legal Status of the Athenian Metic. The verb *metoikein* is not commonly used of "being a metic" in the technical—that is, Athenian—sense of the word until the fourth century. Other words that describe a permanent immigrant include *epoikos, katoikos, paroikos,* and *sunoikos.* For discussion of the date of the introduction of official metic status in Athens, see Whitehead (1986b, 148). For the requirement to register as a metic, see Whitehead (1975, 94 with n. 3; 1986b, 146) and Cohen (2000, 72 with n. 154). For the prosecution of metics failing to register with a guardian or seeking to evade their responsibilities, see Lape (2010, 188–90). For metics granted *isoteleia* and other honors, see *IG* II/III² 7862–81. In contrast to the relative frequency of honorifics awarded to metics, few foreigners were awarded citizenship. For discussion, see Baslez (1984, 93–109) and Demetriou (2012, 205–217). Cohen (2000, 72–73) asserts that "many individuals (or their offspring) ultimately became fully involved in Athenian life, and physically and culturally indistinguishable from the mass of *politai* [citizens]." The law forbidding metics to leave Athens during wartime was probably put into effect some time before the battle of Chaeronea in 338. For foreign deities worshipped in the Piraeus, see Garland (2001, table 3 [p. 109]) with the important revision by Demetriou (2012, 217–27). For leases of sacred properties, see Walbank (1983, part 4, table 1).

The Composition and Size of Athens's Metic Population. Krentz (1980, 305) notes that 19 of the 69 metics whose profession is recorded in *IG* II² 10 were involved in agriculture, 31 in small manufacturing, and 19 in commerce. These figures reflect the fact that the rebellion they joined began in a remote district of Attica. See Garland (2001) for the metic tomb in Kallithea (p. 62 with figure 11) and for the ethnic diversity of Athenian metics (pp. 62–67). For non-Greek metics, see Whitehead (1977, 109–14), who concludes, "The ethnic origin of a *metoikos* was ultimately less important, *de facto* as well as *de iure,* than the fact that he was, precisely, a *metoikos* and not a *politês*, i.e., citizen." No doubt, too, there were many short-term visitors, known as *parepidêmoi* or *parepidêmountes*, who had to register as metics. Finally, a few metics were former slaves who had been manumitted, though these constituted "a distinct subgroup within the metic category, at least socially and economically" (Lape 2010, 47). They include Pasion and Phormion, both of whom were later granted citizenship.

Prejudice against Immigrants. David Whitehead suggests to me that [Xenophon]'s main gripe at *Ath. Pol.* 1.10 is with foreigners in general, rather than with metics per se. For the ideal metic and his opposite, see Baslez (1984, 130–32). Plu. *Sol.* 24.2 states that Solon trusted only "those who had by necessity been thrown out of their homes and those who had left their homes for some purpose." Judging from the titles of their plays, it is probable that the comic dramatists occasionally ridiculed metics, especially those who were non-Greek. There are uncomplimentary references to the Thraco-Phrygian god Sabazius in four Aristophanic comedies, including one in which he and other foreign deities are expelled from Athens (Cic. *Leg.* 2.37). To escape the Thirty Tyrants, Lysias fled to Megara (12.7). When the democracy was restored, he returned to Athens and prosecuted Eratosthenes, one of the Thirty, for causing his brother's death. See Phillips (2008, 153–84) for full discussion of the speech. The verdict in the trial is unknown. Krentz (1982, 129) writes movingly of the metic contribution to the overthrow of the Thirty Tyrants: "Men who did not have the vote fought to preserve Athenian democracy, not because they expected to become voting citizens, but because the radical restructuring of society intended by the oligarchs would have meant either their complete exclusion from Attica or their reduction to a subservient role." For the decree dated ca. 401/400 granting citizen rights to metics who had fought against the Thirty, see *IG* II² 10 = Harding 3; [Arist.] *Ath. Pol.* 40.2; Lys. 31.29. Krentz (1980, 303–4) tentatively suggests that they may have received *isoteleia*. Thrasybulus had originally proposed awarding them citizenship, but this had been blocked. Metic status evidently endured after death. In Eur. *Heracl.*, when Eurystheus, king of Argos and Mycenae, requests burial in Athens, he promises "to lie beneath the earth as a *metoikos* for all time and be hostile to the descendants of these people [viz the Spartans]" (ll. 1032–33). Demetriou's claim (2012, 199–200) that, "The arrival of these non-Athenians contributed to making Peiraieus a multicultural society that may have challenged the Athenian concept of citizenship" is somewhat exaggerated.

Emigrant Workers. See MacDonald (1981, 159–68) and Hornblower (2011, 208–9).

Chapter 10. The Itinerant

Itinerants in Archaic Greece. For the Homeric *dêmiourgos*, see Baslez (1984, 50–53) and Finley (2002, 51–52). It is likely that Herodotus has retrojected the phenomenon of the public physician into the sixth century, since all other examples belong to the fifth century. See Cohn-Haft (1956, 21f., 26, 46f., 53) for physicians specifically.

Itinerants in Classical Greece. See McKechnie (1989, 142–77). Seers have been the subject of a number of important recent studies, including those of Johnston and Struck (2005); Flower (2008); and Johnston (2008). For wandering female seers, see Flower (2008, 211–39). *Agurtês*, like *chrêsmologos* and *magos*, was a term of abuse when applied to a seer. For sophists as celebrity itinerants, see Garland (2006, 79–81). For the variety of cities to which the craftsmen working at Epidaurus belonged, see Burford (1969, 199–201).

Long-Distance Traders. For the beginnings of long-distance trading in the Greek world, see Tandy (1997, 59–83). For evidence of trading contacts with Cyprus from around 1000 BCE onward at Lefkandi, see Popham (1994, 12f.). Winter (1995, 258) is of the opinion that the Phoenicians in the Homeric poems "must be seen as neither historical nor ethnographic entities, but rather as well-crafted literary tropes" (cited in Hall 2002, 117).

Pirates and Brigands. See McKechnie (1989, 101–41); van Wees (1992, 207–17); De Souza (1999, 17–42), and Horden and Purcell (2000, 387–88). For the Phoenicians in the *Odyssey*, see Winter's important article (1995, 247–71), in which she argues that their portrayal is in part the product of "suspicion regarding the consequences of dispersal and mobility" (p. 264). She concludes, "'Homer's Phoenicians' do not represent the world of the Phoenicians; rather, they present a masterful literary construct." For Odysseus's Cretan guise as the son of Castor, see De Souza (1999, 18–21).

Mercenaries. Both Polyb. 11.13.6–8 and Xen. *Hier.* 10 stress the dependency of tyrants on mercenaries. For hoplite mercenaries having to provide their own armor, see Whitehead (1991, 105–13). For the rise of mercenaries in the fourth century and the profound implications that this development had both for the life of the *polis* and for the structure of Greek society, see Marinovic (1988), who notes that this was fostered by "the semi-permanence of warfare, the recrudescence of social conflicts … and the impoverishment of the masses" (p. 3). See also Baslez (1984, 171–75). When Cyrus reviewed the Ten Thousand, they were all wearing crimson tunics (Xen. *Anab.* 1.2.16). For the ethnic composition of the Ten Thousand, see Roy (1967, 302–309) and Marinovic (1988, 32–34). For a vivid description of the rigors attendant upon life as a mercenary, see Lee (2007, 232–54). For the conditions of service, see Roy (1967, 312–16) and McKechnie (1989, 89–93). Hornblower (2011, 200) aptly describes mercenary service as "a kind of alternative to colonization, both being a form of emigration to escape poverty." He suggests, perhaps somewhat fancifully, that it would have done much to erode racial prejudice among Greeks. For the fate of the mercenaries who served under Darius III following his defeat by Alexander, see Badian (1961, 25–28). For Alexander's mercenary settlements, see Bosworth (1994, 866–88). A major recruitment center for mercenaries from the 330s onward was the sanctuary of Poseidon of Taenarum, located at the tip of the Mani peninsula in the Peloponnese (D.S. 17.111.1; cf. RE, *s.v.* "Tainaron," col. 2040f.; Badian 1961, 27–28; Schumacher 1993, 72–74).

Persons of No Fixed Abode. For beggars, see Finley (2000, 52–53). For the poor, see Hands (1968, 62–72).

Chapter 11. Repatriation

L'Esprit de Retour. "Nostalgia" first entered the English language in 1770 to describe what was identified as a disease among a ship's company longing for home (*OED*). Regarding the problem presented by returnees today, Long and Oxfeld (2004, 13) write: "While return is a way to reconcile and heal past conflict, it also gives rise to new tensions and boundaries, sometimes fueling ethnic hatreds"—a fitting comment on Hom. *Od.* 24. For the Paionians, see Demand (1988, 418–19). Xen. *Anab.* is also infused with *l'esprit de retour*. For the repatriation of the Athenian *dêmos* in exile, see Garland (2001, 32–37) and Wolpert (2002, 100–118). In 406 the Syracusan Assembly passed a decree recalling all exiles (D.S. 13.92.4–7).

The "Return" of the Messenians. The invention of tradition to bolster claims of ethnic identity has been extensively researched by historians. A classic work is that edited by Hobsbawm and Ranger (1983). The most thorough investigation of the reality behind the claim of the Messenians to be the heirs of a venerable mythic and historical heritage is by Luraghi (2008, pp. 210–30 for the regional implications of the foundation of Messene; and pp. 245–58 for its ethnic composition). See also Shipley's important entry in Hansen and Nielsen (2004, 561–64).

Mass Enforced Repatriation. See Loraux (2002, 242–44) for further discussion of the return of the exiles from Phlius.

The Exiles' Decree of Alexander the Great. See Badian (1961, 28–31) and Poddighe (2011, 117–19). The claims put forward by Balogh (1943) that Alexander's decree shows him as "the protector of the unfortunate" (p. 68) and that "a serious social evil came to an end, or was at least considerably lessened" (p. 69) are implausible. For extensive discussion of the Tegean Decree, see Heisserer (1980, 205–29) and Lonis (1991, 99–103). Heisserer (p. 221) points out that it implicitly sanctioned the return (among others) of those who had joined the revolt against Macedon orchestrated by Agis III of Sparta in 331 and whose leaders had been exiled in 330, following the suppression of the revolt by Antipater (Curt. 6.1.20). Courts consisting of foreign judges became increasingly common in the hellenistic period, evidence of their effectiveness as a way to settle disputes (Lonis, 1991, 108; Rhodes and Osborne, pp. 530–31). The inscription from Tegea is the only surviving document directly connected with the Exiles' Decree. Other *poleis*, however, may well have made similar pronouncements in an attempt to implement the terms of Alexander's mandate according to local conditions. The only comparable piece of legislation is a decree from Mytilene that was passed in 334 or perhaps a few years later when a change of government in favor of democracy occurred (Tod 201 = Heisserer 1980, 123–31 = Harding 113 = Rhodes and Osborne 85).

The Return of the Samians. See Badian (1976, 289–94); Shipley (1987, 155–68); Habicht (1997, 30–35); and Poddighe (2011, 119–20). Iasus was merely one of several Greek communities that provided the Samian exiles with a refuge during their long years of banishment, as we know from the fact that many other individuals were honored by them (Shipley 1987, 161–63). Evidently their expulsion had caused deep offense throughout the Greek world. In fact even in Athens it had been controversial (Arist. *Rhet.* 2.1384b 29–36). Many Samians had taken refuge at Anaea, the mainland territory opposite the island, which was part of the Samian state. See Badian (1976, 289–94).

APPENDIX A

THE TERMINOLOGY OF DIASPORA

The contemporary debate about migration is bedeviled by semantic imprecision. There are no clear distinctions, for instance, between the terms "asylum-seekers," "illegal" (or "irregular") immigrants, and "refugees." The attempt to establish a classificatory system based on motivation is also flawed, not least because many factors are regularly in play. It is often impossible to differentiate between voluntary and forced migration, or between migration that has a predominantly political motive and that which is fueled primarily by economic considerations. It is also unclear to what extent a collective need is the motivating factor and to what extent individual aspiration or ambition is to the fore.

The difficulties that beset the study of migration in antiquity are even greater, not least because Greek historians habitually fail to indicate whether individuals or groups who leave their homeland have been exiled or have fled voluntarily. This problem is compounded by the fact that the terminology for displacement and migration shows considerable overlap.* There is no linguistic distinction between relocation and deportation, since Greek uses the portmanteau word *metoikêsis* to cover both conditions. Given the brevity of many of the accounts of mass movements in our sources, it is often impossible to determine whether such a movement was voluntary or forced.

The word "refugee," too, is problematic. The 1951 Geneva Convention relating to the Status of Refugees defines a refugee as someone who has a "well-founded fear of being persecuted" in his or her country

* For a useful discussion of the problems presented by the terminology of displacement, see Demand (1990, 6–11).

of origin "for reasons of race, religion, nationality, membership of a particular social group or political opinion" (Article 1.A.2). As has been frequently observed, the Convention does not recognize as refugees those who are escaping from either civil war or famine. Many countries, therefore, have adopted a broader definition—one that includes those who flee from their homeland to escape any kind of violence or disturbance.

It is, of course, impossible to define the refugee in antiquity in accordance with the (fairly) strict definition laid down by the Geneva Convention, since Greek does not possess any word that exactly conforms to the modern meaning of the word. *Phugas* probably comes closest, though this is also used both of a criminal who is escaping from justice and of a slave who is escaping from servitude. Even more problematically, it is used to describe both someone who has been banished in accordance with a judicial or political ruling and someone who has gone into voluntary exile.* Likewise the abstract noun *phugê* means both "exile" (that is, enforced) and "flight" (that is, voluntary). To further complicate matters, we do not always know whether a person described as a *phugas* has been officially exiled or whether he has taken to his heels in advance of sentencing because he fears for his life. Many individuals who underwent *atimia*, which means "loss of civic rights," were probably forced into exile, but there are likely to have been exceptions, particularly in the case of those too old or too sick to travel.† It seems that the Greeks cared little as to whether a person fled or was exiled, or perhaps they surmised that their condition was in most respects identical. Further overlap exists between "evacuation," meaning

---

* The same semantic imprecision pertains to the Latin word *fuga*, which conveys both voluntary and enforced departure.

† MacDowell (1978, 28) renders *atimia*, "outlawry." Rhodes (1993, 158 and 430–31) argues that in the classical period *atimia* became "tamed"—that is, involving "the loss of political and judicial rights but not outlawry." As Todd (1993, 142) points out, however, though an Athenian who was *atimos* could in theory continue to reside in Athens, the loss of his rights might have made his situation so intolerable that he would have chosen "voluntarily" to go into exile. Plu. *Sol.* 19.3 suggests that the *atimoi* whose rights were restored to them by Solon had been exiled as a result of crimes other than homicide. For further discussion see Hansen (1976, 75–82); Grasmück (1978, 16–20); and Forsdyke (2005, 10–11).

the voluntary withdrawal from a country or territory, and "deportation," involuntary removal.*

The Greek language has a number of words that correspond to our word "migrant." *Alêtês*, literally "wanderer," is used to describe a "beggar" by Homer and an "exile" by the tragedians. *Apoikos*, literally "one who is removed from or deprived of an *oikos* or *oikia*," often means "emigrant," whereas *epoikos* means "immigrant." In practice, however, the terms are often interchangeable. In official Athenian terminology *epoikos* also means "a settler dispatched subsequently or sent as a reinforcement" (cf. Figueira 1997, 14–24). *Apoikia*, which is the collective noun for a group of emigrants, is usually translated "settlement" or, less appropriately, "colony," though it can also describe any group of people living abroad. Later sources do not always distinguish between *apoikos*, "settler," and *klêrouchos*, literally "proprietor of a land allotment or *klêros* that is not in one's native land." The term *emporion*, which first occurs in Herodotus with reference to the Greek foundations along the north coast of the Black Sea, is also confusing. Though often translated as a "trading station" or "port of trade," it is not always clear whether an *emporion* is distinguishable from an *apoikia*.†

Another word for a migrant is *metanastês*, which often carries a pejorative meaning (for example, Hom. *Il.* 9.648). The abstract noun *metanastasis*, which occurs first in Thucydides, covers all types of displacement and migration. Isocrates, who wrote scathingly about the dangers posed by migration in the mid-fourth century, favored the portmanteau term *planômenos*, and its synonyms *planês* and *planêtês*, "traveler, wanderer" (for example, 5.96 and 120; 9.9). *Apolis* and *apopolis* describe "one who has no attachment to a *polis*," either because that person has chosen to live outside the *polis* or because he has been either outlawed or banished. *Hiketês*, which is usually translated as "suppliant," identifies a person who has ceased (at least temporarily) to be a refugee and is

---

* Learned Greeks were sometimes troubled by the ambiguities and imprecision of their language. Their debate as to whether "ostracism"—the process by which the Athenians expelled one of their number for ten years without confiscating his property—should or should not be classified as exile is an interesting case in point (earlier, chapter 8).

† For further discussion of the distinction between *apoikia* and *emporion*, see chapter 3.

hoping to be granted the status of a legal immigrant, though the noun can also apply to someone who has committed homicide and is seeking purification on account of his crime.

There are other problems of a conceptual nature. Ancient historians from George Grote (1794–1871) onward have referred to the establishment of settlements outside the Greek mainland from the eighth to the sixth century BCE as a "colonization movement," which suggests that this phenomenon anticipated the now discredited feature of nineteenth-century European imperialism.* But the communities that established themselves along the Mediterranean littoral and elsewhere were driven by the desire neither to disseminate hellenism nor (primarily at least) to enhance the political power of the cities from which they originated. Though it is no doubt true that some migrants were seeking a better life, others, as we have noted, were driven by such basic compulsions as poverty and hunger, and yet others by what may be broadly described as commercial interests.

Political exile as it functioned in the Greek world has no exact modern equivalent. Both individuals and groups might expect to be exiled on a fairly regular basis to serve their enemies' political agenda. As a result they constituted a far larger percentage of the refugee population in Greek antiquity than they do in the modern world. Though they should in theory be regarded as distinct and separate from those who were homeless as a result of natural disaster or war, once they left their homes many of them would have been indistinguishable from refu-

---

* Edmund Burke coined the term "colonization" (from Latin, *colonia*, "a settlement or colony of citizens sent from Rome or the people composing it") in 1770. George Grote first applied it to ancient history in 1849 (Purcell 1990, 56). Its unsuitability for Greek history has been much discussed in recent years. The first to question its applicability was Finley (1976, 174), who noted with regard to early Greek and Phoenician settlements, "Commercial domination, monopoly, even export drives occur and recur in literature, not because the evidence suggests these things but simply because we have acquired the unfortunate habit of callings the settlements "colonies." Tsetskhladze (2006, xxiii–xxviii) points out that the debate often hinges upon what "colonization" actually "was." This, as he goes on to remark, depends largely on an individual scholar's academic training in the varied disciplines of ancient history, archaeology, anthropology, and the like.

gees. Whether or not they retained their status as political exiles would often have depended on whether they succeeded in making common cause with the enemies of the state that had expelled them. Finally, the word *metoikos*, which the Athenians used to describe free, noncitizen foreigners living within their territory, constituted a category without any exact modern equivalent. Though it is commonly equated with a modern resident alien, this conceals the fact that a significant percentage of *metoikoi* would have been short-term residents, since in Athens at least metic status legally defined those who were resident for (probably) only one month at least.

It follows from all this that the study of the Greek diaspora is a highly inexact science. As often as not we can determine whether a person is a refugee, a fugitive, an exile, a deportee, and so on, only by the literary context, though the context, too, often fails to provide adequate detail. In many instances, the best I have been able to do is to apply whichever English word seems most applicable to the Greek.

APPENDIX B

CATALOGUE OF ATHENIAN CLERUCHIES AND COLONIES

This appendix is greatly indebted to the work of Jones (1957, esp. 169–73); Graham (1964, 166–210); Brunt (1966, 71–92); Figueira (1991, Table 4 [pp. 217–25]); and Hansen and Nielsen (2004, Index 27 [pp. 1390–96]).

Aegina

In 431 the Athenians expelled the Aeginetans and sent out settlers of their own to occupy the island. Thucydides variously refers to them as *epoikoi, oikêtores*, and *apoikoi* (2.27.1; cf. 7.57.2; 8.69.3). However, both Plutarch (*Per.* 34.1) and Strabo (*Geog.* 8.6.16 C375) claim that the Athenians divided the land into allotments—that is, converted it to a cleruchy. Scholars continue to dispute the status of the settlement.

Amisus

In the mid-430s Athenians from the Piraeus settled in Amisus, a *polis* on the southern shore of the Black Sea, and renamed it Piraeus. It had initially been founded by Milesians. (Theopompus, *FGrH* 115 F 389 = Str. *Geog.* 12.3.14 C547).

Amphipolis

In 476/5 the Athenians made an unsuccessful attempt to establish a settlement at an Edonian (that is, Thracian) site that they renamed *Ennea Hodoi*, or Nine Ways, close to the future site of Amphipolis. Legend had it that this was the first of nine misfortunes that they suffered before they finally established a viable settlement in the region (Sch. Aesch. 2.31; Ephorus, *FGrH* 70 F 191.10 = *POxy* 13.1610 fr. 6). In 465/4(?) the Athenians sent out "10,000 of their own citizens and whoever else wished to go" from among their allies in their second attempt, but were again thwarted by the Edonians (Thuc. 1.100.3, 4.102; cf. D.S. 11.70.5). They finally succeeded in 437/6, by founding a panhellenic *apoikia*, which they named Amphipolis, just south of *Ennea Hodoi* (Thuc. 4.102.3, 5.11.1).

Andros

In 450 the Athenians sent out 250 settlers, probably cleruchs, to Andros (inference based on reduced tribute paid to the Delian Confederacy in 449 and subsequent years, cf. *IG* I³ 262.i.19; 263.iv.22 with Rhodes [1992, 60]).

Astacus

Probably in 435/4 the Athenians established an *apoikia* at Astacus, an unlocated settlement (perhaps not a *polis*) on the Propontic coast of Asia Minor (Memnon of Heraclea, *FGrH* 434 F 12.3; D.S. 12.34.5; Str. *Geog.* 12.4.2 C563; Hansen and Nielsen 2004, 977).

Brea

In either ca. 445 or 426/5 the Athenians established an *apoikia* at Brea in Thrace with possibly 1,000 Athenian settlers. The decree establishing the colony (*IG* I³ 46 = *ML* no. 49 = Fornara 100) is the subject of detailed investigation by Mattingly (1996, 117–46), who supports the lower date of 426/5. For the site, which has not been identified, see Asheri (1969, 337–40) and Mattingly (1996, 126). Its purpose, Mattingly suggests, was to serve as "a new strongpoint in this vulnerable area" (p. 128). Plu. *Per.* 11.5 contains a possible reference to the local people as "Bisaltae." Nothing is known of the history of Brea, but the settlement was probably short-lived.

Carystus

In 453/2 or 452/1 the Athenians sent out 250 cleruchs to Carystus, a *polis* in Euboea (inference based on reduced tribute paid to the Delian Confederacy, cf. *IG* I³ 259, ii.16; 262, i.23; 263 iv.26 with Rhodes [1992, 60]). See Figueira (1991, 225 note y) for further evidence of the existence of a cleruchy.

Chalcis

In 506 the Athenians compelled the so-called *hippobotai* (horse-breeders—that is, the very wealthy) of Chalcis, a *polis* in Euboea, to hand over their land to 4,000 of their cleruchs, after they had made an abortive attack on Athens in alliance with the Boeotians and Peloponnesians (Hdt. 5.77.2; 6.100.1; Plu. *Per.* 23.2). The number is probably exaggerated. Aelian (*VH* 6.1) puts the figure at 2,000. In 490 the cleruchs withdrew to Oropus when the Persians invaded Euboea. It is not clear whether they returned to Chalcis after the battle of Marathon (Hdt. 6.100–101).

Colophon

In 447/6 the Athenians sent non-Athenian *oikistai* to Colophon, a *polis* in Ionia (*IG* I³ 37.41–2; Hansen and Nielsen 2004, 1078).

Eion

In 476/5 the Athenian general Cimon seized Eion and "handed it over to the Athenians for occupation" (Plu. *Cim.* 7.3, 8.2).

Elaious

Elaious, a *polis* in the Thracian Chersonese, was probably settled by the Athenians in the sixth century. It was certainly in their control in the fifth century (Hdt. 6.140.1; cf. Hansen and Nielsen 2004, 906).

?Eretria

A fragmentary inscription dated 446/5 or 424/3 may have included provisions for the establishment of an *apoikia* at Eretria on Euboea, following the quelling of a revolt (*IG* I³ 39 = Fornara 102).

Euboea

In 453/2 the Athenian general Tolmides established a cleruchy at an unknown site in Euboea for 1,000 citizens (D.S. 11.88.3; Paus. 1.27.5).

Histiaea

In 446 the Athenians deported the inhabitants of Histiaea, a *polis* in Euboea, to Macedonia and occupied it as an *apoikia* (Thuc. 1.114.3; *IG* I³ 41; Plu. *Per.* 23.2). Theopompus (*FGrH* 115 F 387) puts the number of Athenian settlers at 2,000; Diodorus Siculus (12.22.2) at 1,000. A portion of the original population remained in the territory with its own *dikastêrion* (lawcourt) (Koch 1991, 181–83, 192–93; Hansen and Nielsen 2004, 656–67).

Lemnos and ?Imbros

Miltiades the Younger subdued Lemnos and "handed over the island to the Athenians," presumably so that they could send out settlers (Hdt. 6.136.2). Very likely the Athenians settled the neighboring island of Imbros as well. For the possible establishment of an Athenian cleruchy on Lemnos and Imbros in ca. 449 see Figueira (1991, appendix B).

Lesbos

In 427, after crushing the Mytilenean Revolt, the Athenians took control of the entire island of Lesbos, except for Methymna, its second most powerful city, which was democratic and had not revolted. They then divided the land into 3,000 lots and sent out 2,700 cleruchs, reserving 300 lots for the gods (Thuc. 3.50.2). Thucydides does not mention the cleruchs participating in any future military action that took place on the island. It is therefore likely that they were withdrawn as soon as they were no longer needed to keep the islanders in check. Quinn (1981, ch. 3, n. 58, citing P. A. Brunt, *Ancient Society and Institutions*, ed. E. Badian [Oxford, UK: Blackwell, 1966] 81–84) is of the opinion that the cleruchs left "some time before 424." This view is endorsed by Mattingly (1996, 136), who suggests that the decision to recall the cleruchs may have been forced upon Athens by a manpower crisis consequent upon a fresh outbreak of plague. Cf. also *IG* I³ 66: treaty between Athens and Mytilene dated ca. 427/6, indicating that a measure of independence had by now been restored to Lesbos.

Melos

In 416/5, after massacring all the adult males of Melos and enslaving the women and children, the Athenians sent out 500 *apoikoi* to occupy the island (Thuc. 5.116.2–4).

Naxos

In 453–48 Tolmides established a cleruchy of either 500 or 1,000 citizens on Naxos to punish the islanders for their recalcitrance as allies (D.S. 11.88.3; Plu. *Per.* 11.5; Paus. 1.27.5).

Neapolis (Campania)

At an unknown date the Athenians, the Chalcidians, and the inhabitants of Pithecusae "sent out *epoikoi*" to Neapolis (Str. *Geog.* 5.4.7 C246).

Notion

In 428/7 the Athenians sent Athenian *oikistai* to Notion, a dependent *polis* on the west coast of Anatolia, "and settled it according to their own laws, bringing in all the Colophonians from the city-states" (Thuc. 3.34.4).

Potidaea

In 430/29, after expelling the inhabitants of Potidaea, a *polis* in Chalcidice, the Athenians sent out *epoikoi* to occupy it (Thuc. 2.70.4). Diodorus Siculus (12.46.7) puts their number at 1,000. A dedication by these *epoikoi* on the eve of their departure from Athens has come to light (*ML* 66 = Fornara 129). Some seventy years later, in 362/1, the Athenians sent cleruchs to Potidaea, seemingly at the request of the inhabitants. However, by 356 the cleruchs had been expelled by Philip II of Macedon.

Salamis

A decree describing the settlement of Salamis, which has been dated ca. 510–500 on the basis of its letter forms, contains a possible reference to cleruchs who have recently settled on the island (*IG* I³ 1.1 = *ML* 14 = Fornara 44b). If the dating is correct, Salamis would have been the first Athenian cleruchy.

Samos

Horoi (boundary stones) found on Samos have been interpreted as evidence that the Athenians established a cleruchy on the island in ca. 446 to quell discontent prompted by their increasingly high-handed behavior toward their allies. Craterus's reference to the Athenians "expelling the local people" may also refer to this period (*FGrH* 342 F 21). See further Shipley (1987, 114–16). The Athenians reestablished a cleruchy on Samos in or after 365, following the conquest of the island by their general Timotheus (Isoc. 15.111). The cleruchs occupied the island until the Lamian War broke out in 323/2, after which the Macedonian commander Perdiccas "brought the Samians back to their homeland 43 years after they had been deported" (D.S. 18.18.9).

Scione

In 421 the Athenians successfully besieged Scione, a *polis* in Chalcidice, which had attempted to secede from their empire. They put to death all the adult males and enslaved the women and children. They then divided the land into lots and offered it to the exiled Plataeans to inhabit (Thuc. 4.122.6; 5.32.1; D.S. 12.76.3). Scione was returned to its former inhabitants in 405/4 by the Spartan navarch Lysander (Plu. *Lys.* 14.3; cf. Xen. *Hell.* 2.2.3 and 9).

Scylace

Scylace, situated on the Propontic coast in Asia Minor, is said to have had a mixed population of Athenians and Pelasgians—that is, pre-

Greek inhabitants of the Aegean region (Hdt. 1.57.2). It is uncertain whether it was an Athenian foundation.

Scyros

In 476/5 Cimon enslaved the so-called Dolopian (that is, non-Greek) inhabitants of Scyros, an island in the Sporades, and settled it with Athenians (Thuc. 1.98.2; Plu. *Cim.* 8.3–5; D.S. 11.60.2; Ephorus, *FGrH* 70 F 191 line 10 = *POxy* 13.1610 fr. 6). No numbers are given. For the status of the settlement, probably an *apoikia* rather than a cleruchy, see Figueira (1991, 221 note b).

Sestus

Founded by settlers from Lesbos in the seventh century, Sestus, a *polis* in the Thracian Chersonese, was resettled by Athenians in the sixth century (Hansen and Nielsen 2004, 910). In 353/2, after seizing the city and slaughtering the men and enslaving the women and children, the Athenians established a cleruchy (D.S. 16.34.4; *IG* II² 1613.297).

Sinope

In ca. 437 Pericles expelled a tyrant from Sinope, a *polis* on the southern shore of the Black Sea, and passed a decree to the effect that "600 Athenian *ethelontes* [volunteers] should sail to Sinope and settle alongside the Sinopians, dividing up the land and the houses that the tyrants had previously held" (Plu. *Per.* 20.2).

Thracian Chersonese

In 453 or 447 Pericles sailed to the Thracian Chersonese with 1,000 Athenian *epoikoi* in order to "strengthen the cities there with the flower of manhood" (Plu. *Per.* 19.1–2, cf. 11.5; D.S. 11.88.2–3).

Thurii

In 446/5 the Athenians established a panhellenic colony at Thurii on the site of Sybaris, which had been destroyed in 510. Settlers of Athenian origin comprised one-tenth of the mixed population (D.S. 12.9–10; Plu. *Per.* 11.5). Strabo (*Geog.* 6.1.13 C263) states that the Athenians and other Greeks slew the few survivors from Sybaris, who "had collected together and were settling it again." For the importance of Thurii to the Athenians, see Figueira (1991, 163 n. 8).

Torone

In 422 the Athenians captured Torone, a *polis* in Chalcidice, enslaving the women and children and deporting the men to Athens. They may have intended to send out settlers of their own to replace the population and establish an imperial settlement. Instead, when the war ended the following year, they exchanged the deportees for Olynthians who were being held prisoner by the Peloponnesians. In consequence, the deportees returned to Torone (Thuc. 5.3.2–4).

APPENDIX C

CATALOGUE OF DEPORTEES

See, too, Hansen and Nielsen (2004, 1363–64) for instances of expulsion and *andrapodismos*.

546 BCE	When he came to power, the Athenian tyrant Peisistratus expelled the powerful *genos* known as the Alcmeonids. The Alcmeonids returned to Athens in 510 when Peisistratus's son Hippias, who succeeded his father as tyrant, was driven into exile, largely as a result of the machinations of the Alcmeonids (Hdt. 5.62.2; 6.123.1).
496	Citing an oracle, the Athenian general Miltiades the Younger expelled the so-called Pelasgian (that is, non-Greek) inhabitants of Lemnos (Hdt. 6.140; D.S. 10.19.6). The Athenians probably also expelled the inhabitants of Imbros around this date (Hdt. 5.26). No numbers are given.
494	When the Persians captured Miletus after its unsuccessful attempt to revolt, their king Darius, having enslaved the women and children, "did the men no further harm but settled them in the sea called the Erythraean [that is, the Persian Gulf] in the city of Ampe" (Hdt. 6.19.3–20). Since the majority of the Milesian population had been slaughtered by the Persians, those unharmed probably amounted to only a privileged few, viz Persian sympathizers.
491	The *dêmos* and the slaves of Syracuse exiled the *gamoroi* (landowners) to Casmenae. A few years later Gelon defeated the *dêmos* and made himself tyrant of Syracuse, whereupon he invited the *gamoroi* to return (Hdt. 7.155.2).

ca. 490   After destroying Eretria for assisting the Ionians in their revolt, Darius ordered the survivors to be brought before him in chains since he bore a bitter grudge against them. Thereafter, however, he "did them no further harm" and settled them at Arderikka, about 20 miles from Susa (Hdt. 6.119.1–2).

Anaxilas, tyrant of Rhegium, "exiled the inhabitants of Zancle, and settled it with a mixed population and renamed it Messana, after his old homeland" (Thuc. 6.4.6).

ca. 485   To increase the size of Syracuse's population, Gelon, its tyrant, deported thither all the inhabitants of Camarina, half the population of Gela, and the well-to-do of Megara Hyblaea, granting them all citizenship. He also deported the common people of Megara Hyblaea to Syracuse, but these he enslaved and sold abroad (Hdt. 7.156.2; see chapter 5).

480   After the battle of Thermopylae and as a mark of their enslavement, Xerxes branded "the majority of the Thebans" whom he had taken prisoner, before deporting them to Persia (Hdt. 7.233.2).

476   Hieron I, tyrant of Syracuse, deported the entire populations of Naxos and Catania to Leontini. Though Naxos was not resettled, Catania received 10,000 settlers from the Peloponnese and Syracuse. It was renamed Aetna (D.S. 11.49.1; see chapter 5).

464   Following the great earthquake, Sparta's helots revolted and took refuge on Mount Ithome. They eventually surrendered and were permitted to depart from Messenia under a truce. The Athenians invited them to settle in Naupactus (Thuc. 1.103.1–3; see chapter 11).

457   After defeating the Boeotians at Oenophyta, the Athenians deported some of their prisoners, along with (possibly) the people of Phocis. A decade later in 447 the deportees inflicted a heavy defeat upon the Athenians at Coronea. They then returned to their homeland (Thuc. 1.108.3 and 1.113).

446   After putting down a revolt, the Athenians deported the inhabitants of Histiaea in revenge for their massacre of some Athenian prisoners. A local people called the Ellopioi, however, were permitted to remain because, being subject to the Histiaeans, they had not been responsible for the massacre.

The Athenians sent out their own settlers to occupy Histiaea (Thuc. 1.114.3; *IG* I³ 41).

441–40   Possibly after installing a democracy on Samos, the Athenians seized fifty men and fifty boys as hostages and sent them to Lemnos, an Athenian cleruchy. However, a group of Samian fugitives undertook a daring night raid to rescue the hostages and returned with them to Samos (Thuc. 1.115.3–5). The Athenians blockaded Samos and after eight months took the island. They imposed terms that included the seizing of an unknown number of hostages, whom they presumably deported to Athens (1.117.3).

mid-430s?   Some Athenians settled in Amisus and renamed it Piraeus, perhaps expelling the former inhabitants (Theopompus *FGrH* F 389 = Str. *Geog.* 12.3.14 C547).

433   For strategic reasons Perdiccas II, king of Macedon, persuaded the Chalcidians to destroy the cities that they occupied along the coast and to settle inland at Olynthus, making it a strong foundation (Thuc. 1.58.2; see chapter 4).

ca. 431   The popular faction in Epidamnus expelled the *dunatoi* (powerful), viz the oligarchs. The latter joined forces with the barbarians (viz those living in the surrounding territory) and proceeded to plunder their home city. We do not know when the exiled oligarchs returned (Thuc. 1.24–29; see chapter 5).

ca. 431?   The popular faction in Megara expelled the oligarchs (Thuc. 4.66.1; see chapter 5).

431   In response to the Theban attack on Plataea, the Athenians seized all the Boeotians resident in Attica (Thuc. 2.6.2). Their fate is unknown, but it is likely that they were deported.

Shortly after the outbreak of the Peloponnesian War the Athenians expelled the Aeginetans, some of whom fled to Thyrea, a city and region on the east coast of the Peloponnese, where they settled, while others "scattered throughout the length and breadth of Greece" (Thuc. 2.27.1–2; see chapter 5).

430/29   Following the surrender of Potidaea after a two-year siege, the Athenian generals decided to deport the entire population either to Chalcidice (that is, to the region around Potidaea) or "to where each of them could go." The Athenian *dêmos* was severely displeased with its generals for this decision, "since it believed that it could have taken the city on its own terms," viz without striking a deal (Thuc. 2.70.4). We hear no more about the Potidaeans and have no way of knowing what percentage of them survived as refugees. It was a banal occurrence in a bloody war that generated many similar incidents. The Potidaeans were lucky to be deported. It was only because the Athenian army was experiencing hardship as a result of the protracted siege that their generals had accepted the offer of surrender, though the condition of the besieged had been so dire that they had even resorted to cannibalism. Had the Athenians taken Potidaea by siege, they would probably have slaughtered the men and enslaved the wives and children, which is perhaps what the *dêmos* had desired.

429/8   The Athenian general Phormion conducted an operation that was aimed at securing the political allegiance of Acarnania by "expelling persons judged not to be trustworthy from Stratus, Coronta [of unknown location], and other places" (Thuc. 2.102.1). We are not told where the refugees, who presumably included women and children, headed, nor what numbers were involved.

427   After capturing Plataea, the Spartans and their allies massacred some 200 of its citizens and enslaved about 110 women. They then permitted political refugees from Megara who were friendly to Thebes to inhabit the vacant city for about a year and afterwards destroyed its walls (Thuc. 3.68; see chapter 5). In recognition of their alliance with Plataea, the Athenians granted citizenship to the refugees.

424   *Phugades* from Mytilene and other cities on Lesbos, who had presumably fled from the island when Athens imposed a severe settlement on it after putting down the revolt in 427, sought to restore themselves to power "by seeking to subdue the Aeolian cities on the mainland." They were eventually defeated by the Athenians when attempting to fortify Antandrus (Thuc. 3.50, 4.52.2, 4.75.1). We never hear of them again.

The Athenians destroyed Thyrea and deported all the Aeginetans living there to Athens. They then slew them "on account of their previous long-standing hatred" (Thuc. 4.56.2–57; see chapter 5).

The Athenians removed "a few" of the inhabitants of Cythera whom they considered untrustworthy and settled them "in the islands" (Thuc. 4.57.4).

The *dunatoi* of Leontini, with the aid of the Syracusans, expelled the *dêmos* (Thuc. 5.4.2–4; see chapter 5).

424/3   The Spartan general Brasidas, having taken Amphipolis, proclaimed that those Athenians and Amphipolitans who did not wish to remain in the *polis* had five days to depart and could take their property with them (Thuc. 4.105.2). We are not told how many took up the offer nor where they went.

422   The Athenians expelled the Delians from their island, maintaining that "when they had been consecrated as a sacred people they had been impure because of an ancient offence" (Thuc. 5.1). The Persian satrap Pharnaces permitted the deportees to settle in Adramyttium (modern Adramyti) in the region called Mysia on the coast of Turkey. (For possible motives behind Pharnaces' action, see Hornblower [2004, 423–24].) The following year the Athenians restored the Delians to their island, "stirred to do so by their reverses and by an oracle of the god at Delphi" (5.32.1). Not all the refugees returned, however, for in 411 "the chief men among them," who were still living in Persia, were enticed out of Adramyttium by Arsaces, lieutenant of Tissaphernes, Pharnaces' successor. Tissaphernes laid an ambush for them while they were at dinner and had them all slaughtered (8.108.4). It is with this incident that Thucydides' history breaks off.

The *dunatoi* in Leontini, with the assistance of the Syracusans, expelled the *dêmos*, laid waste their city, and migrated to Syracuse. Later, not finding conditions in Syracuse to their liking, they withdrew from the city, came to terms with "the majority of the exiled people," and established themselves between a part of Leontini called Phocaeae and a neighboring settlement called Bricinniae (Thuc. 5.4.2–4).

417   The *dêmos* of Argos overthrew the *oligoi* by "slaughtering some of their opponents and exiling others." The oligarchic *phugades* were received by the people of Phlius, a *polis* in the northwest Argolid, whose territory the Argives plundered shortly afterward "because they had received their exiles." The following year the exiles, now allied to the Phliasians, ambushed the Argives when they invaded Phlius. In the winter of 416/5 the Spartans settled the Argive exiles at Orneae by appropriating some of the territory that was owned by the Orneatae. They then made the Orneatae and the Argive exiles undertake a truce not to harm each other's territory. Soon afterward, however, the Athenians and the Argives began besieging Orneae. The exiles managed to escape by night, and we never hear of them again (Thuc. 5.82.2, 5.83.3, 5.115.1, 6.7.1).

416/5   Alcibiades seized 300 pro-Spartan Argives and deported them "to nearby islands under Athenian control" (Thuc. 5.84.1). The deportees were massacred by the Argives the following year with the connivance of the Athenians (6.61.3).

              The Athenians sailed with some Macedonian *phugades* who had been residing in Athens to Methone and plundered the coastline of Macedonia (Thuc. 6.7.3). It is unclear why the refugees were residing in Athens.

415   The inhabitants of Thurii expelled those who were hostile to the Athenians in advance of the arrival of the Athenian expedition in Sicily (Thuc. 7.33.5).

412   The *dêmos* of Samos executed about 200 of the *dunatôtatoi* and banished 400 others. They appropriated their land and houses (Thuc. 8.21; cf. *IG* I³ 96).

407   The Athenian commander Thrasybulus expelled Spartan sympathizers from Thasos and partly resettled the island with Athenian citizens (Xen. *Hell.* 1.1.32; 1.4.9).

405   As a reward for their loyalty, the Athenians granted citizenship to "all the Samians who stood by the *dêmos* of the Athenians" (*ML* 94 = Fornara 166). We do not know how many Samians accepted the offer and migrated to Athens.

404/3   At the end of the Peloponnesian War the Spartans decreed that all Athenian exiles should immediately return to Athens and be subject to the Thirty Tyrants (Xen. *Hell.* 2.2.23; see chapters 5 and 11).

Following Athens's defeat the Samians capitulated to the Spartan navarch Lysander on condition that "every free person should depart with only a single cloak" (Xen. *Hell.* 2.3.6). An Athenian decree dated 403/2 commends the people of Ephesus and Notus "for having welcomed warmly [those of the] Samians who were in exile" (Tod 97.8 = Harding 5). Probably some of the deportees migrated to Athens (see Shipley 1978, endnote I, for evidence of Samians resident in Attica at this time). Rather than a mass expulsion from Samos, we should perhaps be thinking of "a lopping-off of the highest ears of corn" (Shipley 1978, 132–33).

"More than half of Athens' population" fled from Athens to the Piraeus to escape the violence of the Thirty Tyrants (D.S. 14.5.7).

The Thirty Tyrants compelled "more than 5,000 Athenian citizens to take refuge in the Piraeus" (Isoc. 7.67).

403   With the restoration of democracy Athenian deportees and refugees who had been living in the Piraeus staged a triumphal return to Athens. Those who had been sympathetic to the Thirty Tyrants and feared for their lives were permitted to relocate in Eleusis, which now became a semi-independent polity (Xen. *Hell.* 2.4.38–9; see chapter 5).

401/400   The Spartan king Agis deported "a vast number of slaves" from Elis (Xen. *Hell.* 3.2.26).

Dionysius I of Syracuse enslaved the *dêmoi* of both Catania and Naxos (D.S. 14.15.1–2).

The Spartans expelled the Messenians from Cephallenia and Naupactus "because of their longstanding enmity toward the Spartans." The Messenians "departed from mainland Greece with their arms." Some sailed to Sicily and served as mercenaries under Dionysius I, tyrant of Syracuse; the rest, about

3,000 in all, sailed to Cyrene, where they joined forces with exiles who were seeking to recover the city. In the ensuing conflict, however, almost all the Messenians were slain (D.S. 14.34.2–5).

399   Following an outbreak of *stasis* the Spartans expelled the Oetaeans from Heraclea Trachinia, a *polis* in Thessaly they had founded in 426. The majority fled to Thessaly, but after five years they were restored by the Boeotians (D.S. 14.38.4–5; see Gehrke 1985, 73; Malkin 1994, 221–27; Hansen and Nielsen 2004, 711).

395   The Boeotians and Argives seized Heraclea Trachinia. They slew the Spartan garrison but allowed the other Peloponnesians to depart with their possessions. They then recalled the Trachinians whom the Spartans had expelled and permitted them to reside in the city (D.S. 14.82.6–7).

392   Dionysius I of Syracuse deported most of the Sicels from Tauromenium, a *polis* on the east coast of Sicily (D.S. 14.96.4). We do not know where they subsequently settled.

385/4   After being defeated by a Spartan-led coalition, the inhabitants of Mantinea were forced to raze their city to the ground and return to their original four villages (D.S. 15.12.2; Xen. *Hell.* 5.2.7; see chapter 4).

ca. 385   The inhabitants of Thasos were exiled from their island on the orders of Sparta.

382–79   The *dêmos* of Phlius expelled its oligarchic population. Fearing reprisals from Sparta, it later invited the oligarchs to return and reclaim their property. However, the democrats reneged on the deal, so the oligarchs went into exile a second time. The latter appealed to the Spartans, who successfully besieged the city and restored them to power. An unknown number of democrats were condemned to death (Xen. *Hell.* 5.2.9; 5.3.10. 5.3.25; see chapter 11).

ca. 373   The Thebans made a surprise attack on the Plataeans, destroyed their town for the second time, and annexed their territory. As in 427, the surviving Plataeans sought refuge in Athens. The Thespians, who had also been expelled, begged the Athenians not to leave them "without a city" (Xen. *Hell.* 6.3.1).

ca. 370   At the foundation of the Arcadian League "800 Tegeans fled to Sparta" according to Xenophon (*Hell.* 6.5.10), whereas Diodorus Siculus claims that "1,400 fled, some to Sparta, others to Pallantium" (15.59.2). Those who fled to Pallantium were slaughtered, whereas those who fled to Sparta prevailed upon the Spartans to invade Tegea. The exiled Tegeans participated in the invasion and were probably restored as a result.

365?   The Athenian general Timotheus, while assisting the Persian satrap Ariobarzanes, successfully besieged Samos in order to strengthen Athenian control of the Aegean. The Athenians deported the Samians and established a cleruchy on the island. According to the fourth-century historian Heraclides Ponticus, quoted by Aristotle (fr. 611.35 Rose), the Athenians "exiled everyone." Shipley (1987, 164) states, "The exodus in 365 no doubt ran into many hundreds, possibly thousands." Most of the refugees settled in Ionia, Aeolis, and Caria. See Habicht (1957, 152–237) for a collection of Samian inscriptions thanking the "benefactors of Samos" for their support in their years of wandering. The Samians were still in exile 43 years later in 324, when Alexander promulgated the so-called Exiles' Decree (D.S. 18.8.7; see chapter 11).

363/2   The Athenians decreed that the rebellious Iulietae of Ceos "are to be banished from Ceos and Athens and their possessions are to belong to the *dêmos* of the Iulietae" (*IG* II² 111.41–2 = *SIG*³ 173 = Harding 55 = Rhodes and Osborne 39). The details are not fully understood, but it may be that rebels from Iulis had sided with the Thebans in their attempt to supplant Athens's mastery of the sea (D.S. 15.78.4–79.1).

358–47   After Philip II of Macedon had successfully besieged Potidaea, he "humanely" sent the Athenian garrison back to Athens, sold the citizens into slavery, and handed the city "with all its buildings" over to the Olynthians (D.S. 16.8.5). No numbers are given.

    The Athenian general Chares, having captured Sestos, slew all the adult males and enslaved the remainder of the population (D.S. 16.34.3). No numbers are given.

357   Philip II captured Amphipolis and "*ephugadeuse* [exiled] those who were unfavorably disposed toward him" (D.S. 16.8.2). A decree of the *dêmos* of Amphipolis that exiled leading opponents of Philip may either predate or postdate his capture of the city (Tod 150 = Harding 63 = Rhodes and Osborne 49).

354   After successfully besieging Methone, a *polis* in Macedonia, Philip II permitted its citizens to depart "with one cloak each." No numbers are given, and the fate of the refugees is unknown. Philip then razed the city to the ground and divided up its territory among the Macedonians (Dem. 4.4; D.S. 16.31.6 and 34.4–5).

352   The Phocian general Phaüllus razed to the ground Naryka, a *polis* in East Locris (D.S. 16.38.5). No numbers are given, and the fate of its inhabitants is unknown.

339/8   Timoleon "slaughtered" the Campanians living in Aetna (D.S. 16.82.4) and deported the Syracusans from Leontini (D.S. 16.82.7).

338   After Philip II had exiled the Troezenians, the latter appealed to the Athenians, who granted them citizenship and other privileges. They did so in recognition of the fact that the Troezenians had provided refuge for their women and children before the Battle of Salamis 150 years prior (Hyp. *Ath.* 31–33). No numbers are given.

336/5   Shortly after coming to power Alexander the Great put down a revolt in Thebes. He then ordered the massacre of over 6,000 Thebans. The rest—some 30,000 in all—were sold into slavery "with the exception of the priests, the guest-friends of the Macedonians, the descendants of Pindar, and those who had opposed the vote for revolt" (Plu. *Alex.* 11.6). A decree passed by the so-called League of Corinth included the provision that "Theban *phugades* should be deported from the whole of Greece and no Greek should offer refuge to a Theban" (D.S. 17.14.3).

    The oligarchs in Ephesus expelled the democrats for supporting Alexander the Great. When the king arrived in Ephesus in

334, he recalled the exiles, overthrew the oligarchs, and set up a democracy. Rarely, according to Arrian, did he gain a higher reputation than in consequence of his treatment of the Ephesians (*Anab.* 1.17.10–12).

335?   Certain Chians, who were hostile to the Macedonians, betrayed their city to the Persians and deported their opponents (Arr. *Anab.* 2.1.1). Alexander recovered the island the following year and in an edict probably dated 334 declared that "All the exiles from Chios shall return and the constitution in Chios be democratic" (*SIG*³ 283 = Tod 192 = Rhodes and Osborne 84).

APPENDIX D

CATALOGUE OF EXILES

As noted earlier, it is not always possible to distinguish between exiles, fugitives, and those who choose to "retire" abroad.

Aeschines, Athenian politician: Left Athens and retired to Rhodes after being defeated by his adversary Demosthenes in 330.

Agathocles, tyrant and later king of Syracuse: Exiled from Syracuse in ca. 330 by his oligarchic opponents because of his democratic leanings; recalled by the Syracusan *dêmos* but again exiled by the oligarchs; reinstated in 319/8 in Syracuse, where he ruled as tyrant; remained in control until his death in 289.

Alcaeus of Mytilene, lyric poet: Went into exile from Mytilene in ca. 600 after he was discovered to be plotting against the tyrant Myrsilus, though he remained on the island of Lesbos; went into exile two more times as a result of his opposition to the tyrant Pittacus (fr. 114, 130 B Campbell). For full discussion of the testimonia, see Bowie (2007, 33–34).

Alcibiades, Athenian politician, grandfather of the more famous Alcibiades: Ostracized in 460.

Alcibiades, Athenian politician and general: Fled from Athens to Sparta in 415/4 to avoid prosecution for his involvement in religious scandals; subsequently condemned to death; tried unsuccessfully to engineer his return by obtaining the support of Persia; reappointed general in 411; returned to Athens to a rapturous welcome in 407; withdrew to Thrace in 406 when one of his subordinates was defeated by the Spartans; attempted unsuccessfully to give advice to the Athenians before the Battle of Aegospotami in 405; took refuge with the

Persian satrap Pharnabazus but was murdered on his host's orders in 404/3.

Anaxagoras, Ionian philosopher: Put on trial for impiety in Athens in ca. 450; subsequently retired to Lampsacus in the northern Troad.

Andocides, Athenian politician: Charged with being implicated in the mutilation of the herms and the profanation of the Mysteries in 415; secured immunity by confessing to his role in the mutilation; being debarred from entering sanctuaries or the Agora, he left Athens and became a merchant; made two unsuccessful attempts to regain his citizenship in 411 and 410; took advantage of the amnesty of 403 to return to Athens; successfully defended himself in 400 or 399 against a further attempt to debar him from entry into sanctuaries or the Agora in his famous speech titled "On the Mysteries"; prosecuted for treason because of his role in negotiating terms with the Spartans in 392/1; fled from Athens before the verdict was given, after which nothing more is heard of him.

Androtion, Athenian politician and local historian: Exiled in 346 after being prosecuted for making an illegal proposal; lived out his days in Megara.

Aristides, Athenian politician and general: Ostracized in 482, in part because of his intense rivalry with Themistocles (Hdt. 8.79.2); recalled in 480 when an amnesty was announced in advance of Xerxes' invasion of Greece (Forsdyke 2005, 166–67).

Aristotle of Stagira, philosopher: Settled in Athens in 367 at the age of 17 to study under Plato; left Athens on Plato's death in 348/7 and journeyed first to Assos and then to Mytilene; became tutor to Alexander the Great in 342 at the invitation of Philip II of Macedon; returned to Athens in 335, where he became a metic and established his philosophical school called the Lyceum; fled to Chalcis in 323 to escape the anti-Macedonian sentiment that broke out on the death of Alexander; later claimed that his flight was occasioned by the desire to prevent the Athenians from "sinning twice against philosophy"—an allusion to the trial and execution of Socrates; died in Chalcis in 322.

Cimon, Athenian general and politician: Ostracized in 461, in part because of his intense rivalry with Pericles' political ally Ephialtes.

Cleisthenes, Athenian politician: Forced to withdraw from Athens for a short period by his political rival Isagoras in 508/7.

Cleomenes I, Spartan king: Took refuge in Thessaly after being accused of intriguing against his fellow-king Demaratus; invited back to Sparta, where he allegedly committed suicide, perhaps suffering from paranoid schizophrenia.

Critias, Athenian politician: Exiled in 406, possibly because of his association with Alcibiades; withdrew to Thrace, where he is said to have worked to establish democracy and to have fought on behalf of a servile group known as the *penestai* (Xen. *Hell.* 2.3.36); recalled in 404 in accordance with Athens's peace treaty with Sparta at the end of the Peloponnesian War; became the leader of the Thirty Tyrants; killed fighting against Thrasybulus in 403.

Demaratus, Spartan king: Fled to Persia in ca. 491 as the result of rivalry with his fellow-king Cleomenes I; accompanied Xerxes on his invasion of Greece (Hdt. 6.61–70, 73–75).

Democedes, physician from Croton: Fled from Croton when the city was engulfed in *stasis*; settled in Plataea.

Demosthenes, Athenian orator and politician: Went into voluntary exile in 323 after being found guilty of misappropriating public money; recalled soon afterward; exiled by Antipater, who became ruler of Macedon after the death of Alexander the Great; subsequently condemned to death; under pursuit from Antipater's henchmen, he took refuge in the sanctuary of Poseidon on the island of Calauria, where he committed suicide in 322.

Diagoras, poet from Melos: Condemned to death for impiety by the Athenians; fled first to Pallene and later to Corinth.

Diogenes of Sinope, Cynic philosopher: Sent into exile (or alternatively fled) after 362 because either he or his father had defaced the coinage (D.L. 6.20–1; see Branham [2007, 72–73] for numismatic evidence in support of the testimony); spent the remainder of his life in Athens and Corinth.

Dion, tyrant of Syracuse: Exiled from Syracuse by his nephew Dionysius II in 366; went to live in Athens; returned in 357 to Syracuse, where he established himself as tyrant; became unpopular and went into exile at Leontini; invited to return to Syracuse when Dionysius II sought to reestablish his power; later assassinated.

Dionysius II, tyrant of Syracuse: Withdrew (or was exiled) to Locri Epizephyrii in 356; recovered Syracuse, but in 344 withdrew to Corinth under pressure from Timoleon, who had control of Greek-dominated Sicily.

Ducetius, Sicel leader: Exiled in 450 to Corinth by the Syracusans after being defeated in battle; returned to Sicily in 446; founded Kale Acte on its north coast.

Euripides: Accepted invitation from Archelaus, king of Macedon, to reside permanently at his court in 408, having left Athens possibly on account of his unpopularity.

Harpalus, Macedonian general: Fled from Babylon to Cilicia on Alexander's return from the East, suspected of abusing his position as Alexander's treasurer; fled to Athens in 324, perhaps hoping to stir up a rebellion against Alexander; fled from Athens to Crete, where he was murdered in 323.

Hermocrates, Syracusan politician: Exiled from Syracuse in 410 following a quarrel with the Persian satrap Tissaphernes; returned to Sicily in 409; died in battle in 407 while trying unsuccessfully to secure his return to Syracuse.

Herodotus, historian from Halicarnassus: Possibly exiled as a result of his opposition to the Persian-backed tyrant Lygdamis of Naxos (Sud. *s.v.*; disputed by Dillery [2007, 53–54, 63–64]).

Hipparchus, relative of former tyrant Hippias: Ostracized in 487, the first victim of the procedure.

Hippias, tyrant of Athens: Escaped from Athens to Sigeum in 510 when the Spartans invaded Attica to oust him; took up residence at the court of the Persian king Darius I; remained in Persia for the rest of his life; accompanied the Persians to Marathon in 490, hoping to be reinstated in Athens as tyrant (Thuc. 6.59.4).

Hipponax, Ephesian poet: exiled in ca. 450 from Ephesus by the tyrant Athenagoras and settled in Clazomenae.

Histiaeus, tyrant of Miletus: Being suspected of treason by the Persian king Darius I, he was detained in Susa; eventually allowed to leave

Persia to negotiate an end to the Ionian Revolt; turned to piracy and died in 493.

Hyperbolus, Athenian politician: Ostracized in ca. 417, the last victim of this procedure, when seeking to secure the banishment of one of his political opponents (Forsdyke [2005, 170–74]).

Isagoras, political leader: Withdrew (or fled) from Athens in 508/7 after his attempt to establish a narrow oligarchy had been defeated by his opponent, Cleisthenes.

Leotychidas II, Spartan king: Went into voluntary exile in Tegea in 477 to escape the charge of bribery; remained in Tegea till his death.

Lysias, Athenian orator: Expelled from Thurii in 412/11 because of his pro-Athenian sentiments; resided in Athens as a metic; arrested by the Thirty Tyrants, but escaped from prison; gave support to the democrats in exile; was rewarded with citizenship on the restoration of democracy in 403, but the grant was revoked as unconstitutional.

Megacles, Athenian politician and nephew of Cleisthenes: Ostracized in 486.

Miltiades the Younger, Athenian politician and general: Fled from the Thracian Chersonese to Athens at the end of the Ionian Revolt in 493; elected one of the ten generals for 490/89; tradition held him primarily responsible for the Athenian victory over the Persians at Marathon; fined fifty talents for having failed in an attack on the island of Paros as it supposedly sided with the Persians; died of gangrene in 489 before he could discharge his debt.

Orestes, son of Thessalian king: Fled to Athens, from which in 454(?) he unsuccessfully attempted to make a comeback (Thuc. 1.111.1).

Pausanias, Spartan regent: Accused of treason in 471 or 470, fled to a sanctuary of Athena, where he was starved nearly to death; died outside the sanctuary soon afterward.

Pausanias II, Spartan king: To avoid execution for a military failure, in 395 fled to Tegea, where he died many years later.

Phidias, Athenian sculptor: Fled from Athens to Olympia in 438 after being accused of embezzlement and impiety; murdered in Olympia according to the tradition preserved by Philochorus (*FGrH* 328 F 121), though Plutarch (*Per.* 31.5) reports, less plausibly, that he died in prison.

Philistus, Syracusan historian and politician: Banished by Dionysius I, tyrant of Syracuse, in 386; lived in Epirus, where he wrote a history of Sicily; recalled to Syracuse twenty years later.

Pisander, Athenian politician: Fled to Sparta in 411 when the Council of Four Hundred was overthrown.

Pisistratus, tyrant of Athens: Went into self-imposed exile for ten years in Thrace and Eretria after his second failed attempt to establish a tyranny in Athens; eventually returned to Athens in ca. 546 and established a secure tyranny; died in 528/7.

Pleistoanax, Spartan king: Exiled sometime between 446 and 444 on the charge of accepting a bribe from the Athenians to have him withdraw his army from ravaging Attica during the so-called First Peloponnesian War (Thuc. 1.114.2; 2.21.1); recalled to Sparta in 426; faced ongoing criticism that his recall was responsible for Sparta's reverses (Thuc. 5.16).

Pythagoras, philosopher from Samos: Allegedly fled from Samos in ca. 531 to escape the tyranny of Polycrates; migrated to Croton, where he founded a sect that bore his name; later fled to Metapontum, where he died.

Pythodorus, Athenian general: Exiled from Athens in 424 on the charge of accepting a bribe from the Sicilians (Thuc. 4.65.3).

Sophocles, Athenian general: Exiled from Athens in 424 on the charge of accepting a bribe from the Sicilians (Thuc. 4.65.3).

Themistocles, Athenian politician and general: Ostracized at the end of the 470s; went to live in Argos, from which he "visited other places in the Peloponnese" (Thuc. 1.135.3; Plu. *Them.* 23–4); fled westward to Corcyra and Epirus and then eastward via Macedonia to Persia, where Artaxerxes I made him governor of Magnesia; recalled to stand trial for treason and condemned to death *in absentia*; remained in Magnesia till his death, when his bones were returned to Athens and secretly buried.

Theognis, elegiac poet from Megara: Possibly driven into exile, though the evidence for this claim is based on a single problematic passage in his poetry (ll. 1197–1202; see Lane Fox [2000, 44] and Bowie [2007, 42–43]).

Thrasybulus, Athenian general and politician: Banished by the Thirty Tyrants in 404; fled to Thebes, where he assembled a band of exiles; seized Phyle and later the Piraeus; defeated an army of the Thirty Tyrants; returned to Athens in 403, when an amnesty was proclaimed and the democracy restored.

Thucydides, son of Olorus, Athenian general and historian: Exiled (or fled) to avoid prosecution in 424 for his failure to save Amphipolis from the Spartan general Brasidas; subsequently associated "especially with the Peloponnesians"; remained in exile for twenty years, returning at the end of the war; died a few years after its end (Thuc. 5.26.5).

Thucydides, son of Melesias, Athenian politician: Ostracized in 433 or slightly later, as the result of a clash with Pericles (Plu. *Per.* 14; see Forsdyke [2005, 168–69]).

Timaeus of Tauromenium, historian: Exiled by the tyrant Agathocles in 315; went to live in Athens; took revenge on Agathocles after his death by "defaming him for all time"; may have returned to Sicily in ca. 265 (D.S. 21.17.1; *FGrH* 566 T 4a).

Timotheus, Athenian general: Went into voluntary exile in Chalcis in 355 after being heavily fined for his failure to take Chios.

Xanthippus, Athenian politician, father of Pericles: Ostracized in 484; recalled in 480 when a political amnesty was announced in advance of Xerxes' invasion of Greece.

Xenophanes of Colophon: Went into voluntary exile probably as a result of the Persian conquest in 545; "wandered" for 67 years (fr. 8 *IEG*).

Xenophon, Athenian general: Exiled from Athens in ca. 394 for having fought against his fellow-citizens as a mercenary at the Battle of Coronea; went to live first in a Spartan settlement near Olympia, then in Corinth; permitted to return to Athens in ca. 368 (*Anab.* 5.3.7).

APPENDIX E

CATALOGUE OF THE ENSLAVED

This catalogue includes Greeks who were enslaved by non-Greeks, non-Greeks who enslaved Greeks, and Greeks who enslaved other Greeks. I am much indebted to Pritchett (1991, 226ff.); Rosivach (1999, 131–32); and Hansen and Nielsen (2004, Index 20 [pp. 1363–64]). We know little of enslavement in historical times before Herodotus.

6th century? BCE The inhabitants of Methymna on Lesbos enslaved their fellow islanders inhabiting the *polis* of Arisba (Hdt. 1.151.2).

545? Mazares the Mede captured Priene and enslaved its inhabitants (Hdt. 1.161).

ca. 513 The Persians enslaved the inhabitants of Barce, a *polis* in Libya (Hdt. 4.203.1).

ca. 511? The Persian governor of Lemnos enslaved all the islanders (Hdt. 5.27.1–3).

494 After the Persians had destroyed Miletus, they sent all their prisoners, mainly women and children, to Susa. King Darius I later permitted them to settle at Ampe on the Persian Gulf (Hdt. 6.18–20).

493 Hippocrates, tyrant of Gela, enslaved "most of the inhabitants of Zancle," after previously promising to lend them military assistance (Hdt. 6.23.6).

After suppressing the Ionian Revolt, the Persians castrated the most handsome boys and enslaved the most beautiful virgins. Herodotus (6.32) comments: "In this way the Ionians were reduced to slavery for the third time, first by the Lydians, twice by the Persians."

490	The Persians enslaved "those of the Naxians whom they captured." The remainder "fled to the hills" (Hdt. 6.96).
	King Darius I enslaved the Eretrians after plundering and setting fire to their temples (Hdt. 6.101.3).
ca. 485	When he became tyrant of Syracuse, Gelon "sold the *dêmos* of Megara Hyblaea into slavery for export from Sicily" (Hdt. 7.156.2).
480	Gelon captured, and presumably enslaved, 10,000 Carthaginians before the Battle of Himera (D.S. 11.21.2). After his victory he apportioned "a vast number of prisoners" among his allies. Most were put in chains and used for building public works (11.25.1–2). Of these the majority was apportioned to the Acragantines.
478	The Athenians enslaved the inhabitants of Eïon and Scyros (Thuc. 1.98.1–2; cf. Hdt. 7.107.1–2).
476	Theron of Acragas either executed or deported and presumably enslaved those who had been plotting against his rule in Himera (D.S. 11.48.6–8).
470	The Athenian general Cimon captured 20,000 Persians, whom he presumably enslaved (D.S. 11.62.1).
468	The Argives enslaved the Mycenaeans and dedicated a tenth part of them "to the god" (D.S. 11.65.5).
453	The Syracusan general Apelles took "a multitude of prisoners" from among the Tyrrhenians living on Corsica and presumably enslaved them (D.S. 11.88.5).
450	Cimon captured the crews of 100 Persian ships and presumably sold them into slavery (D.S. 12.3.3).
	As a result of Pericles' citizenship law, "rather fewer than 5,000" were denounced and sold into slavery (Plu. *Per.* 37.3–4).
447	The Athenians enslaved the inhabitants of Chaeronea (Thuc. 1.113.1).
446	The Athenians rescued(?) 2,000 prisoners in their war against Megara (*ML* 51 = Fornara 101; cf. Thuc. 1.114).
440	The Syracusans enslaved the inhabitants of Trinacie, a Sicel town of uncertain location (D.S. 12.29.4).

435	The Corcyraeans enslaved "the *epêludes*" (foreigners), viz a group of Corinthians who had intended to settle on Corcyra (Thuc. 1.29.5).
433	The Corinthians enslaved 800 Corcyraeans (Thuc. 1.55).
430	The Athenians enslaved the Ambraciots (Thuc. 2.68.7).
427	The Spartans enslaved the women of Plataea (Thuc. 3.68.2).
425	The Corcyraeans enslaved the female relatives of the oligarchic insurgents whom they had massacred (Thuc. 4.48.4).
424	The Athenian general Nicias enslaved the inhabitants of Thyrea in Laconia (D.S. 12.65.9).
422	The Athenians enslaved the women and children of Torone (Thuc. 5.3.4).
	The oligarchs of Leontini deported the *dêmos* (Thuc. 5.4.2).
421	The Athenians enslaved the women and children of Scione (Thuc. 5.32.1).
	The Campanians enslaved the inhabitants of Cyme, a *polis* on the west coast of Italy (D.S. 12.76.4).
416/5	The Athenians enslaved the women and children of Melos (Thuc. 5.116.4).
415	The Athenians enslaved the inhabitants of Hyccara, a *polis* in Sicily (Thuc. 6.62.3).
413	The Syracusans enslaved the allied soldiers who had fought against them, except for the Athenians and the Sicilian Greeks (Thuc. 7.87.3). The total amounted to several thousand.
412	The Spartans appropriated slaves belonging to the inhabitants of Meropid Cos (Thuc. 8.41.2).
	After sacking Iasus the Peloponnesians sold its inhabitants, both free and servile, to the Persians for the price of one *statêr* apiece (Thuc. 8.28.4).
411	The Athenians appropriated slaves belonging to the Lampsacenes (Thuc. 8.62.2).
409	The Carthaginian general Hannibal "distributed among his army"(that is, as slaves) the women and children of Himera (D.S. 13.62.4).

The Athenians seized slaves belonging to the Lydians (Xen. *Hell.* 1.2.4).

406   The Spartan navarch Callicratidas sold into slavery the Athenian garrison serving at Methymna on the island of Lesbos. He also auctioned off the slaves whom he captured. However, he resisted appeals from his allies to enslave the inhabitants of the city (Xen. *Hell.* 1.6.15).

405   The Spartan navarch Lysander enslaved the inhabitants of Cedreiae in Caria (Xen. *Hell.* 2.1.15). He also appropriated slaves belonging to the Lampsacenes (Xen. *Hell.* 2.1.18–19) and sold as booty the women and children of Iasus, a *polis* in Caria (D.S. 13.104.7).

404   The Campanians "married" the wives of the inhabitants of Entella, a *polis* in Sicily, after massacring all the men who were liable to military service (D.S. 14.9.9). We do not know what status the women were accorded, though some may have lived in conditions close to slavery.

400   Aristarchus, the Spartan governor of Byzantium, sold 400 of the 10,000 mercenaries who had served in Cyrus the Younger's army because they refused to vacate the city. Cleander, the previous governor, had been looking after the sick and compelling the Byzantines to give them shelter in their homes—seemingly a rare instance of humanitarianism (Xen. *Anab.* 7.2.6). It is possible that Aristarchus sold them to the Persian satrap Pharnabazus, rather than offer them on the open market (Rosivach 1999, 139).

399   Seuthes and Xenophon captured 1,000 Thracians, whom they sold (Xen. *Anab.* 7.3.48, 7.4.2, 7.5.2).

398   The Spartan king Agis appropriated "a vast number of slaves" from Elis (Xen. *Hell.* 3.2.26).

397   The Syracusan tyrant Dionysius I sold as booty the inhabitants of Motya, a stronghold of the Carthaginians (D.S. 14.53.4).

395   Medius, the ruler of Larissa, sold as booty the inhabitants of Pharsalus (D.S. 14.82.6).

The Spartan king Agesilaus displayed for sale naked non-Greek prisoners, whom his army had captured in raiding parties (Xen. *Hell.* 3.4.19).

390 Agesilaus "displayed for purchase" the prisoners he had taken from Piraeum, a peninsula close to the Isthmus of Corinth (Xen. *Hell.* 4.5.8).

389 Agesilaus appropriated "a great many slaves" from the Acarnanians and sold them (Xen. *Hell.* 4.6.6).

387 Dionysius I of Syracuse sold into slavery all of his prisoners from Rhegium who could not pay him one mina as their ransom. They numbered more than 6,000 (D.S. 14.111.4).

384 Dionysius I captured and presumably sold as booty the inhabitants of Agylla (D.S. 15.14.4).

374 The Persians captured and presumably enslaved some Egyptians (D.S. 15.42.5).

373 The Spartan navarch Hypermenes appropriated slaves belonging to the Corcyraeans and "sent them off," presumably for sale (Xen. *Hell.* 6.2.25).

369 The Arcadians enslaved the inhabitants of Pellene (D.S. 15.67.2).

365 After taking 200 prisoners, the Eleans sold into slavery all those who were *xenoi* and slaughtered all those who were exiles. In a separate operation the Argives, Thebans, Arcadians, and Messenians captured over 100 Spartans and *perioikoi* and distributed them evenly among themselves as slaves (Xen. *Hell.* 7.4.26–27).

364 The Thebans sold into slavery the women and children of Orchomenus (D.S. 15.79.6).

ca. 364? Philip II of Macedon "enslaved very many cities" (Theopompus, *FGrH* 115 F 27.3 = Polyb. 8.11.1). His destruction of these cities—over thirty according to Demosthenes (9.26)—was so thorough "that a wayfarer would find it hard to say whether they had ever actually existed."

358/7 Philip II sold the inhabitants of Potidaea into slavery (D.S.16.8.5).

ca. 358/7? Philip II sold the inhabitants of Stagira into slavery, though he later refounded the *polis* as a synoecism "and restored those of its citizens who had either been exiled or enslaved" (Plu. *Alex.* 7.2).

356/5   The mercenary general Nypsius enslaved many Syracusan women and children and appropriated those already enslaved (D.S. 16.19.4).

353/2   The Phocian general Onomarchus enslaved the inhabitants of Thronion, a town of unknown location in Epirus (D.S. 16.33.3). The Athenian general Chares slew the men of military age in Sestus and enslaved the rest (D.S. 16.34.3).

348   Philip II enslaved the inhabitants of Olynthus and sold them as booty (D.S. 16.53.2–3).

346/5   After defeating a band of Elean exiles, the Arcadians and Eleians divided up their captives. This included 4,000 mercenaries, who had been assisting the Elean exiles. The Arcadians sold their share of the captives into slavery, whereas the Eleians, incensed because the mercenaries had plundered the sanctuary at Delphi, executed theirs (D.S. 16.63.5).

344   Philip II captured and enslaved 10,000 Sarnousians, a people living inside the Persian Empire, and deported them to Macedonia (Polyaenus 4.2.12).

340/39   The Corinthian general Timoleon captured "no fewer than 15,000" Carthaginians and presumably enslaved them (D.S. 16.80.5).

335   The Macedonian general Parmenion sold as booty the inhabitants of Grynium, a *polis* on the northwest coast of Anatolia (D.S. 17.7.9).

Alexander the Great sold 30,000 Thebans into slavery for the sum of 440 talents. The only Thebans whom he excluded from this punishment were the priests, the *xenoi* (guest friends) of the Macedonians, and the descendants of the poet Pindar (Din. 1.24; D.S. 17.14.1, 4; Arr. *Anab.* 1.9.9–10; Plu. *Alex.* 11.6).

334   At the battle of the River Granicus, Alexander captured 20,000 Persians, whom he presumably sold as slaves (D.S. 17.21.6). He enchained the Greek mercenaries who had fought in the

battle and sent them to Macedon to do hard labor "because they had fought with barbarians against Greeks" (Arr. *Anab.* 1.16.6). He later enslaved the Persians who had fought to defend Miletus (D.S. 17.22.5).

332   Alexander enslaved the women and children of the Phoenician city of Tyre (D.S. 17.46.4).

330   Alexander enslaved the women of Persepolis (D.S. 17.70.6).

CHRONOLOGY

ca. 770–750 BCE	Al-Mina (modern name of the port, whose ancient name is unknown) is founded at the mouth of the Orontes River in Turkey, possibly as the first Greek *emporion*.
ca. 770	Pithecusae, the island of Ischia in the Bay of Naples, is established by Chalcidians and Eretrians as the earliest Greek overseas settlement in the west.
ca. 750–550	Approximate dates of the so-called Greek age of colonization.
ca. 650	A sizable number of Colophonians and other Ionians partially relocate to Siris in southern Italy.
ca. 621	The Athenian Alcmaeonid *genos* is exiled in perpetuity.
ca. 607/6	The Athenians make an abortive attempt to colonize Sigeum in the Troad.
ca. 555	Voluntary *émigrés* from Athens under Miltiades the Elder settle in the Thracian Chersonese.
ca. 545	The Phocaeans evacuate their city in order to avoid being enslaved by the Persians. A few years later they establish themselves at Elea on the west coast of Italy. The Teans partially relocate to Abdera.
494	The population of Miletus is massacred, enslaved, or resettled on the Erythraean Sea by the Persians.
487	Hipparchus is ostracized from Athens—the first victim of the process.
ca. 485	Gelon, tyrant of Gela, orders the mass transfer of the populations of Gela, Camarina, Megara Hyblaea, and Euboea to Syracuse.
480	The population of Athens is evacuated in advance of the Persian invasion under Xerxes. Themistocles threatens to relocate the *polis* to Siris in south Italy before the Battle of Salamis.

476	Hieron, tyrant of Syracuse, transplants the populations of Naxos and Catania to Leontini and refounds Catania as Aetna.
479	Following their defeat of Persia, the Greeks debate whether to abandon Ionia and resettle its entire population in the west.
ca. 470	Themistocles is ostracized from Athens.
465/4?	Athens sends out 10,000 settlers in a failed attempt to establish a settlement at Ennea Hodoi (Nine Ways). After several other failed attempts, in 437 they found a settlement nearby, which they name Amphipolis.
461	Acragas, Gela, and Himera receive back those exiled during the period of tyrannical rule and expel those who had wrongfully appropriated their dwellings.
457/6?	Athens settles in Naupactus the helots who had revolted from Sparta after the great earthquake.
446	The Athenians found the panhellenic colony of Thurii.
431	In advance of the Peloponnesian invasion Athens's rural population evacuates the countryside and shelters inside the city walls. The Athenians deport the Aeginetans and occupy their island.
429	When their city is being besieged by the Spartans and their allies, 212 Plataean refugees escape to Athens.
427	Megarian oligarchs go into voluntary (or perhaps enforced) exile.
426	The Spartans destroy Plataea. Plataean refugees are given Athenian citizenship.
424	Megarian democrats go into voluntary exile. The historian Thucydides goes into exile.
422	The aristocracy of Leontini, having deported the *dêmos*, migrates to Syracuse and is given citizenship.
ca. 417	Hyperbolus is ostracized from Athens—the last victim of the process.
411	Athens's interim oligarchic government, known as the Four Hundred, exiles a large number of its political opponents.
410/9	Oligarchs flee from Athens after the restoration of democracy in consequence of a decree permitting the killing of those who had participated in the overthrow of democracy by the Four Hundred.

409	The Himerans evacuate half their population on board triremes to Messene; many who cannot be accommodated are either slaughtered or enslaved by the Carthaginians.
406/5	Under siege from the Carthaginians, the people of Acragas are evacuated to Leontini, Syracuse, and southern Italy.
405	Dionysius I, future tyrant of Syracuse, evacuates the populations of Gela and Camarina.
405/4	The Athenians award citizenship to the Samians in recognition of their loyalty during the Peloponnesian War.
405–392	Dionysius I undertakes a mass relocation program in southeast Sicily involving the populations of 14 *poleis*.
404	According to the peace treaty at the end of the Peloponnesian War, the Aeginetans, Melians, and Scionians, whom the Athenians had deported, are permitted to return to their homes. In addition, Athens is required to receive back all its exiles. Most of these are oligarchs, who had been exiled in 411–410. When Athens is taken over by the Thirty Tyrants, many leading democrats flee. Later the Thirty expel an unknown number of democrats, many of whom flee to the Piraeus.
401	Athens passes an amnesty permitting all its political exiles to return. The Persian prince Cyrus the Younger hires 10,000 Greek mercenaries.
395	Dionysius I settles 10,000 mercenaries in Leontini.
379	With Athenian help, returning Theban exiles establish Thebes on a democratic footing and liberate the city from Spartan control.
377–67	Mausolus, satrap of Caria, moves his capital from Mylasa to Halicarnassus by relocating the inhabitants of five of the neighboring towns.
371/370	Mantinea undergoes a resynoecism.
369	The supposed descendants of the helots who revolted from Sparta in 464 found the city of Messene on the slopes of Mount Ithome.
368/7	Megalopolis is founded as a synoecism of twenty Arcadian villages.

ca. 367–54	Dionysius II, tyrant of Syracuse, redistributes populations in thirteen Sicilian *poleis*.
366/5	The inhabitants of Cos relocate from Astypalaea on the southwest tip of their island to a site on the northeastern tip, naming their new city Cos.
365	The Athenians establish a cleruchy on Samos, exiling the entire population.
340	Alexander the Great deports an insurgent people known as the Maedi in the Strymon valley and resettles it with immigrants.
	Timoleon invites 60,000 Greeks to settle in Sicily.
335	Alexander the Great destroys Thebes and drives its entire population into exile.
324	Alexander promulgates the Exiles' Decree, which grants amnesty to all political refugees apart from those who had been exiled as a result of his actions.
333	Greeks who abandoned their settlements in the remotest parts of Alexander's empire are massacred on their way back home.
321	The Samian survivors (and their descendants) return to Samos after 43 years in exile.

GLOSSARY

aeiphugia: the state of being in permanent exile

agêlatein: to expel someone who is polluted

alêtês, alômenos: wanderer

anachôrêsis: relocation

anastasis: return; also expulsion of a people

anastatos: of a people, uprooted, unsettled, expelled; of a town or region, depopulated

andrapodismos: the annihilation and/or enslavement of a population

anistanai: to make a people emigrate; to make suppliant(s) leave a sanctuary

anoikizein: resettle; also, move up country, as in the case of moving away from the sea

anoikos, aoikos: homeless; having no family

apoikia, apoikismos: group of emigrants; foundation consisting of emigrants

apoikos: emigrant

apolis, apopolis, apoptolis, aptolis: one who has no connection with a *polis* either because s/he is an exile or a fugitive or because s/he lives far from a *polis*; a region that is bereft of *poleis* (*aptolis* and *apoptolis* occur mainly in tragedy)

asulia: right of refuge; inviolability of a sanctuary or of an individual in accordance with a treaty or international law (*asulia* means literally "not plundering," viz from a sanctuary)

asulon hieron: part of a sanctuary that afforded temporary protection for a suppliant

atimia: loss of honor; loss of civic rights, often involving exile

dêmos: either the citizen body as a whole or those members of the citizen body who support radical democracy *dikhostasia:* standing apart, dissension, sedition

dioikismos: the state of living apart or in separate communities or villages; the division of a *polis* into its original communities or villages; the opposite of *sunoikismos*

dioikizein: to disperse or cause to live separately

drapetagôgos: one who is employed to recover a runaway slave

drapetês: runaway; commonly, a runaway slave

ekballein: to drive into exile

elaunein: to drive into exile

emporion: a term of doubtful meaning often translated "port of trade"

enoikos: resident, inhabitant

epêlus: immigrant, stranger, foreigner; as opposed to *enoikos*

epidêmeuein: to reside temporarily in a place

epoikos: immigrant; also additional settler—that is, one who becomes a settler after a settlement has already been founded

exoikein: to leave one's home or *oikos* permanently; emigrate

exoikizein: to depart from one's home or *oikos*

exorizein: to drive beyond the borders; expel

hierosulia: the violation of *asulia*

hikesia, hiketeia: supplication

hiketêria: olive branch held by a suppliant

hiketês: suppliant

kataphugas: runaway

kataphugê: place of refuge or, more technically, place of asylum

katelthein: to return from exile

katelthôn: an exile who returns from abroad

kathodos: the return of an exile

katoikos: permanent immigrant (the term commonly used in the hellenistic period)

klêrouchos: one who holds an allotment of land or *klêros* outside his or her native land

ktisma: settlement

ktistês: founder of a settlement

metanastasis: migration

metanastês: migrant

metoikein: to change residence, relocate

metoikêsis: voluntary relocation, often of an entire *polis*; sometimes used as a synonym for *sunoikismos*

metoikos: the preferred Athenian term for a migrant living in Athenian territory for one month at least

mêtropolis: mother-city—that is, a city that sends out a settlement

nostein: to return home

nostos: return home

oikein: to settle, establish one's home

oikistês: leader of pioneering venture to found a new settlement

oikizein: to found a settlement; to resettle or relocate

parepidêmôn: temporary resident in a foreign country

paroikos: long-term immigrant (term commonly used in the hellenistic period)

pheugein: to flee, be in exile

phugadeia: exile or banishment

phugadeion: place of exile or banishment

phugadeuein: to banish; to live in banishment

phugas: fugitive, exile

phugda: in flight (adv.)

phugê: flight, exile

phugimon: place of refuge, asylum

phuza: headlong flight

planês, planêtês, planômenos: traveler, wanderer

poluplanêtos: much-wandering

prostatês: sponsor of long-term immigrant

proxenos: representative and protector of foreign visitors

stasiazô: to be quarrelsome, factious, in a state of *stasis*

stasis: position, state, dissent, discord, faction, sedition, civil strife

sunoikismos: settlement founded by a union between the inhabitants of two or more *poleis*

sunoikizein: to unite into one *polis*; join with others to found a settlement

sunoikos: permanent immigrant; one who joins a settlement on equal terms with its original inhabitants *xenêlasiai:* expulsion of foreigners (noun is usually used in plural as here)

xenia: friendly relations between individuals or states; entertainment given by a host to a guest; guest-friendship

xenos: foreigner, stranger, guest-friend, host, wanderer, refugee; often used in distinction to *astos*, citizen; also used of a mercenary

BIBLIOGRAPHY

A name in square brackets at the end of an entry indicates a collection of sources.

Adler, L. L., and U. P. Gielen, eds. 2003. *Migration: Immigration and Emigration in International Perspective*. Westport, CT, and London: Praeger.

Agnew, V. 2005. *Diaspora, Memory, and Identity*. Toronto: University of Toronto Press.

Amit, M. 1970. "Hostages in ancient Greece." *Rivista di filologia e di istruzione classica* 98, 129–47.

Andreau, J., and R. Descat. 2011. *The Slave in Greece and Rome*. Trans. M. Leopold. Originally published in 2006. Madison: University of Wisconsin Press.

Asheri, D. 1969. "Note on the site of Brea: Theopompus, F 145." *American Journal of Philology* 90, 337–40.

———. 1992. "Sicily, 478–431 BC." In *CAH* V², 147–70.

Asheri, D., A. Lloyd, and A. Corcella. 2007. *A Commentary on Herodotus Books I–IV*. Ed. O. Murray and A. Moreno. 2nd ed. Oxford, UK, and New York: Oxford University Press.

Aubet, M. E. 2012. *Commerce and Colonization in the Ancient Near East*. Trans. M. Turton. Cambridge, UK: Cambridge University Press.

Austin, M. M., ed. 2006. *The Hellenistic World from Alexander to the Roman Conquest: A Selection of Ancient Sources in Translation*. 2nd ed. Cambridge, UK: Cambridge University Press. [Austin].

Austin, M. M., and P. Vidal-Naquet. 1977. *Economic and Social History of Ancient Greece: An Introduction*. London: Batsford.

Badian, E. 1961. "Harpalus." *Journal of Hellenic Studies* 81, 16–43.

———. 1976. "A comma in the history of Samos." *Zeitschrift für Papyrologie und Epigraphik* 23, 289–94.

Balogh, E. 1943. *Political Refugees in Ancient Greece from the Period of the Tyrants to Alexander the Great*. Johannesburg: Witwatersrand University Press.

Barkan, E., and M.-D. Shelton, eds. 1998. *Borders, Exiles, Diasporas*. Stanford, CA: Stanford University Press.

Barrett, W. S. 1964. *Euripides' Hippolytos*. Oxford, UK: Clarendon Press.

Bartels, E. C. "Too many Blackamoors: Deportation, discrimination, and Elizabeth I." *Studies in English Literature 1500–1900* 46(2), 305–22.

Baslez, M.-F. 1984. *L'Étranger dans la Grèce antique*. Paris: Les Belles Lettres.

———. 1996. "Les immigrés orientaux en Grèce. Tolerance et intolerance de la cité." *Cahiers du Centre Gustave Glotz* 7, 39–50.

Bean, G. E. 1980. *Turkey beyond the Meander*. 2nd ed. Revised by S. Mitchell. London: Murray.

Berger, S. 1991. "Great and small *poleis*: Syracuse and Leontini." *Historia* 40, 129–42.

———. 1992. *Revolution and Society in Greek Sicily and Southern Italy*. Stuttgart: Steiner.

Boardman, J. 1999. *The Greeks Overseas*. 4th ed. Ithaca, NY: Cornell University Press.

Boegehold, A. 1994. "Perikles' citizenship law of 451/50 BC." In *Athenian Identity and Civic Ideology*, ed. A. Boegehold and A. C. Scafuro, 57–66. Baltimore: Johns Hopkins University Press.

Bosworth, A. B. 1994. "Alexander the Great. Part 2: Greece and the conquered territories." In *CAH* VI², 846–75.

Bowden, H. 1996. "The Greek settlement at Naucratis: Herodotus and archaeology." In *More Studies on the Ancient Greek Polis*, ed. M. H. Hansen and K. A. Raaflaub, 17–37. Stuttgart: F. Steiner.

Bowie, E. L. 2007. "Early expatriates: Displacement and exile in Archaic poetry." In Gaertner 2007b, 21–50.

Bradley, K., and P. A. Cartledge, eds. 2011. *The Cambridge World History of Slavery: Vol. I, The Ancient Mediterranean World*. Cambridge, UK: Cambridge University Press.

Branham, R. B. 2007. "Exile on Main Street: Citizen Diogenes." In Gaertner 2007b, 71–86.

Braziel, J. E., and A. Mannur, eds. 2003. *Theorizing Diaspora: A Reader*. Malden, MA and Oxford, UK: Blackwell Publishing.

Brenne, S. 2002. "Die Ostrake (487–ca. 416 v. Chr.) als Testimonien (T1)." In *Ostrakismos-Testimonien*, vol. I (= *Historia Einzelschriften* 155), ed. P. Siewert, S. Brenne, B. Eder, H. Heftner, and W. Scheidel, 36–166. Stuttgart: F. Steiner.

Brock, R., and S. Hodkinson, eds. 2000. *Alternatives to Athens: Varieties of Political Organization and Community in Ancient Greece*. Oxford, UK: Oxford University Press.

Brubaker, R. 2005. "The 'diaspora' diaspora." *Ethnic and Racial Studies* 28(1), 1–19.

Brunt, P. A. 1966. "Athenian settlements abroad in the fifth century BC." In *Ancient Society and Institutions: Studies Presented to Victor Ehrenberg on his 75th Birthday*, ed. E. Badian, 71–92. Oxford, UK: Blackwell.

Burford, A. 1969. *The Greek Temple Builders at Epidaurus*. Liverpool: Liverpool University Press.

———. 1972. *Craftsmen in Greek and Roman Society*. London: Thames and Hudson.

Burkert, W. 1992. *The Orientalizing Revolution: Near Eastern Influence on Greek Culture in the Early Archaic Age*. Trans. M. E. Pinder and W. Burkert. Cambridge, MA: Harvard University Press.

CAF. 1800–88. *Comicorum Atticorum Fragmenta*. Ed. T. Kock. 3 vols. Leipzig: Teubner.

CAH III.3². 1982. *Cambridge Ancient History: The Expansion of the Greek World, Eighth to Sixth Centuries BC*. 2nd ed. Ed. J. Boardman and N.G.L. Hammond. Cambridge, UK: Cambridge University Press.

CAH V². 1992. *Cambridge Ancient History: The Fifth Century BC*. 2nd ed. Ed. D. M. Lewis, J. Boardman, J. K. Davies, and M. Ostwald. Cambridge, UK: Cambridge University Press.

CAH VI². 1994. *Cambridge Ancient History: The Fourth Century BC*. 2nd ed. Ed. D. M. Lewis, J. Boardman, S. Hornblower, and M. Ostwald. Cambridge, UK: Cambridge University Press.

Camp, J. M. 1979. "A drought in the late eighth century BC." *Hesperia* 48, 397–411.

Campbell, D. A. 1982. *Greek Lyric*. 3 vols. Cambridge, MA: Harvard University Press. [Campbell].

Canciani, F., E. Pellizer, and L. Faedo. 2005 "*Hikesia/Hikésie/Hikesie/Hikesia*." In *ThesCRA* III, 193–216.

Cartledge, P. A. 1985. "Rebels and Sambos in Classical Greece: A comparative view." *Crux: Essays Presented to G.E.M. Croix on His 75th Birthday*, 16–46. Exeter, UK: Imprint Academic.

———. 2002. *Sparta and Lakonia*. 2nd ed. London and New York: Routledge.

———. 2004. *Alexander the Great*. Woodstock, NY, and New York: Overlook Press.

———. 2009. *Ancient Greece: A History in Eleven Cities*. Oxford, UK, and New York: Oxford University Press.

Cartwright, D. 1997. *A Historical Commentary on Thucydides: A Companion to Rex Warner's Penguin Translation*. Ann Arbor: University of Michigan Press.

Caven, B. 1990. *Dionysius I: Warlord of Sicily*. New Haven, CT: Yale University Press.

Cawkwell, G. 1992. "Early colonisation." *Classical Quarterly* 42, 289–303.

Chadwick, J. 1976. "Who were the Dorians?" *La Parola del Passata* 31, 103–17.

Chaniotis, A. 1996. "Conflicting authorities: *Asylia* between secular and divine law in the Classical and Hellenistic Poleis." *Kernos* 9, 65–86.

Christensen, K.A. 1984. "The Theseion: A slave refuge at Athens." *American Journal of Ancient History* 9, 23–32.

Cieslik, T., D. Felsen, and A. Kalaitzidis, eds. 2009. *Immigration: A Documentary and Reference Guide*. Westport, CT: Greenwood Press.

Clerc, M. 1893 [1979]. *Les métèques athéniens*. Paris: Thorin.

Cohen, E. E. 2000. *The Athenian Nation*. Princeton, NJ: Princeton University Press.

Cohn-Haft, L. 1956. *The Public Physicians of Ancient Greece*. Northampton, MA: Dept. of History of Smith College.

Coja, M. 1990. "Greek colonists and native populations in Dobruja (Moesia Inferior): The archaeological evidence." In Descoeudres 1990, 157–68.

Coldstream, J. N. 1994. "Prospectors and pioneers: Pithekoussai, Kyme, and Central Italy." In Tsetskhladze and De Angelis 1994, 47–59.

Colledge, M. 1987. "Greek and non-Greek interaction in art and architecture." In *Hellenism in the East*, ed. A. Kuhrt and S. Sherwin-White, 134–62. Berkeley: University of California Press.

Cook, J. M. 1982. "The eastern Greeks." In *CAH* III.3², 196–221.

Damsgaard-Madsen, A. 1988. "Attic funeral inscriptions: Their use as historical sources and some preliminary results." In *Studies in Ancient History and Numismatics Presented to R. Thomsen*, ed. E. Christiansen, A. Damsgaard-Madsen, and E. Hallager, 55–68. Copenhagen: Aarhus University Press.

Davies, J. K. 1993. *Democracy and Classical Greece*. 2nd ed. Cambridge, MA: Harvard University Press.

Davis, N. 1967. *Greek Coins and Cities: Illustrated from the Collection at the Seattle Art Museum*. London: Spink.

Delekat, L. 1964. *Katoche, Hierodulie und Adoptionsfreilassung*. Munich: Beck.

Delekat, L. 1967. *Asylie und Schutzorakel am Zionheiligtum*. Leiden: E. J. Brill.

Demand, N. H. 1988. "Herodotus and metoikesis in the Persian Wars." *American Journal of Philology* 109(3), 416–23.

———. 1990. *Urban Relocation in Archaic and Classical Greece: Flight and Consolidation*. Norman: University of Oklahoma Press.

Demetriou, D. 2012. *Negotiating Identity in the Ancient Mediterranean: The Archaic and Classical Greek Multiethnic Emporia*. Cambridge, UK: Cambridge University Press.

Descoeudres, J.-P., and A. D. Trendall, eds. 1990. *Greek Colonists and Native Populations* (= *Proceedings of the First Australian Congress of Classical Archaeology*). Oxford, UK: Clarendon Press.

De Souza, P. 1999. *Piracy in the Graeco-Roman World*. Cambridge, UK: Cambridge University Press.

De Ste. Croix, G.E.M. 1983. *The Class Struggle in the Ancient Greek World*. Corrected edition. London and Ithaca, NY: Duckworth.

Detienne, M. 2001–2002. "The art of founding autochthony: Thebes, Athens, and oldstock French." *Arion* 9 (1), 46–55.

Diels, H. and W. Krantz. 1964. *Die Fragmente der Vorsokratiker*. 3 vols. Zurich and Berlin: Weidmannsche Verl. [*DK*].

Diener, A. C., and J. Hagen. 2012. *Borders: A Very Short Introduction*. Oxford, UK: Oxford University Press.

Dillery, J. 2007. "Exile: The making of the Greek historian." In Gaertner 2007b, 51–70.

Domínguez, A. J. 2006. "Greeks in the Iberian peninsula." In Tsetskhladze 2006, 429–505.

Dougherty, C. 1993. "It's murder to found a colony." In *Cultural Poetics in Archaic Greece: Cult, Performance, Politics*, ed. C. Dougherty and L. Kurke, 179–98. Cambridge, UK: Cambridge University Press.

Douglas, R. M. 2012. *Orderly and Humane: The Expulsion of the Germans after the Second World War*. New Haven, CT: Yale University Press.

Dreher, M., ed. 2003. *Das Antike Asyl. Kultische Grundlagen, Rechtliche Ausgestaltung und Politische Funktion*. Cologne: Bohlau.

Ducrey, P. 1968. *Le traitement des prisonniers de guerre dans la Grèce antique*. Paris: E. de Boccard.

Dummett, M. 2001. *On Immigration and Refugees*. London and New York: Routledge.

Dunbabin, T. J. 1948. *The Western Greeks*. Oxford: Clarendon Press.

Duncan-Jones, R. P. 1980. "Metic numbers in Periclean Athens." *Chiron* 10, 101–9.

Figueira, T. J. 1991. *Athens and Aigina in the Age of Imperial Colonization*. Baltimore: Johns Hopkins University Press.

Finley, M. I. 1976. "An attempt at a typology." *Transactions of the Royal Historical Society* 5(26), 167–88.

———. 1979. *A History of Sicily: Ancient Sicily to the Arab Conquest*. 2nd ed. London and New York: Chatto and Windus.

———. 2002. *The World of Odysseus*. Introduction by B. Knox. 2nd ed. London and New York: New York Review Books.

Fisher, N. 1993. *Slavery in Classical Greece*. London: Bristol Classical Press.

Fisher, N., and H. van Wees, eds. 1998. *Archaic Greece: New Approaches and New Evidence*. London: Duckworth; Oakville, CT: D. Brown Book Co.

Flower, M. A. 2008. *The Seer in Ancient Greece*. Berkeley: University of California Press.

Fornara, C. W., ed. 1983. *Archaic Times to the End of the Peloponnesian War* (= *Translated Documents of Greece and Rome*, vol. 1). 2nd ed. Cambridge, UK: Cambridge University Press. [Fornara].

Forsdyke, S. 2005. *Exile, Ostracism, and Democracy: The Politics of Expulsion in Ancient Greece*. Princeton, NJ, and London: Princeton University Press.

———. 2012. *Slaves Tell Tales: And Other Episodes in the Politics of Popular Culture in Ancient Greece*. Princeton, NJ, and London: Princeton University Press.

Fraser, P. M. 1995. "Citizens, demesmen and metics in Athens and elsewhere," In *Sources for the Ancient Greek City-State*, ed. M. H. Hansen, 64–90. Copenhagen: Munksgaard.

———. 1996. *The Cities of Alexander the Great*. Oxford, UK: Clarendon Press.

Freyburger, G. 1988. "Supplication grecque et supplication romaine." *Latomus* 47, 501–25.

Frost, F. 1980. *Plutarch's Themistocles*. Princeton, NJ: Princeton University Press.

Fuks, A. 1972. "Isocrates and the social-economic situation in Greece." *Ancient Society* 3, 17–44.

Gaertner, J. F. 2007a. "The discourse of displacement in Greco-Roman antiquity." In Gaertner 2007b, 1–20.

———, ed. 2007b. *Writing Exile: The Discourse of Displacement in Greco-Roman Antiquity and Beyond* (= *Mnemosyne, Bibliotheca Classica*, Supplement, vol. 283). Leiden: Brill.

Garlan, Y. 1989. *Guerre et économie en Grèce ancienne*. Paris: Editions La Decouverte.

Garland, R.S.J. 2001. *The Piraeus*. 2nd ed. London and Bristol, UK: Bristol Classical Press.

———. 2006. *Celebrities in Antiquity: From Media Tarts to Tabloid Queens*. London: Duckworth.

———. 2010. *The Eye of the Beholder: Deformity and Disability in the Graeco-Roman World*. 2nd ed. London: Bristol Classical Press.

Gauthier, P. 1972. *Symbola: les étrangers et la justice dans les cités grecques*. Nancy: Université de Nancy.

———. 1976. *Un Commentaire Historique des "Poroi" de Xénophon*. Paris: Minard.

Gehrke, H.-J. 1985. *Stasis: Untersuchungen zu den inneren Kriegen in den griechischen Staaten des 5.und 4. Jahrhunderts v. Chr.* Munich: Beck.

GGM. 1885–61. *Geographici Graeci Minores*. Ed. C. Müller. Paris; republished 2010, Cambridge, UK: Cambridge University Press.

Gibney, M. 2009. "Refugees." In *Encyclopedia of Human Rights*, ed. D. P. Forsythe, 315–22. Oxford, UK: Oxford University Press.

Goldin, I., G. Cameron, and M. Balarajan. 2011. *Exceptional People: How Migration Shaped Our World and Will Define Our Future*. Princeton, NJ: Princeton University Press.

Gomme, A. W. 1945. *A Historical Commentary on Thucydides*, vol. 1. Oxford, UK: Clarendon Press.

Gould, J. 1973. "*Hiketeia*." *Journal of Hellenic Studies* 93, 74–103.

Graham, A. J. 1980–81 [1984]. "Religion, women and Greek colonization." In *Atti del Centro di ricerche e di documentazione sull' antichità classica* 11 (= *Religione e città nel mondo antico*), 293–314. Rome: "L'Erma" di Bretschneider.

———. 1982a. "The colonial expansion of Greece." In *CAH* III.3², 83–162.

———. 1982b. "The western Greeks." In *CAH* III.3², 163–95.

———. 1983. *Colony and Mother City in Ancient Greece*. Revised edition. Chicago: Ares.

———. 1990. "Pre-colonial contacts: questions and problems." In Descoeudres 1990, 45–60.

Grasmück, E. L. 1978. *Exilium: Untersuchungen zur Verbannung in der Antike*. Paderborn: Schoningh.

Green, P. 1996 [1970]. *The Greco-Persian Wars*. Revised edition. Berkeley: University of California Press.

Griffith, G. T. 1935. *The Mercenaries of the Hellenistic World*. Cambridge, MA: Cambridge University Press.

Gruen, E. 2002. *Diaspora: Jews amidst Greeks and Romans*. Cambridge, MA, and London: Harvard University Press.

Guido, M. 1967. *Sicily: An Archaeological Guide*. New York: Praeger.

Habicht, C. 1957. "Samische Volksbeschlussen der hellenistischen Zeit." *Mitteilungen des Deutschen Archäologischen Instituts, Athenische Abteilung* 72, 152–237.

———. 1966. "Athens, Samos, and Alexander the Great." *Proceedings of the American Philological Society* 140, 397–405.

———. 1997. *Athens from Alexander to Antony*. Cambridge, MA, and London: Harvard University Press.

Haley, J. B., and C. Blegen. 1928. "The coming of the Greeks." *American Journal of Archaeology* 32, 141–54.

Hall, E. 1989. *Inventing the Barbarian: Greek Self-Definition through Tragedy*. Oxford, UK: Clarendon Press.

Hall, J. M. 1997. *Ethnic Identity in Greek Antiquity*. Cambridge, UK, and New York: Cambridge University Press.

———. 2002. *Hellenicity: Between Ethnicity and Culture*. Chicago: University of Chicago Press.

———. 2007. *A History of the Archaic Greek World ca. 1200–479 BCE*. Oxford, UK: Blackwell.

———. 2009. "Ethnicity and cultural exchange." In Raaflaub and van Wees 2009, 604–17.

Hammond, N.G.L. 1967. *Epirus*. Oxford, UK: Clarendon Press.

Hands, A. R. 1968. *Charities and Social Aid in Greece and Rome*. London and Ithaca, NY: Cornell University Press.

Hansen, M. H. 1976. *Apagoge, Endeixis, and Ephegesis against Kakourgoi, Atimoi, and Pheugontes*. Odense: Odense University Press.

———. 2004. "*Emporium*: A study of the use and meaning of the term in the archaic and classical periods." In Tsetskhladze 2006, 6–39.

Hansen, M. H., and T. H. Nielsen, eds. 2004. *An Inventory of Archaic and Classical Poleis*. Oxford, UK: Oxford University Press.

Hanson, V. D. 2005. *A War Like No Other: How the Athenians and Spartans Fought the Peloponnesian War.* New York: Random House.

Harding, P., ed. 1985. *From the End of the Peloponnesian War to the Battle of Ipsus* (= *Translated Documents of Greece and Rome,* vol. 2). Cambridge, UK: Cambridge University Press. [Harding].

Heckel, W., and J. C. Yardley, eds. (2004). *Alexander the Great: Historical Sources in Translation.* Oxford, UK: Blackwell Publishing.

Heckel, W., and L. A. Tritle, eds. 2011. *Alexander the Great: A New History.* Chichester, UK, and Malden, MA: Wiley Blackwell.

Heisserer, A. J. 1980. *Alexander the Great and the Greeks: The Epigraphic Evidence.* Norman: University of Oklahoma Press.

Hense, O. 1909. *Teletis Reliquiae.* 2nd ed. Tübingen: P. Siebeck.

Herman, G. 1987. *Ritualised Friendship and the Greek City.* Cambridge, UK: Cambridge University Press.

Higbie, C. 2003. *The Lindian Chronicle and the Greek Creation of Their Past.* Oxford, UK: Oxford University Press.

Hobsbawm, E., and T. Ranger, eds. 1983. *The Invention of Tradition.* Cambridge, UK: Cambridge University Press.

Hodos, T. 1999. "Intermarriage in the western Greek colonies." *Oxford Journal of Archaeology* 118 (1), 61–78.

Hooker, J. T. 1979. "New reflections on the Dorian Invasion." *Klio* 61, 353–60.

Horden, P., and N. Purcell 2000. *The Corrupting Sea: A Study of Mediterranean History.* London: Blackwell.

Hornblower, S. 1982. *Mausolus.* Oxford, UK: Clarendon Press.

———. 1994. "Asia Minor." In *CAH* VI², 209–33.

———. 1997. *A Commentary on Thucydides, Volume I: Books I–III.* Revised edition. Oxford, UK: Clarendon Press.

———. 2004. *A Commentary on Thucydides, Volume II: Books IV–V.24.* Revised edition. Oxford, UK: Clarendon Press.

———. 2008. *A Commentary on Thucydides, Volume III: Books V.25–VIII.109.* Oxford, UK: Clarendon Press.

———. 2011. *The Greek World, 479–323.* 4th ed. London and New York: Routledge.

Human Development Report. 2009. *Overcoming Barriers—Human Mobility and Development.* Ed. United Nations Development Program. New York: Palgrave Macmillan.

Hunt, A. S., and C. C. Edgar, eds. 1963. *Select Papyri,* vol. 2. Cambridge, MA: Harvard University Press. [Hunt and Edgar].

Isaac, B. 2004. *The Invention of Racism in Classical Antiquity.* Princeton, NJ: Princeton University Press.

IEG. 1980. *Delectus ex Iambis et Elegis Graecis.* Ed. M. L. West. Oxford, UK: Clarendon Press.

Jameson, M. H. 1983. "Famine in the Greek World." In *Trade and Famine in Classical Antiquity* (= *Cambridge Philological Society,* suppl. vol. 8), ed. P. Garnsey and C. R. Whittaker, 6–16. Cambridge, UK: Cambridge Philological Society.

Johansen, H. F., and E. W. Whittle. 1980. *Aeschylus: The Suppliants.* 4 vols. Copenhagen: Glydendal.

Johnston, S. I. 2008. *Ancient Greek Divination*. Malden, MA, and Oxford, UK: Wiley Blackwell.

Johnston, S. I., and P. T. Struck, eds. 2005. *Mantikê: Studies in Ancient Divination*. Leiden: Brill.

Koch, C. 1991. *Volksbeschlüsse in Seebundsangelegenheiten: Das Verfahrensrecht Athens im ersten attischen Seebund*. Frankfurt, New York, and Paris: P. Lang.

Koser, K. 2007. *International Migration: A Very Short Introduction*. Oxford, UK: Oxford University Press.

Krentz, P. 1980. "Foreigners against the Thirty." *Phoenix* 34, 298–306.

———. 1982. *The Thirty at Athens*. Ithaca, NY, and London: Cornell University Press.

Kudlien, F. 1988. "Zur sozialen Situation des flüchtigen Sklaven in der Antike." *Hermes* 116, 232–52.

Kuhn, E. 1878. *Über die Entstehung der Städte der Alten, Komenverfassung und Synoikismos*. Leipzig: Teubner.

Kuhrt, A., and S. Sherwin-White, eds. 1987. *Hellenism in the East*. Berkeley: University of California Press.

Kurke, L. 1999. *Coins, Bodies, Games, and Gold*. Princeton, NJ: Princeton University Press.

Lane Fox, R. 2000. "Theognis: An alternative to democracy." In Brock and Hodkinson 2000, 35–51.

Lape, S. 2010. *Race and Citizen Identity in the Classical Athenian Democracy*. Cambridge, UK: Cambridge University Press.

Larsen, J.A.O. 1968. *Greek Federal States*. Oxford, UK: Clarendon Press.

Lattimore, R. 1965. *The Odyssey of Homer*. Translated with introduction. New York: HarperCollins.

Lee, J.W.I. 2007. *A Greek Army on the March*. Cambridge, UK: Cambridge University Press.

Legon, R. P. 1981. *Megara: The Political History of a Greek City-State to 336 BC*. Ithaca, NY, and London: Cornell University Press.

Lemos, I. 2007. "The Migrations to the west coast of Asia Minor: tradition and Archaeology." In *Milesische Forschungen*, ed. J. Cobet, V. von Grave, W.-D. Niemeier, and K. Zimmermann, 713–27. Berlin: Deutsches Archäologisches Institut.

Lévi-Strauss, C. 1962. *The Savage Mind*. English translation of *La Pensée sauvage*, 1966. London and Chicago: University of Chicago Press.

Lévy, E. 1987. "Métèques et droit de résidence." In *L'étranger dans le monde grec*, ed. R. Lonis, 47–67. Nancy: Presses Universitaires de Nancy.

Lewis, D. M. 1992. "Mainland Greece, 479–451 BC." In *CAH* V², 96–120.

Lintott, A. W. 1982. *Violence, Civil Strife, and Revolution in the Classical City, 750–330 BC*. London: Croon Helm.

Lomas, K. 2000. "The *polis* in Italy: Ethnicity, colonization, and citizenship in the western Mediterranean." In Brock and Hodkinson 2000, 167–85.

———. 2006. "Tyrants and the *polis*: Migration, identity and urban development in Sicily." In *Ancient Tyranny*, ed. S. Lewis, 95–118. Edinburgh: Edinburgh University Press.

Londy, P. 1990. "Greek colonists and Delphi." In Descoeudres 1990, 117–27.

Long, L. D., and E. Oxfeld, eds. 2004. *Coming Home? Refugees, Migrants, and Those Who Stayed Behind*. Philadelphia: University of Pennsylvania Press.

Lonis, R. 1991. "La réintégration des exiles politiques en Grèce: la problème des biens." In *Hellenika Symmeikta: Histoire, Archéologie, Epigraphie* (= *Étude d'Archéologie Classique* 7), ed. P. Goukowsky and C. Brixhe, 91–109. Nancy: Brill.

López, I. H. 2006. *White by Law: The Legal Construction of Race*. New York and London: New York University Press.

Loraux, N. 1986. *The Invention of Athens*. Trans. A. Sheridan. Cambridge, MA: Harvard University Press.

———. 2000. *Born of the Earth: Myth and Politics in Athens*. Trans. S. Stewart. Ithaca, NY: Cornell University Press.

———. 2002. *The Divided City: On Memory and Forgetting in Ancient Athens*. Trans. C. Pache and J. Fort. New York: Zone Books.

Losada, L. A. 1972. *The Fifth Column in the Peloponnesian War*. Leiden: Brill.

LSJ⁹. 1996. *Greek-English Dictionary*. 9th. ed. Ed. H. G. Liddell and R. Scott. Oxford, UK: Clarendon Press.

Luraghi, N. 2008. *The Ancient Messenians: Constructions of Ethnicity and Memory*. Cambridge, UK, and New York: Cambridge University Press.

MacDonald, B. R. 1981. "The emigration of potters from Athens in the late fifth century BC and its effect on the Attic pottery industry." *American Journal of Archaeology* 85(2), 159–68.

MacDowell, D. M. 1963. *Athenian Homicide Law in the Age of the Orators*. Manchester, UK: Sandpiper Books.

———. 1978. *The Law in Classical Athens*. London and Ithaca, NY: Thames and Hudson and Cornell University Press.

Maffi, A. 2003. "L'asilo degli schiavi nel diritto di Gortina." In Dreher 2003, 15–22.

Malkin, I. 1987. *Religion and Colonization in Ancient Greece* (= *Studies in Greek and Roman Religion*). Leiden: Brill.

———. 1994. *Myth and Territory in the Spartan Mediterranean*. Cambridge, UK: Cambridge University Press.

———. 2009. "Foundations." In Raaflaub and van Wees 2009, 373–94.

———. 2011. *A Small Greek World: Networks in the Ancient Mediterranean*. Oxford, UK: Oxford University Press.

Marinatos, N., and R. Hägg, eds. 1993. *Greek Sanctuaries: New Approaches*. London and New York: Routledge.

Marinovic, L. P. 1988. *Le mercenariat grec au IVe siècle avant notre ère et la crise de la polis*. Paris: Belle Lettres.

Mattingly, H. B. 1996. *The Athenian Empire Restored: Epigraphic and Historical Studies*. Ann Arbor: University of Michigan Press.

McKechnie, P. 1989. *Outsiders in the Greek Cities in the Fourth Century BC*. London and New York: Routledge.

McKeown, N. 2011. "Resistance among chattel slaves in the Classical Greek world." In Bradley and Cartledge 2011, 153–75.

Meyer, E. A. 2010. *Metics and the Athenian Phialai Inscriptions: A Study in Epigraphy and Law*. Stuttgart: Steiner.

Meyer, M. W. 1987. *The Ancient Mysteries: A Sourcebook*. New York: Harper Collins.

ML. 1988. *A Selection of Greek Historical Inscriptions to the End of the Fifth Century BC*. Revised edition. Ed. R. Meiggs and D. Lewis. Oxford, UK: Clarendon Press.

Montiglio, S. 2005. *Wandering in Ancient Greek Culture*. Chicago: University of Chicago Press.

Moore, J. M. 1975. *Aristotle and Xenophon on Democracy and Oligarchy*. London: Chatto and Windus.

Morel, J.-P. 2006. "Phocaean colonisation." In Tsetskhladze 2006, 358–428.

Moreno, A. 2009. "'The Attic neighbour': The cleruchy in the Athenian Empire." In *Interpreting the Athenian Empire*, ed. J. Ma, N. Papazarkadas, and R. Parker, 211–22. London: Duckworth.

Murray, G. 1934. *The Rise of the Greek Epic*. 4th ed. Oxford, UK: Oxford University Press.

Naiden, F. S. 2006. *Ancient Supplication*. Oxford, UK: Oxford University Press.

Nesselrath, H.-G. 2007. "Later Greek voices on the predicament of exile: from Teles to Plutarch and Favorinus." In Gaertner 2007b, 87–108.

Newman, E. 2003. "Refugees, international security, and human vulnerability: introduction and survey." In *Refugees and Forced Displacement: International Security, Human Vulnerability, and the State*, ed. E. Newman and J. van Selm, 3–30. Tokyo: United Nations University Press.

OCD⁴. 2012. *Oxford Classical Dictionary*. 4th ed. Ed. A. Spawforth, S. Hornblower, and E. Eidinow. Oxford, UK: Oxford Classical Press.

Ogilvie, R. M. 1965. *A Commentary on Livy Books 1–5*. Oxford, UK: Clarendon Press.

Osanna, M. 1992. *Chorai coloniali da Taranto a Locri: Documentazione archeologica e ricostruzione storica*. Rome: Istituto poligrafico e zecca dello Stato, Libreria dello Stato.

———. 1996. *Santuari e culti dell'Acaia antica*. Naples: Edizioni scientifiche italiane.

Osborne, R. 1985. *Demos: The Discovery of Classical Attika*. Cambridge, UK: Cambridge University Press.

———. 1991. "The potential mobility of human populations." *Oxford Journal of Archaeology* 10, 231–52. Reprinted in R. Osborne, *Athens and Athenian Democracy*, 139–67. Cambridge, UK: Cambridge University Press 2010.

———. 1998. "Early Greek colonization? The nature of Greek settlement in the west." In Fisher and van Wees 1998, 251–69.

———. 2009. *Greece in the Making 1200–479 BC*. 2nd ed. London and New York: Routledge.

Osborne, R., and B. Cunliffe, eds. 2005. *Mediterranean Urbanization 800–600 BC*. Oxford: Oxford University Press for the British Academy.

Page, D. L., ed. (1941). *Select Papyri, vol. 3: Poetry*. Cambridge, MA: Harvard University Press. [Page].

Panagopoulos, A. (1978). *Captives and Hostages in the Peloponnesian War*. Athens: Grigoris Publications.

Papastergiadis, N. 1998. *Dialogues in the Diasporas: Essays and Conversations on Cultural Identity*. London and New York: Rivers Oram Press; distributed in the United States by New York University Press.

Parke, H. W. 1933. *Greek Mercenary Soldiers: From the Earliest Times to the Battle of Ipsus*. Oxford, UK: Clarendon Press.

Parker, R. 1983 [1996]. *Miasma: Purification and Pollution in Early Greek Religion*. Oxford, UK: Clarendon Press.

Pedrick, V. 1982. "Supplication in the *Iliad* and the *Odyssey.*" *Transactions of the American Philological Association* 112, 125–40.

Perlman, S. 1976–77. "The Ten Thousand: A chapter in the military, social and economic history of the fourth century." *Rivista Storica Italiana* 6–7, 241–84.

Phillips, D. 2008. *Avengers of Blood: Homicide in Athenian Law from Draco to Demosthenes* (= *Historia Einzelschriften* 202). Stuttgart: Steiner.

Poddighe, E. 2011. "Alexander and the Greeks: the Corinthian League." In Heckel and Tritle 2011, 99–120.

Popham, M. 1994. "Precolonization: Early Greek contact with the East." In Tsetskhladze and De Angelis 1994, 11–34.

Price, M. J. 1991. *The Coinage in the Name of Alexander the Great and Philip Arrhidaeus*. 2 vols. London and Zurich: The Trustees of the British Museum.

Pritchett, W. K. 1991. *The Greek State at War*, Part V. Berkeley and Los Angeles: University of California Press.

Poussou, J.-P. 1994. "De l'intérêt de l'étude historique des mouvements migratoires européens du milieu du moyen âge à la fin du XIXe siècle." In *Le migrazioni in Europa, sec. XIII–XVIII*, ed. D. Cavaciocchi, 21–43. Florence: Le Monier.

Purcell, N. 1990. "Mobility and the polis." In *The Greek City: From Homer to Aristotle*, ed. O. Murray and S. Price, 29–58. Oxford, UK, and New York: Clarendon Press.

Queyrel Bottineau, A. 2010. *Prodosia: La notion et l'acte de trahison dans l'Athènes du Ve siècle: Recherche sur la construction de l'identité athénienne*. Bordeaux: Ausonius.

Quinn, T. J. 1981. *Athens and Samos, Lesbos and Chios 478–404 BC*. Manchester, UK: Manchester University Press.

Raaflaub, K. 1991. "City-state, territory and empire in classical antiquity." In *City States in Classical Antiquity and Medieval Italy: Athens and Rome, Florence and Venice*, ed. J. Emlen, A. Molho, and K. A. Raaflaub, 565–88. Ann Arbor: University of Michigan Press.

Raaflaub, K. A., and H. van Wees, eds. 2009. *A Companion to Archaic Greece*. Oxford, UK: Wiley-Blackwell.

RE. 1883–1980. *Paulys Realenencyclopädie der classischen Altertumswissenschaft*. Stuttgart: Metzler.

Rhodes, P. J. 1992. "The Delian League to 449 BC." In *CAH* V², 34–61.

———. 1993. *A Commentary on the Aristotelian Athenaion Politeia*. Revised edition. Oxford, UK, and New York: Oxford University Press.

Rhodes, P. J., and R. Osborne, eds. 2003. *Greek Historical Inscriptions 404–323 BC*. Oxford, UK: Oxford University Press. [Rhodes and Osborne].

Ridgway, D. 1992. *The First Western Greeks*. Cambridge, UK: Cambridge University Press.

———. 1994. "Phoenicians and Greeks in the west: A view from Pithekoussai." In Tsetskhladze and De Angelis 1994, 35–46.

Romm, J. S. 1992. *The Edges of the Earth in Ancient Thought: Geography, Exploration and Fiction*. Princeton, NJ: Princeton University Press.

Roos, A. G. 1968. *Flavii Arriani Quae Exstant Omnia*, vol. II. New edition edited by G. Wirth. Leipzig: Teubner.

Rose, V. 1886. *Aristotelis Qui Ferebantur Librorum Fragmenta*. Leipzig: Teubner. [Rose].

Rosivach, V. J. 1987. "Autochthony and the Athenians." *Classical Quarterly* 37, 294–306.

———. 1999. "Enslaving *barbaroi* and the Athenian ideology of slavery." *Historia* 48(2), 129–57.

Roy, J. 1967. "The mercenaries of Cyrus." *Historia* 16, 287–323.

Saggar, S. 2003. "Immigration and the politics of public opinion." In *The Politics of Migration: Managing Opportunity, Conflict, and Change*, ed. S. Spencer, 178–94. Oxford, UK, and Malden, MA: Wiley-Blackwell.

Salomon, N. 1997. *Le cleruchie di Atene: caratteri e funzione*. Pisa: Edizioni ETS.

Schaefer, H. 1960. "Eigenart und Wesenszüge der griechischen Kolonisation." *Heidelberger Jahrbücher* 4, 77–93.

Scheffer, P. 2011. *Immigrant Nations*. Trans. L. Waters. Cambridge, UK, and Malden, MA: Polity.

Schlunk, R. R. 1976. "The theme of the suppliant-exile in the *Iliad*." *American Journal of Philology* 97, 199–209.

Schumacher, R.W.M. 1993. "Three related sanctuaries of Poseidon: Geraistos, Kalaureia and Tainaron." In Marinatos and Hägg 1993, 62–87.

Segal, U. A., D. Elliot, and N. S. Mayadas, eds. 2010. *Immigration Worldwide: Policies, Practices, and Trends*. Oxford, UK: Oxford University Press.

Seibert, J. 1979. *Die politischen Flüchtlinge und Verbannten in der griechische Geschichte*. Darmstadt: Wissenschaftliche Buchgesellschaft.

Shipley, G. 1987. *A History of Samos 800–188 BC*. Oxford, UK: Clarendon Press.

*SIG*³. 1915–24. *Sylloge Inscriptionum Graecarum*. 3rd ed. Ed. W. Dittenberger. Leipzig.

Sinn, U. 1990. "Das Heraion von Perachora. Eine sakrale Schutzzone in der korinthischen Peraia." *Mitteilungen des Deutschen Archäologischen Instituts, Athenische Abteilung* 105, 53–116.

———. 1993. "Greek sanctuaries as places of refuge." In Marinatos and Hägg 1993, 88–109.

———. 2003. "Das Poseidonheligtum auf Kalaureia: Ein archäologischer Befund zum antiken Asylwesen." In Dreher 2003a, 107–25.

———. 2005. "*Asylie*." In *ThesCRA* III, 217–36.

Sjöqvist, E. 1973. *Sicily and the Greeks: Studies in the Interrelationship Between the Indigenous Populations and the Greek Colonies*. Ann Arbor, MI: University of Michigan Press.

Snodgrass, A. 2000. *The Dark Age of Greece*. First published in 1971 and reissued with foreword. Edinburgh: Edinburgh University Press.

Sommerstein, A. H. 1997. "Audience, *dêmos*, and Aeschylus' *Suppliants*." In *Greek Tragedy and the Historian*, ed. C. Pelling, 63–79. Oxford, UK: Oxford University Press.

Strauss, B. 2004. *The Battle of Salamis*. New York: Simon and Schuster.

Stroheker, K. F. 1958. *Dionysios I: Gestalt und Geschichte des Tyrannen von Syrakus*. Wiesbaden: Steiner.

Syme, R. 1962. "Lecture on a mastermind: Thucydides." *Proceedings of the British Academy* 48, 39–56.

Talbert, R.J.A. 1974. *Timoleon and the Revival of Sicily, 344–317 BC.* Cambridge, UK: Cambridge University Press.

Tandy, D. W. 1997. *Warriors and Traders: The Power of the Market in Early Greece.* Berkeley and Los Angeles: University of California Press.

TGF. 1887. *Tragicorum Graecorum Fragmenta.* 2nd ed. Ed. A. Nauck. Leipzig: Teubner.

ThesCRA III. 2005. *Thesaurus Cultus et Rituum Antiquorum,* vol. III. Los Angeles: Getty Publications.

Tod, M. N. 1933. *A Selection of Greek Historical Inscriptions.* Oxford, UK: Clarendon Press. [Tod].

Todd, S. C. 1993. *The Shape of Athenian Law.* Oxford, UK: Clarendon Press.

Tsetskhladze, G. R., ed. 2006. *Greek Colonization: An Account of Greek Colonies and Other Settlements Overseas.* Leiden and Boston: Brill.

Tsetskhladze, G. R, and F. De Angelis, eds. 1994. *The Archaeology of Greek Colonization.* Cambridge, MA: Center for Hellenic Studies and Harvard University Press.

Vallet, G. 1968. "La cité et son territoire dans les colonies grecques d'occident." In *La città e il suo territorio. Atti di settimo convegno di studi sulla Magna Grecia,* 67–142. Naples: L'Arte tipografica.

van Wees, H. 1992. *Status Warriors: War, Violence and Society in Homer and History,* 33–80. Amsterdam: J. C. Gieben.

———. 2003. "Conquerors and serfs: Wars of conquest and forced labor in archaic Greece." In *Helots and Their Masters in Laconia and Messenia: Histories, Ideologies, Structures,* ed. N. Luraghi and S. E. Alcock. Cambridge, MA: Center for Hellenic Studies and Harvard University Press.

Verdegem, S. 2010. *Plutarch's Life of Alcibiades: Story, Text and Moralism.* Leuven: Leuven University Press.

Walbank, F. W. 1993. *The Hellenistic World.* Cambridge, MA: Harvard University Press.

Walbank, M. B. 1978. *Athenian Proxenies of the Fifth Century BC.* Toronto: Samuel-Stevens.

———. 1983. "Leases of sacred properties in Attica": Parts 1–4. In *Hesperia 52,* pp. 100–135, 177–99, 200–206, and 207–31.

Walzer, M. 1981. "The distribution of membership." In *Boundaries: National Autonomy and Its Limits,* ed. P. G. Brown and H. Shue, 1–35. Totowa, NJ: Rowman and Littlefield.

Wellman, C., and P. Cole 2011. *Debating the Ethics of Immigration: Is There a Right to Exclude?* Oxford, UK: Oxford University Press.

Wernicke, K. 1891. "Die Polizeiwache auf der Burg von Athen." *Hermes* 26, 51–75.

West, M. L. 1978. *Hesiod Works and Days.* Oxford, UK: Clarendon Press.

Westlake, H. D. 1952. *Timoleon and His Relations with Tyrants.* Manchester, UK: Manchester University Press.

———. 1969. *Essays on the Greek Historians and Greek History.* Manchester, UK: Manchester University Press.

———. 1994. "Dion and Timoleon." In *CAH* VI², 693–722.

Whitehead, D. 1975. "Aristotle the metic." *Proceedings of the Cambridge Philological Society* 21, 94–99.

———. 1977. *The Ideology of the Athenian Metic* (= *Cambridge Philological Society*, Suppl. vol. 4). Cambridge, UK.

———. 1982–83. "Sparta and the Thirty Tyrants." *Ancient Society* 13/14, 105–30.

———. 1984. "Immigrant communities in the classical polis." *L'Antiquité Classique* 53, 47–59.

———. 1986a. *The Demes of Attica 508/7–ca. 250 BC: A Political and Social Study*. Princeton, NJ: Princeton University Press.

———. 1986b. "The ideology of the Athenian metic: Some pendants and a reappraisal." *Proceedings of the Cambridge Philological Society* 32, 145–58.

———. 1990. *Aineias the Tactician: How to Survive Under Siege*. Oxford, UK: Clarendon Press.

———. 1991. "Who equipped mercenary troops in classical Greece?" *Historia* 40, 105–13.

———. 2000. *Hypereides: The Forensic Speeches*. Oxford, UK: Oxford Universtiy Press.

Whitley, J. 2001. *The Archaeology of Ancient Greece*. Cambridge, UK: Cambridge University Press.

Winter, I. J. 1995. "Homer's Phoenicians: History, ethnography, or literary trope?" In *A Tribute to Emily Townsend Vermeule*, ed. J. B. Carter and S. P. Morris, 247–71. Austin: University of Texas Press.

Wiseman, T. P. 1995. *Remus: A Roman Myth*. Cambridge, UK: Cambridge University Press.

Wolpert, A. 2002. *Remembering Defeat: Civil War and Civic Memory in Ancient Athens*. Baltimore and London: Johns Hopkins University Press.

Worthington, I. 2010. "Intentional history: Alexander, Demosthenes, and Thebes." *International History*, 239–46.

Yziquel, P. 2002. "L'étranger en Grèce ancienne." *Pallas* 60, 331–44.

INDEX OF PERSONAL NAMES

INDEX OF PLACE NAMES

INDEX OF SOURCES

This index includes works cited in the main text and further reading section. For abbreviations to the ancient works cited, see relevant entries in *LSJ*.

GENERAL INDEX